STAND & Deliver!

STAND & Deliver!

100 AUSTRALIAN BUSHRANGERS
1789~1901

~ ALLAN M. NIXON ~

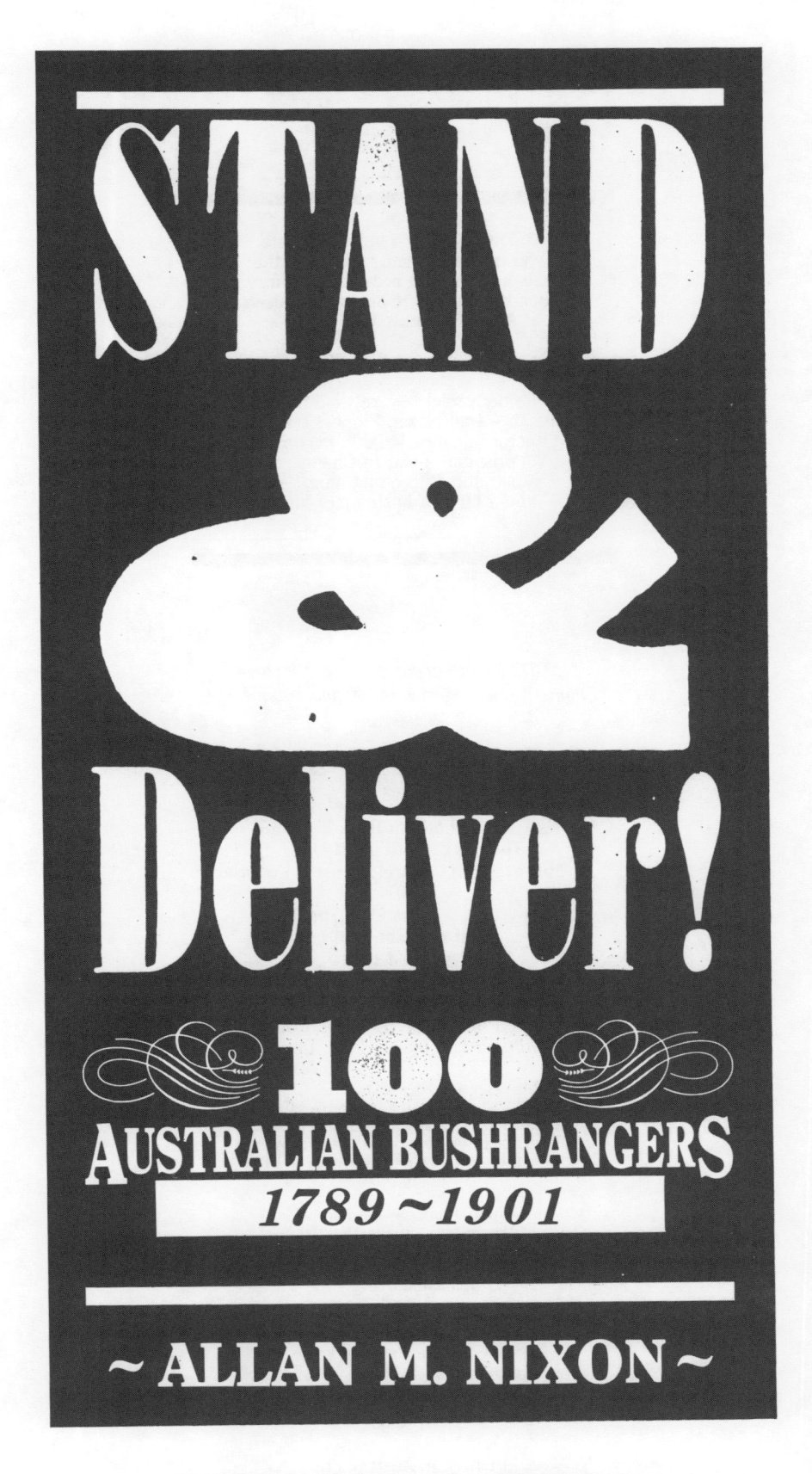

A LOTHIAN BOOK

DEDICATED to a great old mate
who introduced me to Janette, the
air hostess who became my wife,
when he and I were air traffic officers
at Ansett Airlines, Alice Springs:

MAX ('Shep') SHEPLEY,

former camel boy, cattle drover,
bushman – trail blazer, Pioneer bus driver,
actor in Chips Rafferty movies,
prisoner-of-war in Changi,
air traffic officer, and more —
— and a bit of a bushranger himself!

NOTE: Extracts of prison records have been transcribed directly from the original documents, unaltered.

A Lothian Book
Thomas C. Lothian Pty Ltd
11 Munro Street, Port Melbourne, Victoria
3207
Copyright © Allan M. Nixon 1991
First published 1991
Reprinted 1995

Designed by Geoff Hocking
Cover Photograph by Neil Lorimer
Set in Clearface by DigiType, Bendigo

All rights reserved. No part of this publication
may be reproduced, stored in a retrieval system
or transmitted in any form by any process
without the prior permission of the copyright
owner. Enquiries should be made to the
publisher.

National Library of Australia
Cataloguing-in-publication data:

Nixon, Allan M., 1951-
Stand and Deliver!

Includes index.
ISBN 0 85091 447 7.

1. Bushrangers - Australia - History.
2. Australia - History. I. Title.

364.1550994

Printed in Australia by
Southwood Press Pty Limited

CONTENTS

INTRODUCTION	6
WILLIAM ARMSTRONG	11
JAMES ATTERALL	13
WILLIAM BARNES	14
GRAHAM BENNETT	15
BILLY THE PUNTMAN	16
BOGONG JACK	17
ROBERT BOURKE	18
CHARLES BOW	19
JOHN BOW	20
HENRY BRADLEY	22
JACK BRADSHAW	23
MATTHEW BRADY	24
WILLIAM BROOKMAN	27
WILLIAM BRYAN	28
RICHARD BRYANT	29
ARTHUR BURROWE	30
JOSEPH BYRNE	31
JOHN CAESAR	34
MARTIN CASH	35
GEORGE CHAMBERLAIN	37
THOMAS & JOHN CLARKE	38
GEORGE COMERFORD	42
ROBERT COTTRELL	43
PATRICK DALEY	44
ALEXANDER DALTON	46
JAMES DALTON	46
JOSEPH DIGNUM	48
JOHN DONOHUE	50
JOHN DONOVAN	51
BLACK DOUGLAS	52
JOHN DOUGLAS	52
WILLIAM DRISCOLL	53
JAMES DUNCAN	54
JOHN DUNN	56
PATRICK DUNNE	57
GEORGE ELLISON	57
CHRISTOPHER FARRELL	58
JOHN FINNEGAN	60
JOHN FLANIGAN	62
JOHN FOLEY	67
ALEXANDER FORDYCE	68
STEPHEN FOX	68
FRANK GARDINER	71
HENRY GARRETT	74
WILLIAM GARROWAY	76
JOHN GILBERT	77
CHRISTOPHER GOODISON	79
JAMES GOODWIN	80
JIMMY GOVERNER	81
BENJAMIN HALL	84
STEPHEN HART	87
MICHAEL HOWE	88
HENRY HUNTER	90
JOHN JAMES	90
THOMAS JEFFRIES	92
HENRY JOHNSTON	94
GEORGE JONES	94
LAWRENCE KAVANAGH	95
ANDREW KELLY	97
THE KELLY FAMILY	100
FRED LOWRY	112
WILLIAM MACK	113
FRANK MCCALLUM	114
JAMES MCPHERSON	117
HARRY MANNS	118
EDWARD MELVILLE	119
GEORGE MELVILLE	120
DANIEL MORGAN	125
JAMES MORGAN	128
MUSQUITO	129
JAMES NESBITT	130
JOHN NEWTON	132
PATRICK O'CONNOR	133
ALEXANDER PEARCE	135
JOHN PEISLEY	136
GEORGE PENNY	137
HARRY POWER	138
JAMES REGAN	145
CODRINGTON REVINGSTONE	145
JOHN ROBERTS	146
WILLIAM ROBERT ROBERTS	147
THOMAS ROGAN	148
ANDREW SCOTT (Captain Moonlite)	150
WILLIAM SCOTT	157
AARON SHERRITT	158
ALFRED STALLARD	161
OWEN SUFFOLK	162
JOHN VANE	166
FREDERICK WORDSWORTH WARD	168
JOHN WHELAN	171
JOHN WHITEHEAD	172
JACK WILLIAMS	173
THOMAS WILLIAMS 1ST.	174
THOMAS WILLIAMS 2ND.	175
EDWARD WILSON	176
JOHN WILSON	177
ISAIAH WRIGHT	178
JOHN WRIGHT	181
THE BUSHRANGERS	
(Trades or Occupations)	182
(Country of Origin)	182
(Personal Statistics)	183
REFERENCES	184
OFFICIAL GOVERNMENT SOURCES	187
BIBLIOGRAPHY	188
ACKNOWLEDGEMENTS	188
INDEX	189

INTRODUCTION

On 18 April 1854, bushranger Dan Morgan uttered the words 'Stand and Deliver' to one of his victims, hawker John Duff, at a hut near the Victorian gold town of Castlemaine. It was one of many robberies committed by Morgan.

Nearly eleven years later, on 26 January 1865, at Collector in New South Wales, bushranger John Dunn presented a shotgun at Constable Samuel Nelson and called on him to 'Stand'. The policeman kept moving forward and when within about twenty yards he was shot dead.

It would be a scene repeated on many occasions during the wild days of the colonial era. Not all such crimes were bushrangers against police, many victims would be innocent civilians.

Whilst the term 'Bail up' would become the most common term used by bushrangers when holding up coaches or settlers, it should be remembered that this was a colonial term used by the first generation Australian bushrangers. Not all bushrangers were wild Irish catholics with an in-born hatred of the English, as has been the common portrayal of the bushrangers.

Much of our bushranging history in fact has its beginnings on the roads of England when 'highwaymen' roamed and robbed as later bushrangers would roam and rob on the Australian bush tracks. It goes back before the goldrush era in Australia, to the convict period.

The term 'Stand and Deliver' also has its origins on the roads in England when highwaymen such as Michael Howe (in 1811) and George Jones (in 1829) were convicted for 'robbery under arms'. Later, when transported to Australia, they would in time become bushrangers in Van Diemen's Land. Their criminal actions were the same, only the location was different. Many other English convicts, and men of other nationalities, would repeat their 'Stand and Deliver' escapades on Australian soil.

The bushranging era in Australia lasted for well over a century, beginning with such men as Black Caesar, who escaped from the convict settlements established by the First Fleet, and continuing until the exploits of Jimmy Governor in New South Wales early in 1901. My choice of 100 bushrangers for this book has in fact been quite a difficult task because there were so many men who could be called bushrangers, and it would not have been difficult to limit the subject to 100 *Victorian* bushrangers. Over a good many years of research into the subject I have constantly discovered new material about the well-known so-called 'Kings of the Road' and found many clues which could have led me on the track of other men. For example, a report in the *Inglewood Advertiser*, reading 'On 17 January 1865, a holdup was reported at Coutt's outstation Kooyoorah, by a bushranger who had stolen a single-barrelled rifle from Seagrave's Victoria Hotel, Jericho. He stood over them with a loaded gun whilst they prepared him refreshment, after which, when he had received it, he made tracks towards Boort.'

The Police and Government Gazettes of the various colonies are full of notices concerning bushrangers, either known or unknown. As late as 16 June 1888, the Chief

Bushrangers Flight by S.T. Gill, c. 1852-1855.
(Courtesy La Trobe Collection, State Library of Victoria)

Secretary of Victoria offered a reward of £50 because 'at 4.40 p.m. on Friday the 8th June inst. the mail was stopped at Wehla, by a man of low stature, and disguised, and the Wehla, Fenton's Creek and Kuracca West mail-bags stolen and carried away.' Such notices show that the bushranging era did not end with the hanging of Ned Kelly, as many people believe.

Nobody can state, with total accuracy, the total number of Australian bushrangers. Probably they amounted to hundreds, but a great many of them did not receive newspaper attention or the same kind of public interest which surrounded the exploits of men like the Clarkes and Ben Hall. The prison records show that many men were convicted for such offences as 'Robbery under Arms' or 'Highway Robbery', which were categorised as bushranging, but it is very difficult to find out any more about them. The newspapers did not take much notice of them, and the court reports which would give more details of their offences have been lost or destroyed. They remain only as names on prison records.

In this book I have endeavoured to give a cross-section of the bushranging fraternity by including the extremely well-known, such as Ned Kelly; the less known; and those who may in fact be unknown to the majority of readers. During my research into the records of such men, and the official correspondence about them, I have frequently had the pleasure of following tracks neglected by other writers.

For example, Christopher Farrell usually receives little more than a passing mention, but the records show that he was a dangerous and violent criminal who spent about forty years in gaol.

No book on bushranging, to my knowledge, mentions the fact that Harry Power had a sister in Melbourne, who fought for years in a battle for his release from prison. How many people know that there were at least seven criminals with the name Melville operating when Captain Melville was on the rampage, and that Isaiah Wright, was still in trouble with police as late as 1900, twenty years after the hanging of his mate, Ned Kelly?

I know that I have still only just scratched the surface of the rich vein of information contained in records which have been almost forgotten, including such volumes as the Photographic Description Books from which I was able to copy a number of previously unpublished photographs of various bushrangers. My research has enabled various New South Wales researchers to locate the vast collection of official bushranging documents contained in the state archives.

During my prolonged research, I have of course used previously published material, as guide-posts to point the way for me to go. But I have become very conscious of the fact that any writer on matters which happened so long ago and were surrounded by so much public interest may easily become confused by the conflicting stories. It is always possible that some of the most commonly accepted tales about bushrangers had their foundation in someone's fevered imagination rather than reality. The stories of Australian bushrangers have become a part of folklore, which means that they have attracted a certain amount of myth and legend.

One must remember that stories about bushrangers were told by two different types of people: those who admired them, and those who did not. Some recent books published have coloured all bushrangers in the blackest of terms. Nothing is so black and white. In all types of society, there was, as now, good and bad. It should be remembered however, that eventually, crime does not pay.

Obviously the stories would be coloured by the attitude of the teller, and as I continue to research the subject I will not be surprised to find contradictions. In the meantime I hope that my selection of 100 Australian bushrangers will provide a useful addition to the literature on this colourful part of our great country's history.

STAND AND DELIVER

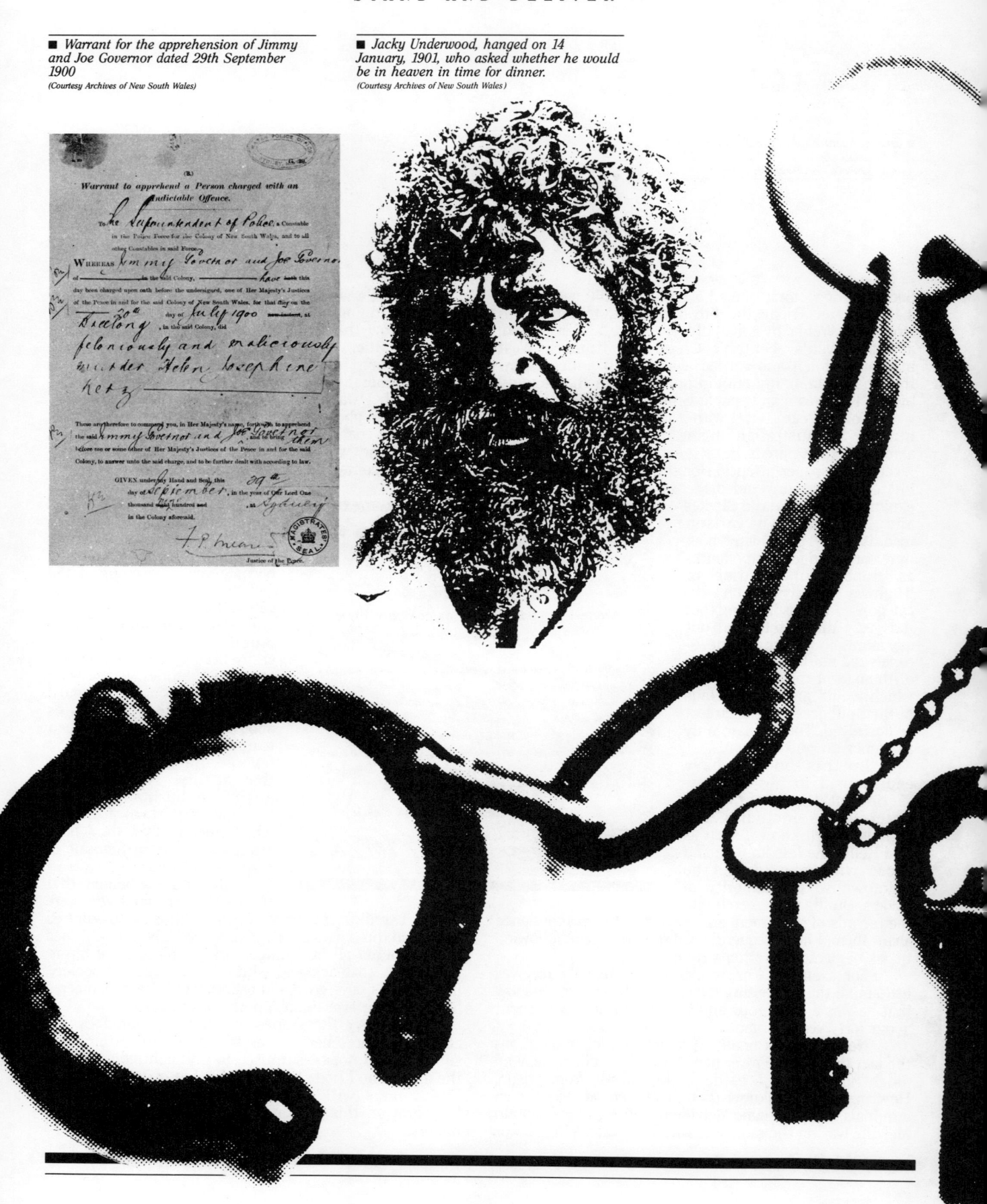

■ *Warrant for the apprehension of Jimmy and Joe Governor dated 29th September 1900*
(Courtesy Archives of New South Wales)

■ *Jacky Underwood, hanged on 14 January, 1901, who asked whether he would be in heaven in time for dinner.*
(Courtesy Archives of New South Wales)

100 AUSTRALIAN BUSHRANGERS 1789-1901

■ *Foster Fyans, Crown Lands Commissioner, Sheriff and Police Magistrate, who sentenced many bushrangers to prison in the second half of the nineteenth century.*
(Courtesy RHSV)

■ *Mounted police officer Montford, one of the captors of bushranger Harry Power.*
(Courtesy Victoria Police PRD)

■ *Leg irons of the type used on convicted bushrangers. A cord was fastened to the central ring and attached to the wearer's belt.*
(Courtesy RHSV)

STAND AND DELIVER

Gold escort attacked by bushrangers — an original lithograph.
(Private Collection)

William Armstrong

> **No.4402**
> Born: 1836
> Native Place: Ireland
> Trade: Labourer
> Religion: Protestant
> Read or Write: Both
> Height: 5ft 4¾ ins
> Complexion: Fresh
> Hair: Brown
> Eyes: Grey
> Nose: Medium
> Mouth: Large
> Chin: Medium
> Eyebrows: Brown
> Visage: Square
> Forehead: Medium
> Particular Marks: scar centre of forehead, scar and mole back of neck, two moles right side of neck, large scar inside lower right arm, a scar back of left hand, large mole centre of back.
> Previous History: Arrived per Saucy Susan to Port Phillip in 1851. Single. No relatives in the colony.
> Sentence: Five years on the roads for Horse stealing.
> Date of Conviction: 24 March, 1859. Supreme Court of Melbourne before Justice Molesworth.

On 5 January 1859, a little party set out through the Omeo district of Victoria on their way to Bairnsdale. They consisted of a young goldbuyer, Cornelius Green; a Miss Mutta, on the first leg of the long journey to England; and Police Constable William Green, who was armed with an old-fashioned pair of single-barrelled horse pistols.

The road from the goldfields was a rough track winding through heavily-timbered hills, which provided excellent cover for anyone with nefarious intent. When the trio were within about four kilometres of the Tongio Mungi Hotel they had to pass through a steep gully, with scrub on both sides of the road. Three men, George Chamberlain, William Armstrong, and George Penny, suddenly appeared out of the scrub and greeted Cornelius Green. They seemed to be on friendly terms with him, but Constable Green had been only a short time in Omeo and did not recognise them.

In the constable's later report of the incident, he wrote 'In a short time after, we reached the inn at Tongio Mungi, where we stopped for the night. I slept in the same room as Mr Green. The gold [which Green had bought in Omeo] was placed on the floor between us. Mr Green remarked that the man Armstrong, who occasionally worked for him, whilst cleaning his revolver the previous day, had rendered it unserviceable.'

The party was joined at the inn by Somes Davis, a storekeeper from Swift's Creek, who went with them when they set off again on the following morning. Green, leading a packhorse carrying the gold, rode ahead with Davis, the policeman and Miss Mutta rode about thirty metres behind them. After a little while Davis and Miss Mutta changed places. Just as they did so, Constable Green heard a shot.

'... thinking it must have been Mr Green's revolver that went off, I looked and saw Mr Green leaning forward in the saddle. I also saw a man on my right armed with a gun. I drew a holster pistol and fired at him, and he either fell or got behind a tree. I was then fired at from a tree on the left side, and was shot through both arms. I did not see the man who fired at me, for the tree was forked with branches interlaced, but he must have been near to me, as several slugs passed through my left arm, carrying strips of my jumper with them. A slug also entered my right wrist, and was held by the skin on the opposite side. Also a slug grazed the skin across my chest.

'My horse turned suddenly and galloped sixty or seventy yards and stopped. I was unable to do anything with him, as both my arms were useless. While the horse was standing I turned around as well as I could, and saw one man standing on the ground, and another standing over him. I saw a man present a gun in my direction and fire, when my horse galloped away and carried me back to the Inn from which we had started in the morning.'

Green raised the alarm and a rider hurried off to the police camp at Livingstone Creek, and returned before nightfall with Inspector Hill and a party of troopers to track down the bushrangers. Constable Green took several men with him back from the inn to the scene of the crime, where they found the goldbuyer's body in a ghastly condition: 'his head riddled with slugs, his nose gashed off, and one of his hands nearly severed from the arm by a tomahawk cut, while there was a terrible gash on the left temple.'

This savage mutilation had been an act of meaningless revenge. The packhorse carrying the gold had bolted during the affray, and returned to the inn. Davis and Miss Mutta were thrown from their horses and ran back to the inn on foot.

Hill's party found two saddle-straps near the site of the hold-up, and these were soon identified as having been sold to Armstrong by a local storekeeper and publican, named Day. Armstrong and Chamberlain had been lodging with Day at the same time as Cornelius Green, and it seemed certain that they had heard about his occupation and valuable cargo while they were there.

Inspector Hill set off on the arduous task of tracking down the bushrangers in the rugged country around Omeo. Weeks went past without success, but Hill and a black tracker named Tommy at last found Chamberlain and Armstrong living in a shanty at Gibbo, about seventy kilometres from Omeo. The shanty was owned by a man named Toake, who was supposed to have been an accomplice.

Hill and his party found the two bushrangers trying to conceal themselves up a tree, but they surrendered without resistance. While Armstrong was awaiting trial he made a startling confession, which read in part: 'About two years ago Toake asked me to join him and a man named "Ballarat" Harry, saying that Harry had £400 with him, and that they would go away prospecting, kill Harry and divide his money. I agreed, but at the last moment refused. Toake than said if you do not "split" I will give you £100 on my return. Toake returned in about two weeks and gave me the money promised, and said he had tomahawked Harry while he slept, burned the body, broke up the bones and scattered them about and then set fire to the bush.'

This case was in fact known to the police. Toake had been charged with the murder of Ballarat Harry because he had gone prospecting with him but returned alone, with plenty of money to spend and no good reason for Harry's disappearance.

He was acquitted for lack of evidence, and his eventual fate is unknown.

Young William Armstrong, who was twenty-three when he made his unsuccessful attempt on the gold of Cornelius Green, was not so lucky. On 2 July 1859 he was convicted of murder, and his brief career as a bushranger ended when he dropped through the gallows trap ten days later.

Also see George Chamberlain, George Penny

JAMES ATTERALL

Born: not known. (Age stated as 20 on this record)
Native Place: not known (one report says native of Lewes, Essex)
Trade: Bread and Biscuit Baker
Height: 5ft 6ins
Complexion: Fair
Head: Small
Whiskers: None
Eyes: Grey
Nose: Broad
Mouth: Large
Chin: Large
Eyebrows: Light brown
Visage: Oval
Forehead: High
Particular Marks: (tattoo) Woman, darts on left hand. Woman, Caroline Ford on right arm. XXOO back of right hand.
Previous History/Remarks: Sussex Quarter Sessions, 2 January 1834. Life. Transported for Felony having been convicted of Felony. Gaol report: convicted before, character bad, connexions good. Hulk report: Good. Single. Stated this offence Highway Robbery stealing money from a man. Once for shoes, 6 months, again for assault. Tried with Cole, Gander and Hawke. Single. Surgeon's report: pretty good, of some use as a teacher. Per Arab 2, 30 June 1834.

*Y*oung James Atterall seems to have been a bad lot. The son of a pastrycook and confectioner, and trained as a baker, he abandoned this innocent background for a career of petty crime in England. It included the theft of a pair of shoes, two cases of assault, and finally a 'stand and deliver' highway robbery, which resulted in transportation for life when he was twenty. In Tasmania, he escaped and joined forces with James Regan, William Davis, and Anthony Banks, and began bushranging in earnest. The gang soon became so notorious that a party of police and Royal Fusiliers was sent after them.

In February 1838 the pursuers heard, at Jerusalem, that the gang had committed yet another robbery and that they were apparently headed for the safety of the thick bush on Brown Mountain. As the police and soldiers slogged after them they heard that the gang had taken the time to rob another settler's property and steal his horse as well as other valuables.

The pursuers reached the summit of Brown Mountain at dusk, and found a hut which they surrounded. The bushrangers realised the game was up and tried to bargain with Captain Mackenzie, the leader of the lawmen, offering to surrender without a fight if Mackenzie would not prosecute them. Mackenzie, of course, refused to bargain.

Atterall, for some reason totally naked, crawled out of the hut and was quickly secured. The others yelled a few threats but also surrendered, and Mackenzie learned that their plan had been to capture the hutkeeper, Tucker, who was employed on the station owned by a Mr Romney. Tucker was considered the best guide in the district, and they had planned to make him guide them through the mountains to safety.

The bushrangers were trussed up and put in a cart, and taken on a painful journey through Richmond to Hobart where they were lodged in the Town Gaol.

Atterall's prison record has suffered from the erosion of time and the bottom section is barely decipherable, but it is possible to read that he was committed to trial for having 'Wilfully and maliciously murdered R. Morley.'

The four men were tried in June 1838 and sentenced to death on 11 June. Apparently Davis and Banks had attempted to plead that Regan and Atterall had forced them into bushranging, because Atterall said when he was sentenced 'I have one observation to make — I should not like to die with the blood of Davis and Banks upon us — I can assure you that they acted voluntarily in all they did, and were not compelled by us, indeed do you think we should be such fools as forcibly to keep these men with us who had every day an opportunity of either betraying or shooting us?'

However the Executive Council did find sufficient entenuating circumstances to commute Davis's sentence to one of imprisonment. As for the others, the *Hobart Town Courier* reported on 22 June 1838 that 'Yesterday morning James Atterall, James Regan, and Anthony Banks suffered the extreme penalty of the law, in the front of the gaol of this town.'

The report commented that Anthony Banks was 'a native youth, born at New Town, and was a remarkably fine handsome-looking youth, he was miserably ignorant and uneducated. We believe that he is the first native-born youth, of English parents, that has suffered an ignominious death of the halter.'

James Regan's last words were 'God bless you all.'

WILLIAM BARNES

William Barnes, together with Edward Wilson, would hardly rate a mention in a book on bushrangers if the *Melbourne Argus* of 8 October 1852 had not described them as 'two of the *Nelson* robbers.'

Various accounts of the daring Nelson robbery have ascribed it to as few as ten men and as many as twenty-one. Exactly how the *Argus* could accuse Barnes and Wilson of participation is hard to deduce. The report went on to say that the Mayor had committed them for trial on a charge of having stolen £15, an order

Born: 1823
Native Place: London
Trade: Stonemason
Religion: Catholic
Height: 5ft 9¼ins
Complexion: Sallow
Hair: Black
Eyes: Hazel
Particular Marks: Star, Wreath, Cross and Sailor on upper left arm, Wreath, Cross and Woman on upper, and Woman on lower right arm.
Previous History: Arrived per Ship Lady Nugent to Van Diemens land 1836. Bond.
Sentence: Six years on the Roads of the Colony for Robbery.
Date of Conviction: 13 October 1852.

for £70, and a receipt for 200 ounces of gold from one James Britton.

Barnes was convicted in October 1852, and sent to the Main Depot, Pentridge, to serve a six-year sentence. The only remark on his record, in November of that year, is that he refused to work at his trade of stonemason.

For this he was placed in irons and made to work in the quarry, and only a month later, on 18 December 1852, he died of 'natural causes.'

Also see Edward Wilson,
John James, the 'Nelson' robbery

Graham Bennett

No. 2172
Born: 1859
Native Place: Yorkshire, England
Trade: Seaman
Religion: Church of England
Read or Write: Both
Height: 5ft 5¾ ins
Weight: 142lbs
Hair: Brown
Eyes: Blue
Previous History: Arrived in colony per ship *Himalaya* in 1877
Previous convictions: Nil Conviction: Murder, before Supreme Court, Sydney. 11 December 1879
Sentence: Death recorded. Commuted to Life on the roads in Irons. ?? years.

Bennett, who was only twenty when he was captured, was one of the wild and foolish young men whom 'Captain Moonlite' seduced into the seemingly glamorous life of a bushranger.

Apparently, like many another British seamen, he 'jumped ship' in Australia to try his luck on the goldfields. How and when he came under the influence of Andrew George Scott, alias Captain Moonlite, has never been ascertained, but it was certainly an evil moment for the youthful ex-seaman.

The story of the battle of Wantabadgery, where Captain Moonlite was brought to book, is told in the section on Scott.

Bennett's arm was shattered by a police bullet and he was tended by Mrs McGlade, one of the captives in the homestead, until the Moonlite Gang surrendered.

Bennett had to suffer the awful experience of having the death sentence passed on him, but it was commuted to life imprisonment working in irons on the roads of the colony.

The records show that he was transferred to Berrima Gaol in 1880 to serve out his time, and after that he fades into the mists of time.

BILLY THE PUNTMAN

One of the bridges over the Ovens River, this one at Porepunkah, which robbed 'Billy the Puntman' of his job as ferryman and turned him into a bushranger.
(Courtesy RHSV)

The official records of Billy the Puntman have vanished, and all we know of him is contained in John Sadlier's book *Recollections of a Victorian Police Officer* and Francis Augustus Hare's *The Last of the Bushrangers*.

Sadlier says that Billy worked the punt crossing the Ovens at Wangaratta. He was notorious for overcharging, and when a protesting passenger pointed out the list of authorised charges his reply was 'Oh, them's out of date. Here's the bloody act, read it for yourself.'

The 'act' consisted of some pieces of dirty paper on which the passenger could not read two consecutive words, and he was forced to pay up. Billy even tried to charge punt fare from the Gold Escort which was entitled to a free passage, and desisted only when threatened with personal violence.

Billy lost his job when a bridge was built across the Ovens, and took to the bush. He soon became known as a confederate of horse and cattle stealers and other lawbreakers, but he escaped detection until he decided to rob the mail.

Billy chose a spot once called Fifteen Mile Creek, close to Greta (which was later the home of the Kelly gang), for the hold-up. Hare, a Wangaratta policeman, had to appear at the Melbourne Supreme Court late in 1855 and was travelling there by coach when the mailman trotted passed it on his horse, leading a packhorse carrying the mail. The coach soon caught up with the mailman again. He was standing on the roadside minus his horses, and he told Hare that Billy had bailed him up with a double-barrelled shotgun.

Hare borrowed a horse from the coachman and tried to follow the bushranger, but lost the trail on stony ground. He had to continue his journey to Melbourne but he advised the Benalla Police about Billy's exploit.

The long arm of the law, in the form of the Victorian mounted police, eventually caught up with Billy at Albury. He was still in possession of some of the property stolen from the mails, and this evidence enabled Judge Forbes, at Beechworth, to sentence him to ten years imprisonment.

Billy made several unsuccessful attempts to escape while he was being escorted to Melbourne to serve his term and finally evaded justice by hanging himself with a strip of blanket in his lonely cell at Donnybrook.

BOGONG JACK

Main Street, Bright
(Courtesy RHSV)

Bogong Jack, sometimes known as Jack-the-Omeo-Butcher, was probably John Payne or Paynter, and he may have arrived from England in 1852. He roamed the wild high country of the Australian Alps; from Bright in the north to Omeo in the south, as far West as the Barry Mountains and east to the slopes of Mount Kosciusko. This is some of the most rugged country in Australia, rising as high as 2300 metres and snow-covered for much of the year.

Some say that Jack was a gold prospector. He was certainly a bushman, and his chief occupation was stealing mobs of horses and cattle. If we believe all we are told in E. Harding's book *Bogong Jack*, then he was a far greater man, bushman, and bushranger than Ned Kelly.

Little is known of him apart from Harding's story and a mention in Sadlier's *Recollections of a Victorian Police Officer*. Sadlier says that Bogong Jack was the leader of a gang of horsethieves who knew the hidden passes in the Omeo ranges. 'Their methods were simple enough. They collected the best of the studs of such breeders as Edward Brook, Robert Firebrace, and William Pearson of Gippsland, drove the horses across the mountains into north-eastern Victoria and Riverina, and, having disposed of them, returned, not empty by any means, but with the best mob of horses they could collect in these districts: and so the game went on.'

Police Sergeant Reid, stationed at Omeo, eventually broke up the gang, but he did not catch Bogong Jack. The mystery of how and when he died is still unsolved, but it seems likely that he was one of the very few bushrangers who got away with his life and liberty.

Old Sydney Hotel, Ovens Street Wangaratta
(Courtesy La Trobe Collection, State Library of Victoria)

Robert Bourke

Like so many bushrangers, Robert Bourke was still in his twenties when he was 'hanged by the neck until he be dead' after a career of violence and crime. After his death in 1868 a claim was made that his real name was Clusky, that he was born in Dublin about 1840, and that he and his sister were sent to Australia in 1854. The same informant claimed that Bourke, or Clusky, had been caught in several acts of dishonesty before he took to bushranging, and that he was interested in 'Mad Dan' Morgan but would not have joined him because Morgan was too bloodthirsty.

However that may be, it is certain that Robert Bourke was sentenced to three years for horsestealing in the Ararat district in 1864. After his release he headed north and for about eighteen months worked as a cook on Mr Broughton's Humewood Station near the Murrumbidgee.

The pleasures of a quiet life soon palled, and with a young man named Quinn he embarked on a series of holdups and robberies: first in the Humewood district and later along the roads near Wodonga and Wangaratta. He was credited with the robbing of the Jugiong-Gundagai coach.

By 4 October 1868 he had made his way down to Robert Hurst's Diamond Creek Station, not far from Melbourne, having shed Quinn on the way. He rode up to Diamond Creek homestead and was met by Hurst's daughter, Ellen. He told her that he had ridden a long way and asked her for a meal.

The dirty and unglamorous aspects of a bushranger's life are illustrated by the fact that Ellen Hurst thought he was a tramp, and had no hesitation in allowing him into the kitchen for a bite to eat. He was sitting at the kitchen table, eating bread and meat, when she noticed for the first time that he wore a pistol in the belt under his coat. She slipped out of the room and told her brother Harry, who loaded a pistol and went with her into the kitchen.

Ellen Hurst said later 'The man was still eating when we entered the room, and I stood nearly behind him, about two yards off. My brother was on the left hand behind the man, and about a yard off. The first thing my brother said was, "Good morning mate, where do you come from?" He answered, "Cape Schanck." My brother said, "And where are you going?" to which he replied, "To Kilmore." My brother said, "The deuce you are, you are going a roundabout way to it".

After a little more questioning Bourke jumped up, lifted his coat to reveal his weapon, and cried 'Do you know who I am? I am a bushranger!'

But instead of drawing his pistol he made a rush at Harry Hurst, while Ellen fled out of the kitchen to call the overseer, Mr Abbott, from the stockyard. Hurst fired, but missed Bourke and almost hit Ellen as she ran out. Bourke then drew and fired but also missed. The two men grappled and another shot was fired, which passed through Hurst's side and into Bourke's thigh just as Abbott ran in and overpowered the bushranger. He dragged him outside and tied him up, and the Hursts sent for the police and for a doctor for Harry. However the young man died about eight hours later.

At Bourke's trial in Melbourne he defended himself with a long statement in which he claimed that Harry Hurst had fired first after insulting him, and that he had shot Hurst in self-defence. The jury did not believe him and he was executed only about five weeks after the unhappy encounter in the Diamond Creek kitchen.

100 AUSTRALIAN BUSHRANGERS 1789-1901

CHARLES BOW

> *No.2458*
> *Born:* 1825
> *Native Place:* Liverpool
> *Trade:* Plasterer
> *Religion:* Protestant
> *Height:* 5ft 5¾ins
> *Complexion:* Fresh
> *Hair:* Brown
> *Eyes:* Grey
> *Particular Marks:* Scar back of right ear, scar under left eye, scar forefinger on right hand, two blue dots between forefinger and thumb left hand, scar on right cheek.
> *Previous History:* Arrived per Ship Bermondsey 1848, Free Ship Adelaide to Port Phillip in 1849, an Exile 10 years, name of 'Jas Clarke', own statement.
> *Date of Conviction:* 23 October 1852, convicted at Geelong.
> *Sentenced:* Six years on the Roads for Highway Robbery.

Charles Bow seems to have been determined to pursue a career of crime, regardless of any opportunities to reform. He arrived in Australia in 1848, but by 1852 he was a full-fledged member of the Eureka Gang and had changed his name from James Clarke to Charles Bow or Bowe.

Led by John Finegan and John Donovan, the Eureka Gang comprised Henry Johnston, John Baylie, and Charles Bow. The gang was very active in central Victoria, where there were rich pickings from the goldminers, and ranged from Melbourne to Bendigo and as far west as Buninyong.

On 4 August 1852, Finegan and Donovan stopped a man named William Cook on the road between Bendigo and Melbourne, while the others watched from a distance. In the usual style of the gang the two bushrangers stripped Cook naked, so that they could pull his clothes apart in search of gold.

As so often seems to have been the case with bushrangers, the gang never accumulated enough loot to enable them to retire from the business. They were still at it when they were caught in Buninyong, and brought before the Geelong court on 23 October 1852. Charles Bow was sentenced to six years for his part in various highway robberies.

He was received at Pentridge on 6 November 1852, and soon tried to escape. On 26 November he was punished for 'Absconding from the Works' by being made to 'wear heavy irons until further orders.'

This made him behave himself, and by 24 April 1854 he earned a good behaviour credit of 169 days and was recommended for Ticket of Leave. This was granted on 23 October 1855, but he was soon back within prison walls again. He was given a month in Geelong Gaol for vagrancy, his Ticket of Leave was cancelled, and he was returned to Pentridge on 24 May 1856.

Bow seems to have been one of those unfortunate men who could behave himself in prison, but quickly went off the rails when he was released. On 17 June 1857 he was given another chance, and again let out on Ticket of Leave. How he managed to sustain himself, nobody knows, but he broke the law by leaving the district to which he was assigned on his Ticket. On 2 February 1858 he was back in Pentridge again, and it was noted that he would have to serve out the rest of his original six-year sentence.

Once more he behaved himself, and his record was free of any misdemeanours such as fighting or absconding. He completed his sentence on 23 October 1858 and was released upon the community.

His hard-learned lessons obviously had no effect. Only four months later, on 21 February 1859, Charles Bow appeared before Mr Justice Barry in the Melbourne Supreme Court on a charge of 'Stealing from the Person' and was sentenced to two-and-a-half years at hard labour.

He served this sentence from 28 February 1859 to 23 March 1861, and might have earned even more remission if he had not misbehaved himself in some way and drawn a punishment of seven days in irons. But the sorry story repeated itself when he appeared before the Chief Justice in Melbourne, on 15 July 1861, for larceny. He was given three years on the roads, and a barely decipherable note on his records says 'Discharge a few days before time, recommendation of Head Officer, per remission to Hobart.'

From that time onwards, Charles Bow disappears from public record. Maybe he reformed or maybe he pursued a more successful career of crime. He was only thirty-six at the time of his last recorded discharge from gaol but he had spent the better part of ten years in prison, and so he had perhaps decided that crime did not pay.

Also see John Donovan and John Finegan

19

John BOW

> *No.5369*
> Born: 1843
> Native Place: Penrith, N.S.W.
> Trade: Labourer
> Religion: Roman Catholic
> Education: Read and Write
> Height: 5ft 10ins
> Weight: 201lbs
> Hair: Fair and bald
> Eyes: Blue
> Particular Marks: Nil.
> Previous History: Sydney Criminal Court, 26 February 1863. Robbery with wounding.
> Sentence: Death. Commuted to Life.

John Bow was a member of the bushranging gang led first by Frank Gardiner and later by Ben Hall. The records made during his various arrests show that he was born in 1842 or 1843 at Penrith in New South Wales, the son of a small farmer, and that he worked either as a labourer or a stockman. He had a respectable upbringing and learned to read and write, but soon after he left school, and began work as a stockman at Burrowa, he became acquainted with the bushrangers Gardiner, Gilbert, and Peisley. He was only a teenager when he began to act as a 'bush telegraph' for the bushrangers, keeping them informed of police movements in the district. They paid him well and he soon attracted notice, young as he was, for his boozing and gambling habits on the Burrowa goldfield.

At some time before his twentieth birthday he must have decided to take up bushranging as a fulltime occupation, but like so many bushrangers his career was cut short when he was still a comparative youngster and, in all probability, the youngest of the Gardiner gang.

The records note that he took part in the robbery of the Gold Escort at Eugowra, New South Wales, on 15 June 1862, which is described more fully in the section on Frank Gardiner. Bow's record states the 'Nature of his offence' was that 'On the 15th June, the gold escort from the Lachlan was attacked at Eugowra between Forbes and Orange by a band of armed men said to be ten in number and described as dressed in red shirts and caps, with their faces blackened, who fired at and wounded the police forming the guard. Opened the mail bags and letters and carried off a large amount of gold dust and money.'

John Bow received some portion of the proceeds, and perhaps it was his freespending habits which led to his arrest only a couple of months later. He was sent to Sydney for trial, and on 26 February 1863 he heard the sentence of death pronounced upon him in the Criminal Court.

At that time there was a public move against the death sentence being imposed upon offenders who had not actually committed murder, and he was fortunate enough to have the sentence commuted to a life sentence of work on the roads, with the first three years to be served in irons. He actually served for eleven years and six months. In August, 1873 the sheriff recommended that he be allowed a conditional pardon, but for some reason Bow 'failed to take advantage' of this clemency. In June 1874 the governor of New South Wales approved another recommendation, for 'liberation within the colony,' and Bow was set free. After that, all we know is that he is supposed to have taken up a selection of land near Lake Cargellico in the Lower Lachlan district.

Prisoner's Name John Bow

NUMBER ON GAOL REGISTER 2569/45   PREVIOUS NUMBER

Portrait on Admission.

Where born	Penrith
Year of birth	1843
Arrived in the Colony { Ship / Year }	—
Trade or occupation previous to conviction	Labourer
Religion	R.C.
Education, degree of	R & W
Colour of { Hair / Eyes }	Fair & Bald / Blue
Height	5ft 10½
Weight { On conviction / On discharge }	201

SPECIAL MARKS AND GENERAL DESCRIPTION.

Nil

Portrait on Discharge.

STAND AND DELIVER

HENRY BRADLEY

Rough sketch of Point Puer, taken from a boat by C.A. Mitchell, 1864.
(Collection: Queen Victoria Museum and Art Gallery, Launceston)

Henry Bradley and his mate Patrick O'Connor had one of the briefest and bloodiest careers of any members of the bushranging fraternity. They started their rampage on 14 September 1853 in Van Diemen's Land, and concluded it on 24 October of the same year on the Melbourne gallows. Either sincerely or sarcastically, Bradley told Justice Williams 'Thank you, my lord, I'm very glad for your sentence — very glad indeed,' when Williams passed the death sentence.

Perhaps he felt that his life had not been worth living. Orphaned at eleven, he had joined one of the gangs of youthful pickpockets which infested London early last century. He was caught and transported to Point Puer, the penal settlement for boys in Van Diemen's Land, and was still described as a 'Prisoner of the Crown' when he joined forces with O'Connor.

Bradley had been in the service of a Mr George McKay, and O'Connor in that of a Mr James Gibson, when they joined forces for their first murderous escapade. The *Launceston Examiner* reported that, on 14 September they proceeded to the hut of Mr Jonathan House, and having tied up two men, took a double-barrelled gun. They then visited the residence of Mr John Spinks, tied up the whole family, and possessed themselves of another double-barrelled gun. After this they left for the farm of Mr Staines, about five miles off in the forest, and after tying Mr Staines and another man together, compelled a servant of the name of Smith to accompany them, saying they were going to Mr John House's — the adjoining farm.'

At House's farm they also tied up the people they found there, except for House who escaped through a window and ran off to obtain help. Bradley fired two shots after him, but missed. When he reported this to O'Connor, The latter replied that 'they would not be disappointed and immediately discharged both barrels at Mr Phillips, through the neck, causing instant death; and this dreadful scene in the bedroom, and in the presence of Mr House's daughters.'

The two men then went on to Atkins' farm, near Black River. Mrs Atkins was alone in the house, but apart from forcing her to cook them a breakfast they did not trouble her. They crossed the river to Medwin's farm and took a gun and some provisions.

The two murderers planned to escape to the mainland, where nobody knew them, and start a career of bushranging. Their first step was successful. At Circular Head they boarded the little schooner *Sophia* and forced the crew, at gunpoint, to sail them across Bass Strait: James Jarvie, mate of the *Sophia* later recalled that on Monday 19 September they forced two seamen to land them by boat near Cape Schanck, but there was 'No account of the boat and the two men belonging to the schooner.'

Bradley and O'Connor then made their way to Brighton, pausing at Mr Balcombe's station but without harming him or his family. At Brighton they followed their usual trick of tying up a Mr King in his farmhouse, and they made his eldest son tell them where the farm horses were to be found.

The horses were being used for ploughing in the paddock, but when the two ordered the ploughman to surrender them he took it as a joke. He told them to 'Come back at dinnertime.' One of the bushrangers immediately shot him dead.

With horseflesh between their knees the two convicts started off on their career of bushranging. According to William Howitt, in his book *Two Years in Victoria,* they were credited with many robberies and they struck terror into the community.

Also see Patrick O'Connor

JACK BRADSHAW

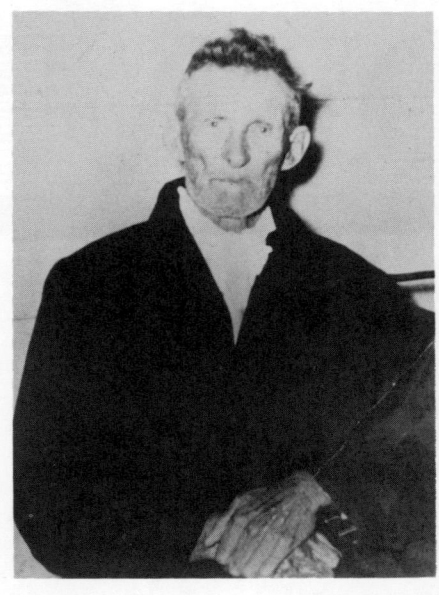

Jack Bradshaw — many years after his exploits as a bushranger. He died in an old people's home.
(Courtesy La Trobe Collection, State Library of Victoria)

Jack Bradshaw may only just qualify for the title of 'last of the bushrangers.' He lived until the 1930s, and as late as 1931, at the age of eighty-five, he was still making a precarious living by hawking his book *The True History of the Australian Bushrangers* from door to door. Roy Mendham, author of the *Dictionary of Australian Bushrangers*, met him in that year. In Mendham's book he remarks that Bradshaw 'wore a neatly clipped moustache, stood erect, and had a vigorous growth of upstanding hair...'

In Bradshaw's own book he says that he had a good home and family in Dublin, where he was born in 1846. Apparently he was brought to Australia in 1860 in care of a relative, but he soon left his arrival port of Melbourne and began roaming through Victoria and New South Wales. He had a number of honest jobs, especially as a shearer and farm labourer, but it seems that he was a born trickster, confidence man, and petty thief.

A typical Bradshaw enterprise was worked with 'Professor' Bruce, who claimed to be able to read people's characters by feeling the shape of their heads. Bradshaw would travel ahead of the 'professor' to a country town, learn as much about the people as he could, and secretly pass the information on to Bruce when he arrived in town. Naturally the 'professor' could amaze people with his knowledge of their lives and backgrounds.

From such comparatively innocent con jobs Bradshaw graduated to more desperate deeds. He teamed up with two characters nicknamed 'Red Lance' and 'After Dark', and the trio planned to rob the Merriwa Bank. However they bungled the effort. Instead of holding up the bank manager on his way to the bank they waylaid a local storekeeper, and fled in panic when they realised their mistake.

Bradshaw drifted on through the bush, picking up a living by fair means or foul, until he met a rascal named 'Lovely' Riley. They stole and sold horses for a while until Bradshaw and Riley held up the Coolah Bank.

This time they managed to get the right man in the right place. They bailed up the bank manager in his living quarters behind the bank and tried to force him to open the safe. The manager's wife was in labour, attended by a midwife, and when the latter heard what was going on she emerged and gave the duo such a tongue-lashing that they turned tail and ran.

In May 1880 they were more successful. They hid near the Quirindi Bank, and when they saw the manager, Mr Allen, walking past them Bradshaw crept up behind him and hissed 'Put your hands over your head or I'll blow your brains out.'

Allen handed over £2,000 and the bank robbers headed first for Currabubula and then to Tamworth, where Riley got drunk and bragged about the robbery. Bradshaw had enough sense to leave in a hurry.

Obviously Bradshaw was a very plausible rogue. He took the name of Davis, travelled on to Armidale with his share of the loot, and soon began to pay court to the daughter of a wealthy landowner living near Mihi Creek. She was so impressed that she married him, but the happy couple had a rude awakening when he was arrested over the Quirindi robbery.

He was sentenced to twelve years in prison, but was released in 1888. His wife stood by him but he could not keep out of trouble. He was caught stealing mail from registered mail bags and sent back to prison.

He was set free again in 1901, at the age of fifty-five, and he soon found a way to profit from his experiences as a 'bushranger.' He made a modest living by writing and lecturing about his own exploits, his knowledge of the bush country and its people, and about other bushrangers. Eager audiences lapped it up, but Jack Bradshaw died in an old people's home.

STAND AND DELIVER

MATTHEW BRADY

Sketch of convict bushranger Matthew Brady.
(Courtesy Archives of Tasmania)

There are many contradictory reports about the character and career of Matthew Brady. Some say he was a ruthless monster who made murder and torture his trade and pillage his hobby. Others say he was a gallant gentleman who never harmed anyone. It is certain that he became such a glamorous figure that when he was sentenced to die there were petitions for his reprieve. Probably, as usual, 'The truth lies somewhere in between.'

Brady was born of Irish parents in Manchester, England, in 1799. He grew into a handsome, well-made young man, able to read and write and a good rider. Employed as a groom, he forged his master's name to a cheque in order to pay off a debt, and on 17 April 1820, at Lancaster, he was sentenced to transportation for seven years.

The Alphabetical Record Book of Convicts' Conduct in Colony, A—B, 1807-30, in the Tasmanian State Archives, spells his name as 'Bready' and shows that he arrived in the colony aboard the *Julianna* in 1820. After preliminary details about his background, which are partly indecipherable, the record goes on to list his offences against good order and discipline. Obviously he was not prepared to submit to the convict system, and as early as 28 March 1821 he received twenty-five lashes for 'Neglect of duty.' This was followed by other punishments for 'Plotting and contriving to escape from the Colony'; for 'Not going to the Convict Barracks with his gang at the regular hour', for which he received another twenty-five lashes; 'Going on board the ship *Castle Forbes* with the intent to escape from the Colony' (fifty lashes); 'Leaving his gang and remaining absent 3 days' (fifty lashes).

Such punishments only served to harden his determination to escape. In June 1824 he was working at the newly-established vegetable farm with about fifteen other convicts, tramping there each morning and returning to the prison settlement each night. In the cold wet winter weather Brady and six of his mates escaped from the gang, seized a boat at Macquarie Harbour, and got clean away.

This was the beginning of Brady's bushranging career. He and his mates armed themselves with stolen muskets and began a series of depredations which kept the colony in a state of apprehension for months.

Their first set-back came at the homestead of a man named Taylor, where the settlers fought back and succeeded in capturing two of the bushrangers, Crawford and Bains. They were hanged at Launceston in September 1824. A squad of soldiers caught up with the rest of the gang in the Jericho district and captured Jeremiah Ryan, and the convict Bryant was caught two weeks later.

Brady and McCabe vanished until November, when Brady alone robbed two settlers at a hut on Black Marsh Road, near Jericho. He disappeared into the bush again for some time, until he and McCabe started on another series of robberies. They appeared in so many parts of the settled areas that the settlers were astonished by their speed of travel.

Obviously Brady had plenty of contacts who kept him informed of the local news and gossip. On 14 April 1825, Lieutenant-Governor Sir George Arthur issued a proclamation in which he offered twenty gallons of rum for the capture of Brady and McCabe. On 20 April Brady suddenly appeared at the Royal Oak Hotel at Crossmarch,

Guard Tower Port Arthur

fastened a notice to the doorway, and galloped off again. The locals were amazed to read 'It has caused Matthew Brady much concern that such a person known as Sir George Arthur is at large. Twenty Gallons of Rum will be given to any person that will deliver this person unto me. I also caution John Priest that I will hang him for his ill-treatment of Mrs Blackwell, at Newtown.'

The administration was not particularly popular with either the settlers or the convicts, and this mocking gesture helped to build up the fast-growing legend of Brady the Bushranger.

He and McCabe soon drew other escaped convicts and malcontents into their company: such men as Cowen, Callaghan, Murphy, and the sixteen-year-old youngster Williams. They were also building up a considerable intelligence network and range of supporters, including Thomas Kenton who was a deserter from a whaling ship. He was living in a hut in the bush country, and in 1826 Brady and McCabe went to visit him. As they rode up to the hut they saw a white cloth hanging from its window, the usual sign that the coast was clear, but Kenton had turned traitor. A squad of soldiers was hidden in the bush and they charged out on the unsuspecting bushrangers.

McCabe escaped by running up the hill but the soldiers caught Brady and tied him up. They left him with Kenton and went off in pursuit of McCabe, but Brady

25

worked free of his bonds. He must have been tempted to put an end to Kenton but he satisfied himself with getting free.

Brady now regarded himself as a sworn enemy of the administration and the establishment. He and his gang appeared and disappeared on well-planned raids throughout the settled areas, including those on Flexmore's property Glenfern, at Kempton, and Robert Bethune's property Thornhill, at Pittwater.

The Thornhill robbery preceded the raid on the gaol at Sorell. After a meal at Thornhill the gang rode on to Sorell and reached it after dark. They burst into the gaol guardroom, took the guards captive, and set the prisoners free from their cells. Laing, the governor of the gaol, was roused by the commotion, and he ran from his quarters across the yard to fetch Lieutenant Gunn. The two officers armed themselves and approached the guardhouse, but the bushrangers brought Gunn down with a volley of bullets. One shattered his right arm and another entered his chest. He fell, apparently dead, but survived his wounds.

The Brady gang escaped from Sorell but now the hunt was really up. So far they had not killed anyone during their exploits, but Brady could not forget Kenton's betrayal. When he heard that Kenton was at the Cocked Hat Inn (probably the inn later known as the Woolpack) he went looking for him. He found him in a bedroom, early in the morning of Sunday 5 March 1826, and after telling him just why he was going to die he shot him through the head.

But time was running out for Matthew Brady. Cowen and Callaghan gave themselves up to the police, and turned traitor. Brady, shot in the leg during one of his raids, was slowed down by the festering wound. Cowen and Callaghan led the police to the remnants of the gang, and Cowen killed young Williams with a shot through the head. For this, he collected £100 reward and a free pardon.

John Batman, the noted bushman and adventurer, who had captured the cannibal bushranger Jeffries, was now on Brady's trail. At the moment of confrontation Brady surrendered without a struggle, and said he didn't mind giving in to Batman but would never have surrendered to the redcoats. He protested only when he was imprisoned in Launceston Gaol with Jeffries and then sent with him in chains to Hobart. He was disgusted by having to associate with the cannibal.

On 25 April 1826 he and the remnants of his gang were brought before the Supreme Court at Hobart on a strange mixture of charges: stealing a musket and bayonet from William Andrews on the highway, maliciously setting fire to the dwelling house of William Effingham Lawrence and stealing three mares and a gelding from the same man, and so on. The most serious charge against Brady was that of murdering Thomas Kenton. Almost as though he was glad that everything was coming to an end, he did not even attempt to defend himself. He pleaded guilty to the charge.

Matthew Brady was hanged on 4 May 1826, protesting bitterly against having to stand on the same gallows as cannibal Jeffries. One of his mates, Bryant, hanged on the same day, and Tilley, Brown, Hodgetts and Goodwin were executed on the following day.

Brady was buried in the old Roman Catholic cemetery, where a stone cairn marked his grave for many years. This was removed at some time during the 1870s, and the definite location of his grave has now been forgotten.

Brady must surely have spoken for all bushrangers when he said, shortly before his death, 'A bushranger's life is wretched and miserable. There is constant fear of capture and the least noise in the bush is startling. There is no peace day or night.'

When he was asked why he had not terminated this miserable existence by giving himself up, he said 'Because I knew it would end this way and I wanted to live as long as I could.'

■ *Matthew Brady and some of his bushranging accomplices.*
(Courtesy Archives of Tasmania)

WILLIAM BROOKMAN

No.1039
Born: 1851
Native Place: Tumut, N.S.W.
Trade: Carpenter
Religion: Church of England
Education: Read and Write
Height: 5ft 9ins
Weight on Discharge: 151lbs
Hair: Light brown
Eyes: Blue
Particular Marks: Scar between the eyes
Prison History: Deniliquin C. Court, 14 January 1868- Wounding with intent to Murder. 15 years Roads. Death formerly.

Portrait on Discharge.

William Brookman was a mere youth of seventeen, said to be 'very boyish in appearance' when he carried out a daring bushranging raid in company with Edward Kelly (no relation to Ned), John Payne, and John Williams. The latter is believed to have been a bullock driver who sold his team, and turned to the more exciting business of bushranging.

Brookman is said to have come from a respectable family, and there is no clue as to why he took to bushranging at such an early age. After two or three raids in conventional bushranging style he and his mates planned an unusual type of hold-up.

On 24 November 1867, a race meeting had been organised at William Whittacker's store, near Mossgiel Station on the Willandra Billabong. About fifty bushfolk had assembled to join the fun and they were quite unprepared for the sudden appearance of young Brookman and his mates.

They took a 'considerable amount' from the race crowd, but after that it appears that Payne and Kelly made their escape while Brookman and Williams went looking for more trouble. They found it in the form of Constable McNamara, who was stationed at Booligal but happened to be visiting Mossgiel on duty. Brookman and Williams, revolvers in hand, bailed him up on the verandah of the store, but he made a rush at Brookman and grappled with him. In the struggle they blundered inside the store, where Brookman's pistol went off and shattered McNamara's wrist. Another shot wounded him in the back of the head.

Williams and Brookman were carrying five loaded revolvers between them, but this armament did not prevent Peerman, the Mossgiel overseer, and a Mr Edward Crombie from rushing in to help McNamara and overpowering the two bushrangers.

When they were captured they were in possession of a total of £116.12.6d, but it is not known whether this was the proceeds of the race meeting robbery or whether some of it may have been derived from earlier exploits.

The two men were secured in a hut under guard until they could be taken to Deniliquin to be charged, while the police went in hot pursuit of Payne and Kelly. They caught Payne first, and he led them to a camp where Kelly lay wounded from an earlier clash with the law.

The four bushrangers were convicted on 16 January 1868. Kelly drew thirty years and Payne twenty, while Brookman and Williams were sentenced to death. It is said that Brookman responded 'Thank you' when the judge passed the death sentence on a charge of 'Wounding with intent to murder.'

The sentence was later remitted to fifteen years on the roads, not life imprisonment as some accounts state.

On 3 July 1874 a lengthy debate on bushranging opened in the Legislative Assembly of New South Wales, with the names of various bushrangers being mentioned including Brookman and Gardiner.

Obviously the legislators were inclined to mercy, because they decided that both men should be released on 8 July 1874. But the final entry on Brookman's prison record states: '8 March. 1875. Sentence remitted.' After that, nothing more is now known about the young bushranger.

William Bryan

No	Year of birth	Native Place	Trade or calling	Rel.	Personal Description				Particular Marks
					Height	Complx	Hair	Eyes	
693	1825	Ireland	Laborer	Prot	5	2	Fresh	Brown	Blue	Scars on right knee

William Bryan, and his mate John Douglas, were typical of the young men whom the goldrush tempted into a career in bushranging. They abandoned their dull jobs as labourers in order to roam the roads between Ballarat and Geelong, and bailed up travellers at Muddy Creek and elsewhere. However they were not very successful or very defiant bushrangers. They were very soon caught, tried, and sentenced to five years on the roads. They were received at Collingwood Stockade on 14 June 1853.

Bryan 'kept his nose clean' while he was in prison. The only mention of his conduct was made on 23 April 1854, which recorded that an amount of task labour credit gained totalled 114 days and that he would be entitled to a Ticket of Leave on 26 April 1855.

He was released after serving two years of his sentence and, unlike many others of that period, must have decided that one taste of imprisonment was enough. He vanished into obscurity and does not appear again on the criminal records of the period.

Also see John Douglas

100 AUSTRALIAN BUSHRANGERS 1789-1901

RICHARD BRYANT

Richard Bryant's principal claim to fame is that he was one of those who murdered Inspector-General John Price, who was notorious for his cruel and inhumane treatment of convicts.

In his early twenties, Bryant teamed up with William Mack for a bushranging career. After various minor thefts they hit the jackpot when they held up J. Jackson's store at Mount Alexander early in 1853. They bailed up the storeman, robbed the till and stole a quantity of gold dust, bundled up as many valuable articles as they could find, and headed for Melbourne.

They enjoyed only a brief taste of affluence before Constable Bloomfield arrested them. For two charges of robbery in company, Bryant received savage sentences totalling twenty years on the roads.

No.532
Born: 1836
Native Place: Dublin
Trade: Sawyer
Religion: Roman Catholic
Height: 5ft 10½ins
Complexion: Dark
Hair: Brown
Eyes: Hazel
Particular Marks: Scar on right side, upper lip, MNV on right arm.
Previous History: Arrived per ship *Moffatt* 1837. Bond.
Sentence: Two charges of Robbery in Company. Twelve years on the Roads, 1st Two years in Irons (1st charge). Eight years on the Roads, 1st year in Irons (2nd charge).
Date of Conviction: (1st charge) 10 February 1853. (2nd charge) 11 February 1853, at Melbourne.

For most of the first four years of his sentence he suffered the appalling conditions of the prison hulks *President*, *Sacramento*, and *Success*, before being sent to Melbourne Gaol on 6 April 1857. His record shows a series of charges for minor offences such as improper language, misconduct, and disobedience of orders.

The hulks and the prison were overflowing with hardened criminals who had come to the mainland from Tasmania, lured by the prospect of good pickings in the gold rush. Bryant was influenced by these, and he joined a prison mutiny in which a number refused to work. When John Price came amongst them to discover the cause of their grievances they battered him to death with their tools.

Bryant was one of the murderers, who died on the gallows on 29 April 1857.

■ *Castlemaine (Mt Alexander) haunt of Richard Bryant.*
(Courtesy of Castlemaine Art Gallery & Historical Museum)

ARTHUR BURROWE

> **No. 695**
> **Born:** 1821
> **Native Place:** England
> **Trade:** Seaman
> **Religion:** Protestant
> **Height:** 5ft 8¼ins
> **Complexion:** Fresh
> **Hair:** Brown
> **Eyes:** Grey
> **Particular Marks:** Pockpitted, Large scar on left knee, Scorbutic marks on left arm and cheek.
> **Previous History:** Arrived per *Sophia Moffatt* 1852, Adelaide. Free. Proper name.
> **Date of Conviction:** 26 April 1853. Geelong Circular Court.

Arthur Burrowe, as his name is spelt on his prison record, also has been referred to as Barrow and Burrow. One book uses these two spellings as though they referred to two different men, but these two bushrangers were in fact the same person.

Burrowe and his companion William Garroway carried out various acts of bushranging, in some of which they were joined by two unnamed companions. These two may have been John Douglas and William Bryan, who appeared with Burrowe and Garroway in the same court on the same day and were listed in the prison records with consecutive numbers. It is known that both pairs ranged the area near Ballarat at about the same period.

Burrowe and Garroway's exploits included an attack on William Henry Mitchell at Pennyweight Flat, near Ballarat. They stopped him and asked the way to the township, then asked him to shout them a drink. When he refused, Garroway hit him with a pick handle and Burrowe threatened him with a pistol. They robbed him of his gold and left him bleeding on the road.

Another of their victims was a Scotsman, Alexander McLean, who was a tougher nut to crack. They stole his gold, but he apparently organised the posse which tracked them down and captured them.

On 26 April 1853, Arthur Burrowe was sentenced to ten years for assault and robbery, the first year to be served in irons. On 4 July he was received in the prison hulk *Success*, and he was later transferred to the hulks *Lysander* and *Sacramento*.

His experience of these hell-ships seems to have sobered him down, because he received 72½ days credit on 24 April 1854. But four months later his Ticket of Leave was delayed one month for misconduct, and he received various short periods of solitary confinement.

After his transfer to the Collingwood Stockade, on 16 July 1856, he was taken out of irons on 19 July. He behaved himself comparatively well in the stockade and was released on Ticket of Leave on 27 August 1858, to the district of Swan Hill.

Also see William Garroway

Joseph Byrne

> John Sadleir having been duly sworn saith I am Superintendent of Police for the Colony of Victoria. I was present when the body now at the police station Benalla was taken into Jones' public house. It is quite stiff encased in the iron armour. It has a bullet wound on the inside of the right thigh, which caused death.

■ *The well-known photo of Joe Byrne's body strung up for display after his death at Glenrowan.*

■ *Superimposed is part of a letter by police officer Sadliers' report of how Byrne's body was recovered from the burnt-out Jones Hotel.*
(Courtesy Public Record Office, Victoria)

Reward notice for the Kelly Gang.
(Courtesy Victoria Police, PRD)

(Opposite) Full details of the scene at which Joe Byrne's body was placed on display. The man at left in coat, holding papers is Julian Ashton ('The Vagabond') who would write many newspaper articles, including 'A Month in Pentridge' — where he interviewed bushranger Harry Power.
(Courtesy La Trobe Collection, State Library of Victoria)

Joe Byrne has been presented as one of the most glamorous of the Kelly gang; the handsome colonial boy who was an expert bushman, a crack shot, well-educated, successful with the ladies, and daringly defiant of the police. All his gallantry did not stand in the way of his cold-blooded murder of his friend Aaron Sherritt when Sherritt was believed to be a police informer. Joe certainly believed Aaron had betrayed him, and Joe thought he had the proof, but Aaron's betrayal of the gang has never been proved beyond doubt.

According to J.J. Keneally, in *The Inner History of the Kelly Gang*, Byrne was the son of a miner, with a good knowledge of alluvial goldmining which made him useful on the Kelly and Hart mining venture on the Stringybark and Kelly's Creeks. John Sadlier, in *Recollections of a Victorian Police Officer*, says that 'he had lived much with the Chinese and had picked up their language.'

Joe Byrne, who was only twenty-three when a police bullet killed him, grew up on the Woolshed diggings near Beechworth. He seems to have been one of the hard-riding, hard-drinking, rough-and-tumble youngsters of the bushland in the last half of last century. He was however said to be quite well educated, his family was poor but respectable, and he was considered 'quiet' and 'well-behaved' by most folk who knew him, a well-dressed young man who, with Ned Kelly, passed as a squatter during their horse stealing stunts.

There would have been plenty like him in the 'Kelly Country': first-generation Australians descended from Old Country battlers who could not offer their sons much of a living. He was known to the police for various minor acts of larrikinism, and the whole picture is that of a high-spirited youngster who would probably have settled down if he had not fallen in with the Kelly Gang.

His niche in Australian history was earned by the manner of his death. John Sadlier writes of the final scene in the Glenrowan pub, 'We were told that Byrne had been firing, and was in great spirits, boasting of what the gang was going to do. The work was hot, and he went to the counter for a drink. Finding that the weight of the armour prevented him throwing back his head to swallow the liquor he lifted the apron-shaped plate with one hand while with the other he lifted the glass to his mouth. In this attitude a chance bullet struck him in the groin, and spinning round once he fell dead.'

Other accounts say that, a moment before the bullet struck him, he offered the toast 'Here's to the bold Kelly Gang!', and yet another version states that he said 'many more years in the bush for the Kelly Gang!'.

After the pub had been set on fire it was entered by Father Gibney, a priest visiting the district. He walked to the front door holding a crucifix. He entered the blazing building endeavouring to assist those inside. He would later give evidence before the Royal Commission in 1881 '... I first found the body of Byrne ... lying there in a strangled kind of way, quite stiff'.

Gibney found the bodies of Hart and Dan Kelly. The police managed to drag the body of Joe Byrne clear but the fire had taken hold and they could not reach the other two bodies.

On the following day, Tuesday, 29 June 1880, Joe Byrne's body was allowed to be hung on the door of the Benalla lock-up so photographers and curious on-lookers could see the end of one of the Kelly Gang. Eyewitnesses at the time wrote that the spectacle, however, was repulsive. The hands were clenched and covered with blood, whilst blood also covered the clothes.

Joe Byrne had only outlived his murdered mate Aaron Sherritt by two days. He was given a pauper's grave within hours of Aaron's own burial.

Also see Ned Kelly

V. R.
£8000 REWARD
ROBBERY and MURDER.

WHEREAS EDWARD KELLY, DANIEL KELLY, STEPHEN HART, and JOSEPH BYRNE have been declared OUTLAWS in the Colony of Victoria, and whereas warrants have been issued charging the aforesaid men with the WILFUL MURDER of MICHAEL SCANLON, Police Constable of the Colony of VICTORIA, and whereas the above-named offenders are STILL at LARGE and have recently committed divers felonies in the Colony of NEW SOUTH WALES; Now, therefore, I, SIR HERCULES GEORGE ROBERT ROBINSON, the GOVERNOR, do by this, my proclamation issued with the advice of the Executive Council, hereby notify that a REWARD of £4,000 will be paid, three-fourths by the Government of NEW SOUTH WALES, and one-fourth by certain Banks trading in the Colony, for the apprehension of the above-named Four Offenders, or a reward of £1000 for the apprehension of any one of them, and that in ADDITION to the above reward, a similar REWARD of £4000 has been offered by the Government of VICTORIA, and I further notify that the said REWARD will be equitably apportioned between any persons giving information which shall lead to the apprehension of the offenders and any members of the police force or other persons who may actually effect such apprehension or assist thereat.

(Signed) HENRY PARKES,
Colonial Secretary, New South Wales.

(Signed) BRYAN O'LOGHLEN,
Attorney General, Victoria.

Dated 15th February, 1879.

BLACK CAESAR
— JOHN CAESAR —

Apparently the convicts who landed from the First Fleet included at least one black man: a giant ex-slave from the West Indies named John Caesar and commonly known as Black Caesar. Somehow he had escaped from slavery on the West Indian plantations and reached London, but he could not find work and so became a petty thief and pickpocket. Capture, trial, and a sentence of transportation to Botany Bay followed almost inevitably, and he stepped ashore with the other poor wretches in January 1788.

The convicts came very close to starving on their meagre rations, and it was even harder for Black Caesar than for the others. His enormous size and physical power demanded extra fuel, and it was perhaps in desperation that he decided to 'bolt' into the bush and see if he could do better by foraging for himself. He stole a musket, an iron cookpot, and some rations, and headed into the depths of almost unknown territory.

He was joined by other 'bolters' and they managed to survive on fish and whatever game they could catch, possibly with the help of some of the Aborigines.

The escapees never retained their freedom for very long, and Black Caesar was soon recaptured and sent back to the convict gangs. But he escaped again, and was recaptured again, and repeated the process until Governor Hunter issued a Government and General Order offering a reward of five gallons of rum to the person who could secure the convict Caesar and return him to custody.

Strictly speaking, Caesar cannot be called a bushranger because he stole only to keep himself alive, but he fits the *Encyclopaedia Britannica* definition of bushrangers as 'Men who lived, during the 19th century, in the Australian bush on the proceeds of robberies.'

Five gallons of rum was a substantial incentive in a colony which used rum as currency, and it prompted a free settler named William Blakehurst to set off after Caesar. Despite the black's giant size he apparently surrendered meekly whenever he was hunted down, and Blakehurst managed to trap him and receive the reward. He and his mates started a drinking spree which soon turned into a violent quarrel. Blakehurst drove an axe into the skull of one of his companions and then fled into the bush, soon to have a price of five gallons of rum on his own head.

But Caesar escaped again and Governor Hunter posted another offer of reward. This time it was taken up by a man named Wimbow. After a few days tracking, in company with another settler, he found Caesar in the bush near Concord.

It was the quiet summer evening of 15 February 1796, but Wimbow shattered the silence when he aimed and fired without warning. The black giant fell and did not rise again.

It had been a case of live or die for Caesar: live a life of misery in the convict system, or die in a desperate desire for freedom. The place where Wimbow shot him was known, ironically enough, as Liberty Plains.

100 AUSTRALIAN BUSHRANGERS 1789-1901

MARTIN CASH

■ *Martin Cash, as he appeared late in life, his convict and bushranging days long gone.*
(Courtesy La Trobe Collection, State Library of Victoria)

Martin Cash, like many another arrival during the early colonial days, was a young Irishman. He never saw Ireland again after the convict ship *Marquis of Huntley* sailed out of Cork Harbour on 29 September 1827, with the eighteen-year-old Martin Cash aboard. Sentenced to seven years transportation for house-breaking, he landed in Sydney four months later.

When he was released on Ticket of Leave he worked as a stockman in the Hunter Valley and took up with a woman named Bessie Clifford, who left her husband to live with the young Irishman. Apparently he made the Hunter Valley too hot to hold him, because he and Bessie left for Tasmania in 1837 under a cloud of suspicion for cattle stealing. They lived on various homesteads as a working couple but were soon in trouble again, this time for stealing eggs and other farm produce. Cash was sentenced to a further seven years, and the details recorded at that time accompany this biography.

He escaped from custody and tried to make his way to Melbourne, but was recaptured and sentenced to an additional two years. On his Tasmanian record, under the heading 'Report,' the following notes appear: 'Malcolm's Hut [in Cambridge-Richmond area] on probation for one year. Conduct to be reported vide Lieutenant-Governor's decision, 10th April 1840. *July 1st 1840.* Crown/larceny under £5. Existing sentence of transportation extended two years. *Same date* larceny under 5/12 months hard labour/three months of that period in chains. 1st offence approved vide Lieut-Governor's decision, 10th July, 1840. 2nd offence approved Jerusalem Chain Gang, 3 months afterwards to Green Ponds for remainder of sentence vide Lieut-Governor's decision 10th July 1840...'

Martin Cash had become a hard case, and he soon found himself in that home of hard cases, Port Arthur. There, he met Lawrence Kavanagh and George Jones. The trio would become known as 'Cash, Kavanagh, & Jones,' or simply as 'Cash & Company.' They planned an escape from Port Arthur, and succeeded in evading the guards and guard-dogs on 26 December 1842. Their bushranging careers were about to commence in earnest.

For the next twenty months they ran riot through the settled areas of Tasmania, robbing homesteads, inns, and travellers and always managing to keep one jump ahead of the parties of police and soldiers sent out in pursuit.

During 1843, Martin heard that Bessie Clifford was no longer faithful to him. Apparently she was tired of seeing Martin only by sneaking into the bush to meet him, with one eye always open for the police. But Martin was furious and determined to kill her and the new man in her life, Joe Pratt.

He and Kavanagh disguised themselves as sailors and went to Hobart to find Bessie, but they were recognised. They escaped the attempt to arrest them, but Kavanagh either was wounded in the affray or, as some accounts have it, fell on his weapon. In any case he decided to give himself up.

Cash returned to Hobart to find Bessie and Joe, but on the night of Tuesday 29 August 1843 he was recognised by two constables. Cash was noted for his fleetness of foot, and as the constables fired after him he fled down Murray Street and into Melville Street. He might still have escaped, but Melville Street was a deadend blocked by the wall of the Prisoners' Barracks, or Penitentiary.

Peter Winstanley, a former Ticket of Leave holder who had become a police constable, was drinking in the bar of the Old Commodore when he heard the commotion. He ran outside, saw Cash with a pistol in his hand, and grappled with him. Cash fired his pistol and the bullet ploughed through Winstanley's left breast and lung and lodged in his spine. He died shortly afterwards.

The other constables, helped by some civilians threw themselves on Cash. He fired again, and the bullet passed through the fingers of a man named McDonald and struck another man, Oldfield, in the nose, disfiguring him for life. The group threw Cash to the ground, but he fought furiously until one man kicked him in the face and another clubbed him with a pistol butt and knocked him out. They dragged their captive into the Prisoners' Barracks, and then took him to the gaol in Davey Street handcuffed and in leg-irons.

Five days later, on 4 September, Cash and Kavanagh were brought before Justice Montagu and the jury at the Hobart Town Criminal Sessions. Cash was charged with wilful murder, Kavanagh with robbery under arms.

They were both sentenced to hang on Monday 14 September, with Cash's body to be handed over to the surgeons for dissection. But, only an hour before the time of execution of this sentence, Judge Montagu arrived at the gaol and handed a warrant of postponement to Sheriff Bennett. Cash and Kavanagh had to wait another two months and twenty days before they were told that they would be transported to Norfolk Island, that most dreaded penal settlement reserved for men who had become too hard to handle in New South Wales and Tasmania. Escape from Norfolk Island was virtually unknown, and both Cash and Kavanagh could look forward to ending their days on the remote island.

They reacted to this prospect in different ways. Kavanagh remained rebellious, and was eventually hanged for his part in an abortive escape plan. Cash became a changed man. Even though the other prisoners looked up to him as one of the greatest of the bushrangers, and he could have exerted a considerable amount of bad influence, he behaved himself and kept out of trouble. In 1852, aged forty-four, he was considered by the authorities to be a 'trusty' and was appointed a convict overseer. On 24 March 1854 he married Mary Bennett, a convict assigned as a domestic servant to one of the government officials on the island.

Times were changing in the convict system.

MARTIN CASH

Born: 1808 (10 October)
Native Place: Wexford (Ireland)
Trade: Labourer
Religion: not recorded
Height: 5ft 9¾ins
Age: 30
Complexion: Florid
Head: Small and round
Hair: Curly and carroty
Whiskers: Small
Eyes: Small and blue
Nose: Small
Mouth: Large
Chin: Small
Visage: Small
Forehead: Low
Particular Marks/Remarks: 'MC' and crucifix tattooed inside right arm, cut on ball of thumb on left hand, long feet, large scar over right temple, large scar top of head, stout made man, breast very much freckled.
Previous History: Transported on the Francis Freeling. Tried Launceston Quarter Sessions, 24 March 1840.
Sentence: 7 years

Transportation of convicts to the eastern colonies had ceased in 1853, and there was a spirit of reform in the air. The convict settlement on Norfolk Island was to be closed down and the remaining convicts transferred to Tasmania, while the island itself was given to the descendants of the *Bounty* mutineers from Pitcairn Island. In this atmosphere, Martin Cash was appointed a constable on 31 July 1854, and on 19 September he was granted a Ticket of Leave. Soon afterwards he returned to Tasmania with his wife.

His bushranging days were behind him and he was a totally reformed character. He could have been a constable in Hobart but he preferred an appointment as overseer in charge of the gardeners in the Government Domain, where he settled down in a neat cottage. In 1855 a son, also named Martin, was born to Martin and Mary Cash.

On 24 June 1856 the ex-bushranger received a Conditional Pardon, confirmed as a Free Pardon on 11 July 1863. By that time he had left his job in Hobart and purchased sixty acres on the banks of Montrose Creek, where he planned to spend the rest of his life. But his son died of rheumatic fever on 6 July 1871 and this affected Cash so much that he became an alcoholic. On 10 August 1877 he fell sick while at the Lord Rodney Hotel, where the end came for the celebrated bushranger on 27 August. Despite all the hardships of his life he had lived to be sixty-nine.

GEORGE CHAMBERLAIN

Born: 1836
Native Place: New South Wales
Trade: Butcher
Religion: Roman Catholic
Education: Read and Write
Height: 5ft 6¼ins
Complexion: Dark
Hair: Black
Eyes: Grey
Nose: Large
Mouth: Large
Chin: Medium
Eyebrows: Black
Visage: Oval
Forehead: Medium
Particular Marks: Ears very small, right ear appeared to be pierced. Top joint of little finger broken, lower front teeth very uneven.
Previous History: Overland to Port Phillip. No relatives in the Colony. Father and Mother living at Camperdown near Sydney.
Sentence: five years on the Roads for Horse stealing.
Date of Conviction: 24 March 1859. Before His Honour Mr Justice Molesworth, Melbourne Supreme Court.

George Chamberlain was one of a gang of four which roamed the Omeo district. The others were William Armstrong, George Penny, and a man whose name is unknown.

Chamberlain must have embarked early upon a life of crime. At twenty-three, when he was in the Omeo district, he already had a sentence of five years for horsestealing behind him, but had probably earned some remission for good behaviour.

In January 1859, the gang heard that the goldbuyer Cornelius Green was travelling from Omeo to Bairnsdale with a load of gold purchased from the miners. Green had remarked that it was to be his last trip as a goldbuyer: a prophecy which was to come tragically true.

Chamberlain and his mates shot and killed him, and then mutilated his body in angry frustration because the packhorse carrying the gold had bolted.

After a long chase, Chamberlain and his mates were tracked down and captured. He was lodged in the Collingwood Stockade until 28 June 1859, when he was transferred to Melbourne Gaol to await trial.

He did not have long to wait. On 2 July he was found guilty of murder and sentenced to death, and he was hanged on 12 July.

A full account of the Cornelius Green murder may be found in the story of William Armstrong.
Also see William Armstrong, George Penny

37

STAND AND DELIVER

THOMAS & JOHN CLARKE

*T*homas and John Clarke, with their relations and friends, comprised a bushranging gang which was more active and more deadly than most. The Clarke exploits received little publicity in modern times until John O'Sullivan published his book *The Bloodiest Bushrangers*. Apart from being the bloodiest, the Clarke Gang may well have been the busiest. From the time that Thomas Clarke escaped from Braidwood Gaol, where he was being held for armed robbery, on 3 October 1865, the list of offences stretches almost continuously over the period until 27 April 1867 when Tom and John Clarke were besieged in a hut in the Jindera Ranges. They

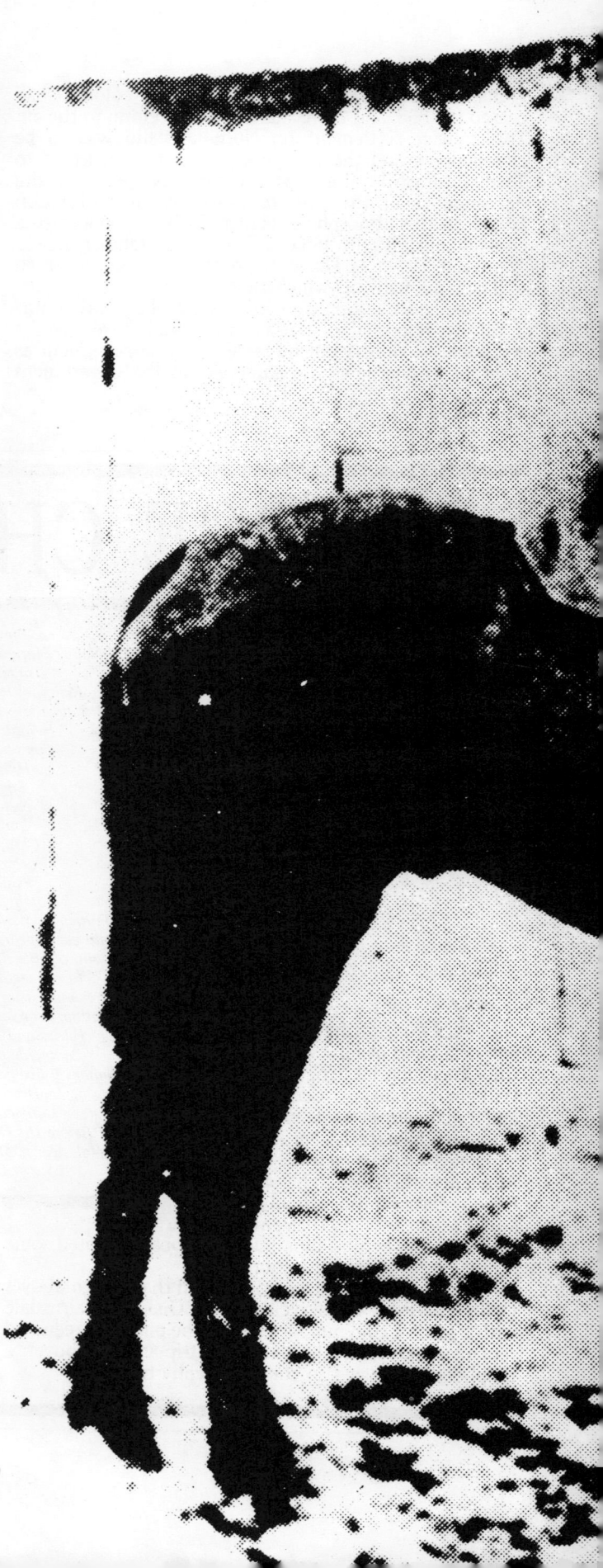

Thomas Clarke on his horse 'Boomerang', one of his fine race horses.
(Courtesy NSW Police, PRD)

The shoot-out between the Clarke Gang and the police at Nerregundah, New South Wales, in April 1866.
(Courtesy La Trobe Collection, State Library of Victoria)

exchanged shots with fifteen police until they surrendered.

The Clarke gang, or perhaps 'group' would be a better word since a number of them acted mainly as supporters, fences, spies on police movements and so on, comprised the brothers Tom, John, and James, their uncle Patrick Connell, their friends or relations Jane, Ellen, Patrick, and Margaret Clarke; John, Michael, Jane, and Ellen Connell; James Fletcher, William Berriman, William Scott, James Griffin, James Dornan alias 'Long Jim the Tailor,' and some others. It is alleged that the Clarkes killed Scott, after he had been wounded in a clash with the police, because they thought he might betray them, and that Griffin actually did betray them.

The whole group lived in the Araluen area, near Braidwood in New South Wales. The Clarkes were country boys brought up to ride and shoot well, but with little prospect of any profitable employment. They turned to 'gully raking,' or stealing horses and cattle, early in their career, and soon made the transition to bushranging.

After Tom escaped from Braidwood Gaol he went on a rampage which terrorised the whole area and made travellers afraid to move along the roads. Between then and April 1867, he and his gang committed at least forty-nine offences. They stole horses, robbed stores, stations, post offices, and houses, bailed up the mail coaches eight or nine times, robbed travellers on the roads, and clashed again and again with the police parties who kept doggedly on their trail.

The gang did not carry out all these exploits without having their own share of casualties. When Thomas, Patrick Connell, and James Fletcher robbed Pollock's store at Nerregundah on 9 April 1866, Fletcher was shot dead in an exchange of shots with Constable Miles O'Grady, who was killed by the other two. William Berriman was caught in September 1866. Constable Kelly killed Patrick Connell on 17 July 1866. Another accomplice, Alexander Bradley, was caught in October 1866, and Thomas Connell in November. James Dornan was found with his skull fractured, perhaps by accident, on Guys Range in February 1867.

The Braidwood Gaol entrance book shows that the women were as guilty as the males. Jane, Ellen, and Margaret Clarke, and Jane and Ellen Connell, were received at one time or another, as were various male members of the families. After Thomas Clarke and Patrick Connell had been proclaimed outlaws, on 5 June 1866, John Clarke had to face the unusual charge, on 16 July, of 'Giving sustenance to an outlaw.'

When a man was proclaimed an 'outlaw,' in the traditional English style, it meant that he was denied the protection as well as the rigours of the law. Anyone who spotted Tom and Patrick could kill them on sight. But there seemed little likelihood of this happening. As the police parties toiled and sweated through the bush-clad hills they may well have thought that everyone in the area was against them.

Eventually they turned to subterfuge. A party of four men, Aeneas MacDonnell, John Carroll, Patrick Kennagh, and John Phegan, were sworn in as special police. They pretended to be surveyors and camped near the Clarke homestead, where they made friends with the mother and sisters of the Clarke boys. But the girls were too cunning to be taken in for long.

One of them must have slipped away to the camp of their bushranging brothers and told them about the 'surveyors.' On 5 January 1867 police visiting the area found the four special constables dead in the bush.

The police caught Michael Connell and James Griffin in January 1867 and it is alleged that Griffin turned traitor and told them that the special constables had been murdered by Tom Clarke and William Scott. The government reacted by posting a reward of £5,000, which was an enormous sum of money in those days, for information leading to the arrest of the Clarkes. The gang's response to this offer was to launch a fresh series of raids.

They bailed up the Yass-Goulburn and Goulburn-Sydney mails, robbed stores and public houses, and robbed numerous people on the roads.

■ *Surrender of the brothers Clarke, at Jindera, New South Wales, 1867.*
(Courtesy La Trobe Collection, State Library of Victoria)

But the days of the Clarke gang were running out. The government was under attack for its failure to deal with this outbreak of bushranging, which had virtually brought trade and travel to a halt in that part of New South Wales. A heavily-armed party of fifteen police, possibly acting upon 'information received' from someone tempted by the reward, cornered Tom and John in the hut in the Jingera Ranges.

The exploits of the Clarke gang had received so much publicity that enormous crowds turned out to see the brothers brought to Sydney. They were amazed to see simple-looking country youngsters instead of the villainous desperadoes whom they had expected. John was only twenty-two, and Thomas twenty-eight. Their father, committed for murder, and their brother James were already in gaol. Their father died before he could be sentenced, and the two young men warned James that 'Crime does not pay.'

There seems to be some doubt that John Clarke actually killed anyone, but the public thirst for revenge was so intense that there was no hope of him escaping the extreme penalty. He and Tom were hanged on 25 July 1867.

GEORGE COMERFORD

George Comerford and Joseph Dignum, who is described later in this book, may have the dubious distinction of being the first bushrangers in the colony of Victoria, which was then a part of New South Wales.

Early in 1837, Dignum and two other convicts took to the bush after escaping from Yass, New South Wales. Later they were joined by six more escapees, including Comerford.

Dignum took charge of the gang with Comerford as his lieutenant, and they made their way to the infant settlement of Melbourne. They robbed isolated homesteads in the region and soon attracted the attention of the tiny Melbourne police force of seven men, but instead of fighting it out they decided to set off for South Australia. They set off on foot, so uncertain about their destination that they soon began to quarrel about the route. By the time they reached Mount Alexander they were running short of provisions. Disgruntled and weary, they settled down for the night in a circle around a big campfire, with guns within easy reach.

But Dignum had decided to quit himself of his quarrelsome crew, and he played possum until he thought all the others were sleeping. Perhaps he had plotted their murder with Comerford. However this may be, it is certain that when he rose stealthily from his blanket, Comerford stood up also. Possibly he had sensed Dignum's intentions or perhaps he had a similar plan of his own. In any case they soon killed all the others with their axes, and threw their bodies onto a huge fire of logs.

They gave up their overland march and returned towards Melbourne, and found jobs with a squatter. For some reason they soon left him and went to work for another squatter, but the first one had them arrested for breaking their agreement. Before he could get them into court they escaped with a couple of muskets and again took to the bush.

After an other round of robberies they decided on another sally towards South Australia, but Dignum determined that 'he travels fastest who travels alone' and took a shot at Comerford as they travelled through the bush. He missed and Comerford took to his heels and returned to Melbourne, where he turned Queen's Evidence and helped the police to capture Dignum. The two men were taken to Sydney because Melbourne had no suitable court for the case, but it seems that the authorities could hardly believe Comerford's story of the Mount Alexander massacre. They took him back there in handcuffs, escorted by Sergeant Tomkins and three constables.

Comerford's tale was proven by skulls, bones, and clothing which had not been consumed by the fire, and the party set off back to Melbourne. Comerford complained of having to walk in handcuffs, and they took them off during the daytime.

One day they found they had left their tea and sugar at the previous night's campsite, and Tomkins sent two men back to fetch these items. But he made the fatal mistake of leaving his carbine standing against a tree, and Comerford grabbed it and turned it on him. His second mistake was to make a rush at Comerford, who fired and killed him and escaped into the bush.

Comerford returned to his old haunts near Melbourne, and became such a menace that the government offered a reward of £50 for his capture and a free pardon for any convict who secured him. This news spread quickly. When he entered a hut at a cattle station and asked for food and a smoke he was recognised by a convict named Kangaroo Jack. While the bushranger was lighting his pipe Kangaroo Jack felled him with a terrific blow, and the other men in the hut fell on him and trussed him up. He was taken by bullock dray to Melbourne and hanged for the murder of Tomkins.

100 AUSTRALIAN BUSHRANGERS 1789-1901

ROBERT COTTRELL
— ALIAS 'BLUE CAP' —

Cottrell's name has been spelt as Cotterall or Cotterill, but the Darlinghurst Gaol Entrance Book shows it as Cottrell. Very little is known about his background or even about the number of his robberies. Some have been documented but he seems likely to have committed a good many more. There is not even any certainty as to why he was called 'Blue Cap,' although the obvious answer is that he affected this type of headgear. Most of his robberies took place near Wagga Wagga in New South Wales, where the well-known writer Rolf Boldrewood (T. A. Browne) was among his victims. Browne adapted the incident for use in one of his books, *Ups and Downs*, in which he used the name of 'Red Cap' for the bushranger.

Boxall gives a brief description of his trial. 'On April 20th, 1868, Robert Cotterall, alias Blue Cap, was tried at Wagga Wagga for having stuck up and robbed Carl Seeman at Rock Station, Reedy Creek, in June, 1867, and William Marshall, Jeremiah Lehane, and several others at various places between July 15th and October 24th. The prisoner had made a hard struggle when run down by police, and had been wounded. He was still very ill when brought to trial. He was deathly pale, and wore a green shade over his eyes. He looked very little like the popular idea of a bold bushranger.'

He was sentenced to ten years imprisonment, of which he served a part at Port Macquarie Gaol. The final entry on his record reads 'Robert Cotterell, alias Blue Cap, for robbery, being armed; convicted 20 April, 1868; term of sentence, 10 years on roads; period served, 6½ years; previous convictions, none. Recommendation of the Sheriff — Not a case for liberation; may be allowed a conditional pardon. Decision of His Excellency — approved; H.R. 1st October 1873.'

Thomas Alexander Browne (1826-1915) *received wide acclaim under the pen-name of Rolf Boldrewood, and is primarily remembered for his book 'Robbery Under Arms'. He published numerous novels and articles over a forty-year period, but is remembered for one book — a classic of Australian literature, most of the book based on actual events.*

He wrote to a friend saying that he was 'writing rather a sensational novel', and that 'a man with eight children and a limited income must do all he can to supplement the income'.

T.A. Browne (he added the 'e' to his surname in the 1860s) arrived in Australia when five years old, on board his father's ship which was delivering a cargo of convicts to Hobart Town.

Privately educated — he would grow to become a pastoralist — one of the 'squatter class' — he had properties at various stages near the wealthy Western District of Victoria, between Port Fairy and Portland, later at Murrabit near Swan Hill on the Murray — but was forced to sell during bad seasons. He then ran a station near Narrandera, N.S.W. until he gave up squatting due to droughts.

He became a police magistrate and goldfields commisioner, occupations that spanned about twenty-five years, the same time spent as a squatter.

He received some criticism for his competence as gold commisioner, due to his lack of mining regulation knowledge. He sued a newspaper editor for libel, but magnanimously sought leniency of sentence for his libeller.

Not everyone thought his writing was of note. In later years Australian author Frank Clune launched a scathing attack on his work, saying the only reason why T.A. Browne changed his name to Rolf Boldrewood was that no self-respecting police magistrate would happily admit to working as a professional liar (a fiction writer) in his spare time.

Strong words from an author whose own work, for so many years regarded as factual research, is now itself coming under more scrutiny and being found to be as much from Clune's own fervent imagination, as from factual archives.

Rolf Boldrewood, however, is now remembered with affection — '...a gentleman...a good staunch friend, courteous, unassuming.'

His work in which it was once said 'romantic spirit is skilfully combined with realistic detail', lives on.

Both his wife and daughter were also published authors. He often asserted he was proud to be an Australian.

He died on 11 March 1915 and was buried in the Brighton Cemetery, in Melbourne, Victoria.

STAND AND DELIVER

PATRICK DALEY

When Patrick Daley was brought into Forbes on 11 March 1863, and charged before Magistrate W. D. Irving with having broken into the police barracks at Pinnacle Station on 7 February and stolen firearms, and shot with intent to kill at Police Sub-Inspector John Oxley Norton near Wheogo on 1 March, the newspaper *Lachlan Observer* remarked 'There is nothing in Daley's physiognomical expression outwardly to denote the degraded villain.'

Frank Clune, in his book *Wild Colonial Boys*, says that Daley was a 'mild youthful, whiskerless person' when he was captured in March 1863. He was in fact only nineteen years old. Like so many bushrangers he was certainly a 'wild colonial boy,' of the generation which had succeeded the early breed of bushrangers who were principally ex-convicts. Those early bushrangers often were fierce callous men, brutalised by the convict system, whereas the men of Daley's generation often were youngsters brought up in the wild freedom of the bush; highspirited, reckless, and defiant of law and order. A number of them were of Irish descent, with an inherent antagonism towards the English and Scottish Protestants who dominated the colonial administration.

According to Clune, Patsy Daley was little more than a boy when he travelled from Arramagong in company with Johnny O'Meally, to a cattle muster fifteen miles from Wheogo. Among the settlers and stockmen gathered there were some men who would go down in bushranging history: Ben Hall, John Vane, Alex Fordyce, Harry Manns, Pat Connors, Fred Lowry, and Jimmy Dunleavy. Most of them were men from the Weddin Ranges, where they had been brought up in the cattle properties hacked out of the bush. The discovery of gold in the area had completely transformed its lifestyle and brought thousands of newcomers flocking in.

Young Daley became associated with Ben Hall's gang and took part in some of Hall's adventures, but his career as a bushranger was to be comparatively brief. By 1863, the government of New South Wales was determined to crack down on bushranging and Sir Frederick Pottinger had been appointed as police inspector in charge of the Western Division, which included the Weddin Ranges. Pottinger was to be the downfall of Daley as he was of so many other bushrangers.

Pottinger had had a somewhat romantic career. Born in England in 1831, he came from a wealthy family and he joined Britain's finest regiment, the Grenadier Guards. He soon became a compulsive gambler and he accumulated enormous debts, and so he disappeared to Australia, dropped his title, and tried to recoup his fortune on the goldfields. But he had no luck on the diggings and he joined the NSW Police by way of making a living. Like most well-born young Englishmen of that era he was a splendid rider, and his army experience had accustomed him to discipline and organisation. He soon achieved promotion and Trooper Pottinger became Inspector Sir Frederick Pottinger. A bold and determined leader of men, he harried the bushrangers relentlessly.

On 7 February 1863, Patrick Daley was with Ben Hall in a cheeky raid on the Pinnacle Police Station while it was unoccupied. They stole a rifle, a carbine, a pair of saddlebags, and a bridle. This exploit was followed by the holdup of Myer Solomon's store at Big Wombat, where Daley and others stole horses, guns, clothing, food, and money. During the robbery a young boy grabbed a revolver and pointed it at the bushrangers, but one of them had a gun at Mrs Solomon's head and he threatened to kill her unless the boy dropped the gun. It is said that Daley then knocked the boy down and kicked him.

> Born: 1844
> Native Place: Yass, N.S.W.
> Trade: Labourer
> Religion: Roman Catholic
> Education: Read and Write
> Height: 5ft 11½ins
> Weight: 173lbs
> Hair: Brown
> Eyes: Blue
> Particular Marks: Cut on right arm.
> General Description: Convicted with Jamieson and Cummings.

The police were in almost constant pursuit of Ben Hall and his men and the noted blacktracker Billy Dargin led Inspector Norton to O'Meally and Daley on 1 March 1863. There was an exchange of shots and the bushrangers cornered Norton but let him go unharmed.

Pottinger then took up the pursuit. With Dargin to help him, and a squad of troopers, he picked up Daley's tracks. They led to the shaft of a goldmine where a horse stood tethered at the top. The police yelled down the shaft for whomever was down there to come up and surrender, and when there was no answer they threw burning bushes down until Daley came coughing and spluttering up the ladder. When he was brought before the magistrate at Forbes, Inspector Norton could not make a positive identification but Billy Dargin exclaimed 'Mine know it, Patsy Daley like it brudder!'

On 23 September 1863, the Goulburn court sentenced Patrick Daley to fifteen years on the roads for two charges of robbery. It was a savage punishment for his brief excursion into bushranging but it reflected the government's determination to make an example of anyone they could catch.

He served some time in Darlinghurst Gaol before being transferred to Cockatoo Island on 4 February 1864, and the last entry on his record reads '15 October, 1873 ... Sentence Remitted ... Discharged.'

100 AUSTRALIAN BUSHRANGERS 1789-1901

Prisoner's Name *Patrick Daly*

NUMBER ON GAOL REGISTER 2121/68   PREVIOUS NUMBER

Where born .... Yass. N.S.W.
Year of birth 1844
Arrived in the Colony { Ship ....
                       { Year ....
Trade or occupation previous to conviction ...... Labour
Religion .... R. Catholic
Education, degree of .. Read & Write
Colour of { Hair ...... Brown
          { Eyes ...... Blue
Height 5ft 11½in
Weight { On conviction
       { On discharge .. 173b

SPECIAL MARKS AND GENERAL DESCRIPTION

Lance Cut on right arm

Connected with Sannesin and Cummins

ALEXANDER DALTON

Alexander Dalton had been a soldier, and the fact that he was transported for some crime committed at Gibraltar suggests that he was part of the garrison there. His record shows that he was a rebellious prisoner and was among the first to be sent to Macquarie Harbour — the 'Western Hell,' as it was known by the convicts in Tasmania when it was opened as a penal station on 3 January 1822. Between that date and May 1827, when the settlement was moved to Port Arthur, no less than 112 convicts escaped. Of that number seventy-four are said to have 'perished in the woods.' The best known of these escapees was Alexander Pearce, who is said to have been the original of Mat Gabbett in the famous novel *For the Term of his Natural Life*. The only prospect for those who survived the dreadful hardships of the escape routes was that of becoming bushrangers, either on their own account or by joining the gangs which already infested Tasmania.

Despite Dalton's own rebellious attitude he had at one stage

> Age: 23 (in 1818)
> Native Place: Kilkenny (Ireland)
> Trade: Soldier
> Height: 5ft 6½ins
> Hair: Brown
> Eyes: Grey
> Where Convicted: Gilbraltar
> Date of Conviction: 18 November 1818
> Sentence: 14 years. A few decipherable details on his record state:
> 12/12/1820 Drunk and disorderly... 14 days for Government in his own time.
> 22/5/1821 Beating his overseer....50 lashes and labour the ????? for 3 months, to be confirmed at nights.
> 6/7/1822 Wilful and corrupt... 100 lashes and remainder of his sentence at Macquarie Harlour.
> 21/8/1822 Neglect of Duty...25 lashes.

volunteered to be a flogger, to inflict punishment upon his companions in misfortune.

Late in 1822, he was one of a gang of eight convicts who escaped from Macquarie Harbour. The others were Alexander Pearce or Pierce, Thomas Bodenham, William Kennelly, Robert Greenhill, James Brown, John Mathers, and Mathew Travis or Travers.

They could find nothing to eat in the dense bush through which they struggled, and they were close to starvation when some of the gang began to whisper about the obvious answer to their problem. Greenhill suggested that they kill Dalton, the ex-flogger, and eat him.

Greenhill killed Dalton with an axe while he was sleeping, and Travers acted as butcher. He cut Dalton's throat to bleed him, dragged the body away and cut it up. He and Greenhill part-cooked the heart and liver and ate them, while the others watched in repugnance. They were still unable to bring themselves to cannibalism, but on the next day they took part in the horrid feast.

The incident illustrates the dark side of bushranging, and the callousness of some of the men who, having taken to the bush, had to live or die by their decision.

Also see Alexander Pearce

JAMES DALTON

James Dalton was one of the hardest of the many hard cases transported from the British Isles to Australia. He arrived while he was in his early twenties, under a sentence of seven years for larceny but his behaviour was so bad that this sentence was extended over and over again. The list of offences recorded against him show that he was one of those men whom even the brutal convict system could not subdue. He arrived on 10 December 1835 and only thirteen days later he committed his first offence. This was the theft of a Bible valued at one shilling and sixpence, for which his sentence was extended eighteen months.

He made several attempts to escape, was repeatedly disobedient and insolent and even threatened to cut an overseer's throat, and he stole whatever he could lay his hands on. He was flogged again and again, loaded with irons, and put in solitary confinement. but nothing broke the spirit of this hard and rebellious man. In 1846 he was sent to Norfolk Island, and almost immediately attempted to seize a boat and make his getaway. On 14 August 1849 he raped an eleven-year-old girl, Mary Willis, and received yet another spell of hard labour in chains.

By the early 1850s the Norfolk Island convicts were being returned to Tasmania, with James Dalton among them. He showed a better side of his nature when he worked hard with the rescue crews during the 1852 floods at Ross, and was rewarded with the cancellation of a four-months spell of hard-labour, but this did not affect his determination to escape.

On 28 December 1852, he and five or six other convicts escaped from Port Arthur and evaded the ferocious dogs and armed soldiers by swimming past Eaglehawk Neck to the unguarded coastline. All but two of them drowned in the attempt, the survivors being James Dalton and Andrew Kelly.

They soon armed themselves with stolen weapons and began their bushranging career. In January 1853 they robbed the Halfway House near Campbelltown and on the following day bailed up thirty people at Simeon Lord's house, Bona Vista. They included the District Constable of Avoca, the watchhouse keeper, and another constable. They shot and killed the watchhouse keeper, collected more than £100 in cash plus watches and jewellery, and galloped away from the scene on two fine horses stolen from Lord's stables.

During the next couple of weeks they made a number of daring raids and collected more money, jewellery, and provisions. On one of these raids they bailed up a hut full of men including Constable Buckmaster, one of those in pursuit of the bushrangers. Buckmaster made a rush at Dalton who killed him with a single shot.

They soon made the South Esk area too hot to hold them and determined to make a break for the mainland. They tried to commandeer the schooner *Jane and Elizabeth*, lying in the Forth River, but her crew defied them and they seized a whaleboat belonging to a local publican and made four miners take them across the Bass Strait. They landed at a lonely spot near Westernport and decided to make their separate ways to Melbourne, with the idea of getting aboard ships bound for England.

News of their brief bushranging career, and of their escape

> Born: 1819?
> Native Place: Browness, near Carlisle
> Trade: Labourer
> Religion: not recorded
> Height: 5ft ¼ins/5ft ½ins
> Age: 16/25
> Complexion: Fresh freckles
> Head: Large
> Hair: Light brown
> Whiskers: Light brown
> Eyes: Dark blue
> Nose: Small
> Mouth: Medium
> Chin: Medium
> Eyebrows: Dark brown
> Visage: Large round
> Forehead: Medium
> Particular Marks/Remarks: Face freckled — small scar over right eyebrow.
> Previous History: Many details including: Transported for Larceny. Tried Cumberland 6/1/1835... 7 years. Arrived 10 December 1835
> 23/12/1835... 6 months extention.
> 15/1/1838... 6 months extension.
> 6/3/1838... 2 years extension. Oct. 1839... 2 years extension. The above details come from two prison records, thus giving varied information

from Tasmania, had gone before them. A reward of £500 was posted for their capture and the Melbourne police had their eyes open for the two escapees, but Dalton's capture was almost accidental.

He found a boatman who agreed to put him aboard the ship *Northumberland,* lying off Port Melbourne, and went with him late one night into a coffee-shop on Bourke Street to change some Tasmanian banknotes into gold, presumably to pay the passage money.

The proprietors of the coffee-shop said that they did not have enough gold on hand to cash the £70 which Dalton offered in notes of the Launceston Bank, but one of the customers observed the affair, said he was a goldbroker, and offered to make the exchange.

Dalton agreed, but his luck had run out. The 'goldbroker' was an ex-cadet of the Melbourne police, named Brice, and he suspected there was something wrong about Dalton. The bushranger handed over the notes and Brice asked him to come along to his 'office'. He led Dalton and the boatman into Little Collins Street and through the back door into the yard of the Police Court. The night was so dark that Dalton could not see where he was being taken.

Brice opened another door, into his 'office,' and Dalton found himself in the clerk's room of the Swanston Street watchhouse. Several plainclothes detectives and other officials were in the room, and Brice showed them the banknotes. The astute Brice challenged Dalton saying he suspected Dalton of having come by them wrongfully.

Dalton, nonchalantly smoking a cigar, said coolly that the accusation was rubbish. The watchhouse keeper told Brice that he could not accept a charge on such slight evidence and gave the notes back to Dalton. He was about to leave the office when Detectives Williams, Murray, and Eason pounced on him. They had recognised him from a circularised description.

Dalton tried to pull out one of the three pistols he carried under his coat but he was overpowered. He said 'You have got the reward of £500. My name is Dalton!'

The police found and arrested Andrew Kelly on the following day and sent both men back to Tasmania. They were tried for the murder of Constable Buckmaster and hanged on 26 April 1853.
Also see Andrew Kelly

JOSEPH DIGNUM

Kyneton — a town en route to the Bendigo and Mt. Alexander goldfields.
(Courtesy La Trobe Collection, State Library of Victoria)

With George Comerford, whose story is told earlier in this book, Dignum's principal claims to fame are those of having been one of Victoria's first bushrangers and bloodiest murderers.

Life was hard and brutal for the convicts of early Australia. There seemed little future as they worked cruelly long hours, under the constant threat of the lash, and so it is no wonder that some of them decided that freedom as a bushranger was a better alternative... even if it led eventually to the gallows.

The brutalising life of the convict gangs, and their earlier existence in the slums of English cities, made such men astoundingly callous.

When Dignum began to quarrel with his gang, it was natural for him to see that the easiest way out of the situation was to kill all of them.

His lieutenant, young George Comerford, was a tall and personable young man, but he was just as callous as Dignum. Neither of them had any hesitation in taking an axe to their companions in crime.

The scene at the Mount Alexander campsite must have been horrifying as the two men set about the bloody business. Four of their mates died immediately, but three others staggered to their feet bleeding from ghastly wounds and had to be despatched by shots or further axe-blows.

The irony of the whole incident is that, after Comerford betrayed him, Dignum escaped with his life. He was punished with life imprisonment on Norfolk Island, but since that convict settlement was abandoned less than twenty years later it is possible that he received remission of sentence. But Comerford, still desperate for freedom, was hanged for the murder of a police sergeant during another escape.

Perhaps the difference in the sentences shows the comparative values held by the authorities in those days. Comerford died for the murder of one of their own kind, whereas Dignum only received a prison sentence for his part in murdering seven convicts.

Also see George Comerford

THE AUSTRALASIAN SKETCHER

No. 75. — VOL. VI.   MELBOURNE, SATURDAY, DECEMBER 21, 1878.   WITH LARGE COLOURED SUPPLEMENT   PRICE 6d.

Outlaws in Camp, 1878.
(Courtesy La Trobe Collection, State Library of Victoria)

BOLD JACK DONOHUE

John Donohue

The popular picture of Bold Jack Donohoe is of a handsome devil-may-care rascal, a kind of Robin Hood figure who was the hero of the oppressed convict gangs. In reality he was a little man, for some reason nicknamed 'The Stripper': perhaps because he stripped his victims of all they possessed. When a reward of £20 was offered for his capture he was described as '22 years of age, 5 feet 4 inches in height, brown freckled complexion, flaxen hair, blue eyes, and has a scar under his left nostril.' J. O'Brien, in his book *Men of '38*, described him as 'An undersized specimen with weak eyes... not much more than five feet tall. Like most of his contemporaries he was no hero in any sense.'

Born in Ireland, he arrived in the ship *Ann and Amelia* on 2 January 1825, aged about nineteen and under a life sentence of transportation for 'Intent to commit a felony.' He was assigned first to John Pagan of Parramatta, but must have misbehaved himself because he drew a spell on the chain gang before being assigned to Major West, a Parramatta surgeon with an estate at Quaker's Hill. He soon absconded from West's employment and took up with two men named Kilroy and Smith. The trio robbed a number of bullock drays on the Sydney-Windsor road before they were caught, tried, and sentenced to death. Donohoe escaped while he was being taken from the court to the Sussex Street gaol but his companions were hanged.

In company with William Underwood and some others he enjoyed nearly three more years of the bushranging life. They covered a good deal of territory, ranging from the Hunter River Valley to Liverpool and Illawarra and from Yass and Bathurst to Burrangong, Campbelltown, and Liberty Plains.

Bushrangers were common in that era but the depredations of Donohoe and his gang particularly exasperated the administration. They seemed to bear a charmed life, and even the offer of 'An Absolute Pardon and Free passage to England, or a grant of land' to any person who could turn them in was not enough to secure their arrest.

A confidential letter from Major Lockyer, Superintendent of Police at Parramatta, to the Colonial Secretary, dated 30 August 1830, concerning the problems of bushranging, suggests that no more Tickets of Leave should be granted to convicts until Donohoe and his gang were taken. Lockyer obviously thought that other convicts would betray Donohoe if they thought he stood in the way of their freedom, but a note in the margin of the letter says 'This might have the desired effect, but I feel it would be considered cruel.'

The story of Jack Donohoe has been obscured by so much myth and legend that no one knows what he was really like. Some reports say he tormented his victims, and even that he burnt one squatter alive.

The end came at last, as it did for most bushrangers, when the pursuers caught up with Donohoe and his gang. In the afternoon of 1 September 1830 a detachment of soldiers surrounded Donohoe in the Bringelly scrub near Campbelltown. The young Irishman was certainly game to the last, and he taunted the soldiers with 'the most insulting and indecent epithets' until Private Muggleston shot him through the head.

The legend of Bold Jack Donohoe flourished in the song bawled out in colonial taverns until the authorities banned it as being seditious. Nevertheless it persisted, with the name changed to 'Jack Doolan,' and was eventually called 'The Wild Colonial Boy.' Its words give a romantic view of bushranging which most certainly would not have been held by those who suffered at the hands of Donohoe and his gang.

JOHN DONOVAN

> Born: 1826
> Native Place: Cork (Ireland)
> Trade: Shoemaker
> Religion: Roman Catholic
> Height: 5ft 4¾ins
> Complexion: Fresh
> Hair: Dark brown
> Eyes: Hazel
> Particular Marks: Large mark lower right jaw, blue mark on left arm.
> Previous History: Arrived per ship Anson 1843. Bond. 7 years, same name. To Victoria 1851
> Sentence: Twelve years Hard Labour on the roads; first two years in Irons, for Highway Robbery
> Date of Conviction: 23 October 1852, at Geelong Court.

John Donovan and John Finegan were considered to be the leaders of the notorious Eureka Gang, which haunted the road between Melbourne and Bendigo and ranged through other parts of that area. Nobody seems to know why they adopted the name 'Eureka.' It could not have had anything to do with the Eureka Stockade incident, because that did not occur until more than a year after the gang had been defeated.

It consisted of Donovan, Finegan, John Baylie, Charles Bow and Henry Johnston. The rough road from Melbourne to Bendigo was the only track to and from the Bendigo diggings and so there were plenty of opportunities for the gang, although some of their robberies were of remarkably small sums of money.

Their *modus operandi* was for a couple of the gang to bail up a traveller, while the other three sat on their horses in hiding in case they were needed. After the two on the road had held up some unfortunate man, they stripped him naked so that they could search every nook and cranny of his clothing and also, it is said, of his body.

Many of their robberies were fairly paltry affairs. When they bailed up William Cook at Aitken's Gap, on 4 August 1852, they stripped him in the usual way and took a pistol and £2.14.0 from his pockets. Finegan wanted to steal everything but Donovan was in a generous mood, and returned Cook's clothing and all but £1 of the money.

Later that month they robbed Wesley Anderson near Buninyong. Their habit of practising their profession in and around the same part of Victoria soon betrayed them, because the police caught them in the Crown Hotel at Buninyong and Wesley Anderson identified Donovan and Baylie as the men who had bailed him up. Other evidence was soon forthcoming and when the gang was put on trial at Geelong on 23 October 1852 they were all found guilty. Donovan and Finegan, as leaders, received twelve-year sentences and their accomplices were given six years apiece.

Donovan was sent to the hulk *President* on 16 December 1852, and was later transferred to the hulk *Success*. Apart from some fairly minor punishments for misconduct his record shows that he behaved himself fairly well as a prisoner, and he was rewarded by release on Ticket of Leave on 23 October 1858, for the district of Bourke.

But John Donovan could not keep out of trouble for long. On 8 June 1859 he stood once more in the dock of the Geelong Court, on a charge of assault and robbery. He was sentenced to eight years on the roads.

He served six years of this sentence and once more behaved himself fairly well, apart from six charges on such offences as talking, idleness, improper language, leaving work, and improper behaviour. He received his second Ticket of Leave, for the district of Stawell, on 15 August 1856.

Five prison records exist under the name of John Donovan and there are similarities in some of the facts, but the dates seem to show that they apply to other men of the same name. John Donovan appears to have been a reformed character after his second spell of imprisonment.

BLACK DOUGLAS

According to James Flett's book *Dunolly: The story of an old gold diggings,* 'Black' Douglas was a mulatto Indian. Possibly his colouring was the reason for his nickname. If there is any other then it has been lost in the mists of time.

Flett says that Douglas operated during 1855 in the vicinity of Maryborough and St Arnaud, as the leader of a gang of cut-throats, and that he once shot a woman in the face because she refused to give up her purse. His favourite haunt was the area known as the Black Forest. The hillsides of the goldfields region, smothered with thick forests and dense scrub, provided ideal cover for men waiting to pounce on diggers travelling down to Melbourne with their hard-won gold.

By 1855, the whole gold-fields region was so infested with bushrangers, and the small police force was so greatly over-extended in its attempts to deal with them, that many of the diggers took their own precautions. They banded into groups to form their own 'gold escorts' to take their gold down to the city. Apparently Douglas and his men heard about one of these groups and planned an attack on them. They waited until the diggers had made camp before they galloped out of the bush, but met with unexpectedly strong resistance. Douglas and his men killed one digger and wounded three others but they could not make the party surrender. They turned away and made for another group of travelling diggers.

This second group was even better prepared for bushrangers. Each man carried a little of his gold on his person, but most of their nuggets were packed into chamois bags and hidden in four small compartments cut into the wooden axle of the dray which carried their baggage and other gear. They covered the compartments with close-fitting lids and concealed them with clay plastered over the axle.

Apart from taking these precautions the diggers were well armed, and they welcomed Douglas and his men with a volley of shots from pistols and muskets. Foiled once again, the bushrangers retreated into the forest. Next day they raided a roadside inn, but their luck had run out. A party of troopers arrived while the raid was in progress and the bushrangers surrendered. Flett says that Douglas was sentenced to fourteen years, but the records dealing with his trial and imprisonment seem to have disappeared.

JOHN DOUGLAS

Some stories about John Douglas spell his name as 'Douglass,' but the prison records all use the single 's'. He joined forces with William Bryan to roam the road between Ballarat and Geelong, and they may at one time have worked with Arthur Burrowe and William Garroway.

Douglas was twenty-three when he and Bryan were caught at Muddy Creek and convicted in Geelong. Douglas was sent to the main depot on 15 June 1853, and he stayed out of further trouble until he was transferred to the hulk *President* for insubordinate language to a constable.

Born: 1830
Native Place: Scotland
Trade: Carpenter
Religion: Roman Catholic
Height: 5ft 7ins
Complexion: Fresh
Hair: Light brown
Eyes: Light hazel
Particular Marks: Woman and child on right arm (tattoo). Two scars centre of forehead. Scar under lip, small mole right cheek. Fleshy mole right side of neck. Scar inside right wrist. Scar outside right wrist. Several moles on left shoulder. Three fleshy moles on left breast. Boil mark right elbow. Several boil marks on back, hairy mole right calf. Two boil marks outside left calf.
Previous History: Free. John Thomas to Adelaide, 1847. Absconded from Adelaide with James McGrath alias Dobbs. He was known by the name of 'Scotty' Armstrong. Information supplied by prisoner G. Thomas.
Sentence: Five years on the Roads for Robbery from the Person.
Date of Conviction: 21 April 1853. Geelong Circular Court.

After that he was in and out of trouble. He absconded from Pentridge, and he spent time amongst the hardened criminals imprisoned aboard the prison hulks *Success, Sacramento,* and *Lysander.*

For escaping from Pentridge he was given three months hard labour and it seems that this quietened him down. No further punishments were recorded against him and on 26 January 1858 he was released on Ticket of Leave for the district of Gippsland. After that he apparently became a reformed character.

Also see William Bryan

100 AUSTRALIAN BUSHRANGERS 1789-1901

WILLIAM DRISCOLL

Born: not recorded
Native Place: St. Giles, London
Trade: Top Sawyer
Religion: not recorded
Education: not recorded
Age: not recorded
Complexion: Florid
Hair: Light brown
Head: Round
Whiskers: None
Eyes: Blue
Nose: Short
Mouth: Small
Chin: Round
Eyebrows: Light brown
Visage: Square
Forehead: High
Particular Marks/Remarks: (tattoos)- Two pigeons, compasses, rose, shamrock, thistle, M'Connor, fish wreath of laurels, bust of woman on right arm, a full rigged ship on left arm, ring second finger of right hand.
Previous History: Tried at Middlesex, 17 June 1833. Transported for 14 years for Larceny from the Person. Single. Stated this offence, Highway Robbery, Stealing from the Person of a child's book, one handkerchief. Surgeons report: Flogged on board for disorderly conduct very bad. Per Norfolk to Australia, arrived 28 August 1835. Tried again at Hobart Supreme Court, 24 October 1843, Life. Tried again at Launceston Supreme Court, 7 April 1847, Life.
9/5/1836 Absent from Divine Service and Muster... 5 days solitary on bread and water.
15/8/1836 Bathing, thereby endangering himself and making use of most insolent and improper language to his overseer... 7 days solitary confinement.
11/4/1837 Absconding for 2 days... 25 stripes on the breech.
29/9/1838 Violent conduct towards fellow prisoner also striking his overseer...25 stripes on the breech.
14/11/1839 Being illegally at large... 12 months hard labour.
25/11/1839 For misconduct in throwing stones at his overseer... 30 stripes on the breech.
8/4/1844 Absconding... 100 stripes on the breech.
22/1/1845 Idleness... 1 month hard labour in chains.

Driscoll was flogged for bad behaviour aboard the prison ship even before he reached Australia, and he was to suffer a total of 340 lashes as a prisoner. He escaped several times but was always caught and punished again. He was constantly in trouble and became the subject of a great deal of correspondence with the Lieutenant-Governor's office, but it seems that even the most savage conduct would not break William Driscoll.

On 20 February 1855 he made a successful escape with a man named George King, who was described as 'About 5 feet, aged 32, complexion rather dark, hair brown, eyes black, native place Leicester, small scar on forehead.' He was under a life sentence of transportation. At the time of their escape, Driscoll and King had been released from prison and were working as assigned servants: Driscoll for F. Cotton and King for Robert Clerk. Amongst their numerous robberies, the two men bailed-up Robert Clerk at gunpoint nearly opposite Story's Tavern on the Avoca Road.

Driscoll and King, and then Driscoll and another escaped convict named Wilson, were to become notorious. Rewards of £100 apiece were posted for the apprehension of Driscoll and King, plus a conditional pardon for any convict who could claim the reward.

As so often happened, a bushranger's career was brief insofar as Driscoll was concerned. He was caught in bed by the troopers in pursuit of him, and it is said that when they arrested him he fell on his knees begging for forgiveness.

When William Driscoll was brought before the Hobart Supreme Court in January 1856 he made a peculiar confession, stating that although he had been transported under the name of William Driscoll his real name was William Timothy. This made no impression upon the judge and jury and on 22 January he was sentenced to death for assault and robbery.

But the Lieutenant-governor not only commuted this sentence to five years imprisonment in Port Arthur, but said that he should be released on Ticket of Leave if he behaved himself for two years. Driscoll took the hint and was granted a Ticket of Leave on 8 September 1857 and a conditional pardon on 16 February 1858.

53

> Born: 1824
> Native Place: London
> Trade: Stonemason
> Religion: Protestant
> Height: 5ft 6¼ins
> Complexion: Fresh
> Hair: Light brown   Eyes: Grey
> Particular Marks: Two cuts on right cheek, slightly pockpitted, a Mermaid with nine dots on left arm.
> Previous History: Arrived per ship Lord Lyndoch in 1840. Bond on arrival. States he was free on arrival.
> Sentence: Fifteen years on the roads; first three years in irons, for Robbery from the ship Nelson.
> Date of Conviction: 28 May 1852. Melbourne.

James Duncan

James Duncan served his apprenticeship as a bushranger on the Keilor Plains and in the Black Forest region of Victoria, as one of the many who preyed upon the diggers and other people travelling to and from the goldfields. It was there, in the early days of the goldrush, that he became acquainted with James Morgan and John James, alias Johnston, and consequently became involved in the massive gold robbery from the ship *Nelson*. The full story of that exploit is told in John James' biography in this book.

The police dragnet soon rounded up the majority of the *Nelson* gang, which has been variously defined as consisting of between fourteen and twenty-two bushrangers. The surviving records are strangely at variance on this point, and so it is possible either that some of the bushrangers got away or that some of the reports owed more to imagination than accuracy.

Duncan and Morgan were soon arrested while still in bed at the Ocean Child Inn, Williamstown, and on 28 May 1852 the former was sentenced to fifteen years on the roads of the colony, the first three years to be served in irons.

Then aged twenty-eight, he quickly proved himself to be a most reluctant prisoner. For the first six years of his sentence his record shows a constant sequence of offences and punishments: misconduct, insolence, disobedience of orders, disorderly conduct, violent and insubordinate language, striking a warder, abusive, violent, and obscene language, and so on. He endured his first spell of solitary confinement in March 1853 and it was to be followed by many more.

Late in 1858 he must have decided that he was playing a losing game, and decided to keep out of trouble. In December 1859, after a year of unblemished behaviour, his record stated: 'Good conduct and industry. To apply

Melbourne 1855, as seen from the north, near the road to Mt. Alexander. A lithograph by Henry Burn.
(Courtesy La Trobe Collection, State Library of Victoria)

in February next for indulgence.'

His application for 'indulgence,' in February 1860, was successful, and on 27 March of that year he was released on Ticket of Leave to the district of Keilor.

Nothing is known about his life for the next five years. Perhaps he obtained honest employment or perhaps he contrived to make a dishonest living without being apprehended. In any case it is obvious that six years of prison and the hulks had not been enough to convince him that honesty is the best policy. On 15 September 1865 he appeared before Justice Molesworth in the Supreme Court, Melbourne, on a charge of Burglary and Stealing. Molesworth sentenced him to four years hard labour and stipulated that he must serve a minimum period of three years and ten months.

In June 1866 he was caught during an attempt to escape and given six months in irons, which quietened him down for a little while. He was in and out of trouble during the rest of his sentence and experienced further spells of solitary confinement, but despite this misbehaviour and Justice Molesworth's stipulation he was set free on 3 February 1870.

One would think that two such spells of imprisonment would be enough for any man, but Duncan apparently was set in his ways. Almost immediately after his release he stole a cheap pair of blucher boots from outside a shoe store, and on 17 February 1870 he was back inside again on month's sentence for larceny.

Perhaps he thought he had got away so lightly that he would try it on again. On 16 May 1870 he was once more in court, this time before the Chief Justice in the Melbourne Supreme Court. He had burgled a jeweller's shop in Bourke Street, near the Theatre Royal. The sentence was ten years on the roads, although his record also bears the statement '9 years 9 months & 20 days.'

On 7 June 1870 he was transferred from Melbourne Gaol into Pentridge to serve out this sentence. He was forty-six and had by that time spent a substantial portion of his life in gaol. Perhaps he was at last reconciled to the idea that he must endure the harsh and primitive conditions of nineteenth century imprisonment and that he could not 'beat the system.' During the next five years, until January 1875, he was only twice in trouble with the authorities: once for having a pipe and once for giving tobacco to a fellow prisoner.

James Duncan's prison record has suffered from water damage and so it is impossible to read any entries after January 1875. Perhaps his good behaviour would have resulted in a recommendation for a Ticket of Leave, but it was James Duncan's fate to end his life in gaol. The last official record of his life is that of the inquest held after his death on 16 December 1875, showing that he had died from 'Abscess on the liver.'

Also see John James, James Morgan

STAND AND DELIVER

JOHN DUNN

Young Johnny Dunn was yet another of the tearaway boys of the bush who could have lived out a contented life if he had not been seduced by the false glamour of bushranging. In his case, it was his fate to live at the time, and in the place, of Ben Hall's bushranging adventures.

Johnny was one of nine children of Mick and Maggie Dunn, and he was born on the leased run of Cumbermurra, to the north of Yass, on 14 December 1846. He began work in his early teens as a stableboy, groom, and occasional jockey on various stations in the district. He became a noted rider and won many races at bush meetings, including the main event at the Yass races in 1864. He rode the Binnalong bred horse *Ringleader* to victory.

In October 1864, when he was only seventeen years and nine months old, he worked irregularly with Ben Hall, John Gilbert, Frank Gardiner, and other notorious 'gentlemen of the road'. Young Johnny was not entirely innocent of crime. He and a mate, Jerry Ryan, had already bailed up a Chinese man on the road near Burrows. They were too well known in the district to get away with this minor piece of bushranging, but for the same reason they were granted bail. On the date of their trial Johnny failed to appear and a bench warrant was issued for his arrest.

So young John Dunn was already a marked man when he enlisted with more experienced bushrangers, and joined them in exploits of the type mentioned under their names in this book. Johnny, unfortunately, seemed to feel that he must show himself as tough and ruthless as the other men, and this characteristic led him to commit the most serious crime of all.

On 26 January 1865, he was with Hall and Gilbert when they moved into the township of Collector to hold up Kimberley's Inn. Hall and Gilbert went into the inn while John Dunn remained on guard outside.

Someone ran to tell Constable Nelson, the only policeman in town, about the holdup. Nelson, a married man of thirty-eight with eight children, his wife, Elizabeth, three months pregnant, promptly loaded his carbine and hurried from the police station to the inn.

Dunn, who was armed with a shotgun and a revolver, was standing on the verandah of the inn. When he saw Nelson coming he dodged behind a paling fence, aimed his shotgun, and fired.

The shotgun blast hit Nelson in the stomach and brought him down, and young Johnny finished the job by firing two revolver shots. These hit Nelson in the face and he died immediately.

Apparently the murderous youth thought that this killing was the final passport into the bushranging

> No. 53 John Dunn
> Country: New South Wales
> Age: 22 years
> (actually born 14/12/1846)
> Former Calling: Stockman
> Religion: Roman Catholic
> Particulars: Mate of Gilbert, Hall
>
> No. 15, 1866 John Dunn Arrival:
> Born in colony
> Bond or Free: Free
> Native Place: Young
> Religion: Catholic
> Trade: Labourer
> Admitted: 19 January 1866. Dubbo.
> Disposed of: Forwarded on escort to Sydney 1/2/1866.
> Crime: Murder

fraternity, because he bragged of it to Hall and Gilbert when the shots brought them running out of the inn. They were less than enthusiastic about the exploit, especially when a notice in the *Government Gazette* of April 1865 linked their names with Dunn's as murderers of Nelson and called on the trio to surrender themselves at Goulburn Gaol on or before 29 April 1865. When they failed to do so they were proclaimed as outlaws.

The year 1865 was a disaster for Ben Hall's gang. Hall and Gilbert would die before it ended and the police would destroy the bushranging nuisance of the region. John Dunn, wounded in the arm in the fight which killed Gilbert, still escaped from the scene, made his way to a station where he demanded food, medical attention, and a horse. After that he was on the run for eight months, picking up a living as a horse-breaker but moving on all the time. The police had not forgotten him and they finally tracked him down on Christmas Eve 1865. In the shootout he was wounded in the foot and by a bullet which entered the lumbar region of the back and paralysed the sciatic nerve.

This caused persistent excruciating pain, but even after he had been locked in Dubbo Gaol he managed to escape on 14 January 1866. He was recaptured on the following afternoon and taken down to Bathurst and then to Sydney, where he was lodged in Darlinghurst Gaol.

On 19 February he appeared in the Central Criminal Court. The verdict was a foregone conclusion and he was sentenced to death. It is difficult to understand why, as a proclaimed outlaw, he had not used his eight months of freedom to get far away from the district where he was so well known, but the records show that he may even have attempted another holdup three days before his capture. On 22 December 1855 a bushranger robbed Blackett's store at Wanbandry, sixty miles from Dubbo, and the victims believed that the robber was John Dunn.

On 19 March 1866, about sixty people witnessed John Dunn's execution. Attended by the Reverends McCarthy and Dwyer, he was led pinioned to the gallows and the white hood drawn over his face. The executioner pulled the lever and young Johnny Dunn dropped through the trap to his death. His body was left hanging for ten minutes. His godmother, Mrs Pickard, was the only mourner present when his body was buried in the Devonshire Street Cemetery. The land was however, reclaimed to build Central Station, so all remains were dug up and reinterred in the Botany Cemetery.

Also see John Gilbert, Ben Hall

PATRICK DUNNE

*P*atrick Dunne was for a short period a member of Matthew Brady's gang, but he did not establish his own vile reputation until he had struck out on his own.

The trouble with Dunne was that he was not content simply with robbing his victims. He delighted in hurting people. When he decided that he wanted a woman, he tried to take one from her Aboriginal husband. The latter objected and so Dunne killed him with a musket shot, but the woman refused to leave the body of her husband. Dunne decided that the answer to this problem was to take the dead man with them, and so cut the head off the corpse, pierced this ghastly relic with a string, and hung it around the woman's neck.

During his brief career in the year 1826 the savagery of his assaults on his victims made him the terror of Tasmania and the subject of hot pursuit. When the troopers caught up with him, and he was committed for trial on 9 November 1826, the charge was 'Cutting and maiming George Bowd and Joseph Price.'

On 13 November he was sentenced to death for this offence, and on the following day brought before the court once more. This time it was for 'Stealing in the dwelling house of W. de Gillern at the Coal River in January last.' He had stolen a silver watch, valued at £5 and other articles.

For this offence he received a second sentence of death. But a man can only die once, and the monstrous Patrick Dunne was hanged on 8 January 1827.

GEORGE ELLISON

*W*hen John Atkins walked up to the bar of the Cross Keys Hotel in Melbourne, he was unfortunate enough to stand beside George Ellison. Ellison asked him what he had done with the gold he had brought from the diggings, and called him a liar when he claimed that he had not any. Ellison said that the colour of his moleskin trousers, stained with dirt and clay like those of all diggers, showed he had come down from the goldfields and so he must have gold with him.

The argument became heated and the landlord ordered Atkins out of the hotel. Ellison and another man followed him, knocked him down and stole the gold which he was in fact carrying on his person.

Atkins quickly reported the assault and theft and the police soon caught up with Ellison, who was sent to the hulk *President* on 4 July 1853 and later moved to the *Success*. Obviously he was an inveterate smoker, because he was punished again and again for having a pipe and tobacco in his possession, and for other minor offences. On 2 March 1858 he was released on Ticket of Leave to the district of The Ovens.

One would think that freedom would have tasted sweet to George Ellison, after a spell in the hulks, but a year or so later he was in trouble again. On 25 May 1859 he was brought before the Beechworth court on a charge of stealing from the person and sentenced to twelve months on the roads.

Released a year later, on Ticket of Leave to Beechworth, he was soon charged again. This time it was for breaching the Ticket of Leave regulations, and he was sent back to prison to serve out the remainder of the sentence he had received for robbing John Atkins.

He was released again, on Ticket of Leave for the district of Carisbrooke, on 28 May 1861, and it would seem that after that he mended his ways.

> *Born:* 1823
> *Native Place:* Birmingham
> *Trade:* Nailmaker
> *Religion:* Protestant
> *Height:* 5ft 8ins
> *Complexion:* Fresh
> *Hair:* Light brown
> *Eyes:* Hazel
> *Particular Marks:* Scar on right cheek. 'W' on right arm.
> *Previous History:* Arrived per ship Canton 1839. Bond. Lady Lyndoch to Van Diemen's Land 1840 10 years. name George Allison, per Yarra Yarra to Victoria 1852. Brother James, and sister Louisa Allison in the colony, residence unknown. Tried May 1859 as George Allan.
> *Sentence:* Ten years on the Roads, first year in Irons for Assault and Robbery
> *Date of Conviction:* 10 February 1853. Supreme Court, Melbourne.

STAND AND DELIVER

Christopher FARRELL

Christopher Farrell and Owen Suffolk, whose story is told separately in this book, were two of the most turbulent characters of Australia's early criminal history. Their stories have been touched on by other bushranging historians but could not be fully told until recent research unearthed their prison records.

Farrell arrived in 1848 and got himself into trouble very quickly. On 16 November 1848 he appeared before the Melbourne court for 'Robbery from a hut,' and was sentenced to three years hard labour. Obviously Farrell was determined to serve his time the hard way. On 17 February 1849 he received fourteen days in the cells for fighting, and later in the year he was given three months in irons for seriously injuring a constable with a blow from a stone. He did not profit from this lesson and in February 1850 he received twenty-one days in the cells for gambling and being absent from muster. Further charges followed, for insolence and fighting, but nevertheless he was released on Ticket of Leave on 1 March 1851.

But his freedom was shortlived. Only four days later his ticket was cancelled for some unstated reason and he was returned to the Pentridge Stockade, where he remained until he was set free on 15 April 1851.

It is almost certain that he met Owen Suffolk during his time in prison. Suffolk was convicted for horsestealing in December 1848, and both prisoners were sent to Cockatoo Island, Sydney. Probably they planned a future criminal career and joined together as soon as they were both at liberty, because they carried out a classic bushranging operation less than six weeks after Farrell's release.

On 23 May 1851 (not 23 June as Boxall records) the two men bailed up the mail coach between Portland and Geelong at Bruce's Creek. The full story of the exploit is told in Suffolk's biography in this book. They robbed the mail and passengers and made a successful getaway, but the much maligned police did not take long to catch up with them. Some records state that they were caught within forty-eight hours of the robbery. Suffolk was arrested while strolling along the beach near the Geelong wharf, and Farrell was found in a boarding-house not far away. The exact length of time that it took the police to catch up with the bushrangers is not known, but they appeared before the Geelong court on 20 June and so it could not have been long.

Each man was sentenced to ten years on the roads of the colony for Highway Robbery with Arms, and received in the Pentridge Stockade on 7 August 1851. Almost immediately, they displayed their attitude towards imprisonment by refusing to work on 13 August, and had two months added to their sentences. This made no impression on Farrell, who escaped and was recaptured on 29 August and received 100 lashes.

The gaolers may have thought that this savage punishment had broken Farrell's spirit. He kept out of trouble until May 1854, when his violent and rebellious nature once more asserted itself. From then onwards his record carries a series of punishments for various infringements of the regulations: 'Insolence and the use of profane language, tearing his blankets, telling a falsehood, idleness and insolence, looking over a cell door', and 'attempting to set all authority at defiance.' His punishments ranged from a caution to spells of solitary confinement on bread and water, and he spent a great deal of his prison time in irons. He served his sentence in Pentridge Stockade, the Melbourne Gaol, and aboard various prison hulks.

Farrell was close to the murder site when the convicts killed Inspector General John Price and it is perhaps a miracle that he was not involved in the murder. In the book *The Life and Death of John Price*, J. V. Barry writes 'At muster two prisoners, King and Farrell, were missing, and were later found in a cunningly concealed excavation not far from the scene of the "rush". Despite later suggestions that their attempt to escape was connected with the plot to murder Price, it is clear that it has nothing to do with the spontaneous assault on Price and the officials, for the two men had gone into hiding before Price arrived.

In June 1857 the Medical Officer ordered Farrell's leg irons to be removed and he almost immediately attempted to escape. An addition of two years hard labour to his sentence did not stop him from assaulting another prisoner in December, and drawing twenty days in solitary confinement.

The fact that he had not joined in Price's murder was seen as being in his favour, and he was eventually released on Ticket of Leave on 19 April 1859. But, by this time, he seems to have been a complete delinquent.

The prison records covering the rest of his criminal career are often brittle and faded with time, and almost illegible, but it is possible to trace a sad and violent story. He was soon back in Pentridge again, having been sentenced at Kilmore, on 26 October 1859, for Robbery in Company. The records between 1860 and 1865 carry thirty-two notations of his prison offences and the resultant punishments, but on 19 September 1865 he once more smelt the fresh air of freedom with a Ticket of Leave for the McIvor district.

A concise note dated 2 April 1866 states 'Illegally at large. Recommend that Ticket of Leave be cancelled,' and on 8 May 1866 the gates of Pentridge opened once more to admit Christopher Farrell. After that it was the same dreary story of offences and punishment until he was released again in December 1868.

After that he either behaved himself for nearly twenty years, or had become so skilful a criminal that the police did not catch him. There is a long gap in the records until 13 October 1887, when he was brought before Fitzroy Petty Sessions for being 'In possession of housebreaking implements.' Four days later he was brought before Mr Justice Hobroyd, in the Melbourne Supreme Court, for 'Shooting with intent to do grievous bodily harm.'

This brought a sentence of twelve years penal servitude, which may have seemed like a deathblow to Farrell. He was then in his fifties, after a life of almost continuous hardship.

But his spirit was not broken yet. He went to Melbourne Gaol, thence to Pentridge, and was transferred to Geelong Gaol on 6 July 1889. On 8 October 1889 he made a last desperate escape, and was free for eight days before he was recaptured. The authorities added another two years of hard labour to his sentence.

He was never to be free again. He was returned to Geelong Gaol and he died there on 30 August 1895. The inquest papers give the cause of death as 'pneumonia and debility.'

Also see Owen Suffolk

No.267

Born: 1827
Native Place: London, Liverpool
Trade: Printer/Mason
Religion: Roman Catholic (from N.S.W. record)
Height: 5ft 7ins/5ft 8ins
Complexion: Fresh
Hair: Light hazel
Eyes: Brown
Particular Marks: Scar on front part of right arm above the elbow.
Previous History: Arrived at Port Phillip per ship Marion an exile from Pentonville Prison, in 1848. An exile from Parkhurst under sentence of 10 years.
Sentence: (First) Three years Hard Labour on the Roads of the Colony, for Robbery from a hut.
Date of Conviction: 16 November 1848, at Melbourne (Details combined from two records)

John Finnegan

John Finnegan is supposed to have been the leader of the Eureka Gang, of which the story is told in the biography of John Donovan in this book.

The Eureka Gang ended its brief career when its members were caught in the Crown Hotel at Buninyong. Wesley Anderson identified Baylie and Donovan as the men who had bailed him up on a Sunday in August 1852, and the police soon found other witnesses to identify the rest of the gang.

However there is a possibility that they were blamed for some crimes which they had not committed. When the jury had returned a verdict of guilty against the five members of the gang, and the judge asked whether they had anything to say before he passed sentence upon them, one exclaimed 'Do you think we are crows? . . . Here's one man says we stuck him up at Aitken's Gap, another at the Porcupine, another near Mount Egerton, and others at other places, and the police says they caught us in the Crown Hotel, Buninyong. Why, your Honour, horses couldn't get over the ground in the time.'

But the judge was not impressed by his pleas and he sentenced Finegan and Donovan to twelve years imprisonment, the first two to be served in irons, while Baylis, Johnston, and Bow received six years apiece.

By December 1852, John Finegan was beginning to sweat out his time aboard the hulk *President*. He kept out of trouble to begin with, although for some reason he was transferred first to the hulk *Success* and then to the *Sacramento* during 1853. His first prison offence was on 31 December 1853, when he was given thirty days in solitary for tampering with his irons and other misconduct, and he drew another five days solitary confinement in February 1854 for using obscene language.

In February 1855 his irons were removed but he was placed in 'lighter chains,' and he stayed in these until 14 July 1856. He wore them until May 1857, but they did not prevent him from having four more brushes with the authorities. Two of these resulted only in reprimands, but the other acts of misconduct were bad enough — at least in the eyes of his gaolers — to earn him a total of sixty more days in solitary confinement.

On 4 December 1858, after six years of his twelve year sentence, he was told that he would be granted a Ticket of Leave, and he was released ten days later.

His Ticket of Leave stipulated that he must live in the district of Geelong, but he soon ignored this and went up to Ballarat. Only two months after his release, on February 1859, he was charged with 'Stealing from a Dwelling' in Ballarat, and returned to prison to serve another eighteen months.

Apparently this second lesson taught him the error of his ways. He behaved himself well and in July 1860 he was granted a second Ticket of Leave. Released on 14 August 1860, he did not appear again on the criminal records of Victoria.

Also see John Donovan

Born: 1832
Native Place: Dublin
Trade: Bootmaker
Religion: Roman Catholic
Height: 5ft 2¼ins
Complexion: Fresh
Hair: Light brown
Eyes: Grey
Particular Marks: 'VFt' on right arm, some blue marks on left arm.
Previous History: Arrived per ship Adelaide in 1848. To Adelaide, free. To Victoria per Flash in 1852 - proper name Jn. Finnegan.
Sentence: Twelve years on the Roads of the Colony, first two years in Irons, for Highway Robbery.
Date of Conviction: 23 October 1852, at Geelong Court.

■ *Crown Hotel Bunninyong, 1862, centre of photo.*
(Courtesy Bunninyong Historical Society)

By His Excellency CHARLES JOSEPH LA TROBE, *Esquire, Lieutenant Governor of the Colony of Victoria and its Dependencies.*

TO ALL TO WHOM THESE PRESENTS SHALL COME:

KNOW YE that I, the Lieutenant Governor aforesaid, in pursuance of the power and authority in me vested, do hereby direct the removal from *the Hulk "Success" in Hobsons Bay* of the undermentioned Prisoners confined therein to *the Hulk "Sacramento" off Geelong* there to be kept for the residue of their sentence, or until removed by legal authority.

NO.	NAME.	SENTENCE.	DATE OF CONVICTION.
503	William Carr	Twelve years 1st 2 in Irons	10th December 1852
511	Cornelius Gilbert	Ten years 1st in Irons	9th Do
365	Amos French	Three years, extended 3 mos	18th September 1852
269	James Katon (alias Caton)	Ten years	26th June 1852
454	John Finnegan	Twelve years 1st 2 Irons	23rd October "
168	Felix Daley	Twelve years 1st 3 in Irons	19th March "
153	Francis Coffey	Ten years 1st 3 in Irons	16 February "
640	John Fagan (alias Fulton)	Three years in Irons	23rd March 1853
383	William Jones (2)	12 years 1st 2 in Irons	21st September 1852
679	John Dyson (alias Thomas)	Seven years	18th April 1853
599	James Baker	Three years in Irons extended 3 months	3rd March 1853
151	William Wilson	10 years. 1st 3 in Irons	16 February 1852
694	William Garroway	10 years 1 year in Irons	26th April 1853
352	Alfred Jones	10 years 1st two in Irons	21st August 1852
484	William Thomas (2)	10 years	16th December 1852
612	John Burns	Eight years	17th March 1853
608	John Johnson	Eight years	15th March 1853
671	William Potts	7 years 1st in Irons	16th April 1853
574	Francis Clarke	10 years 1st in Irons	10 February "
699	Nalley Smith	7 years	27th April "
580	John Greenhall	10 — 1st in Irons	10 February "
659	John Davis '5'	7 —	12 April 1853
695	Arthur Burrows	10 — 1st in Irons	26 " "
652	Daniel McGowan	7 —	26 March "
814	John Martin	two years Hard Labn	19 May "
182	Thomas Haines	10 years 1st 3 in Irons	21st April 1852
255	William Hatfield	10 —	28 May "
707	Charles Sullivan	8 —	19 March 1853
542	William Jones (4)	10 — 1st in Irons	10 February "
183	William Johnson	12 — 1st 2 in Irons	21 April 1852
494	James Haddon	10 —	16 December "
399	Edward Wilson	10 —	18 October "
280	Charles Halliday	10 —	28 May "
696	John Reilly	7 —	27 April 1853
396	John Chesley	10 — 1st in Irons	16 October 1852
508	George Thomas	12 — 1st in Irons	9 December "
171	Henry Brookes	10 — 1st 2 in Irons	19 March "
545	Michael Farrell	5 years and 5 years	11 & 12 February 1853
653	William Smith 5	8 —	26 March 1853
681	George Allison	10 —	18 April "

GIVEN under my Hand, at the Government Offices, Melbourne, Victoria, this day of *October* in the year of our Lord 1853.

■ An original 'removal' document dated October 1853. List includes convicted bushrangers Finegan, Garroway, Clarke (Gardiner) and Burrowes.
(Private Collection)

Lieutenant Governor.

John FLANIGAN

> **Born:** 1827
> **Native Place:** Dublin
> **Trade:** Sailor
> **Religion:** Roman Catholic
> **Height:** 5ft 3½ins
> **Complexion:** Fresh
> **Hair:** Brown
> **Eyes:** Blue
> **Particular Marks:** Scar under right eye.
> **Previous History:** Arrived per ship Richard Webb 1842, to Van Diemen's Land. Bond. 7 years, same name. Brother of John Gibney. Proper name Owen Gibney. To Victoria per City of Melbourne 1851.
> **Sentence:** (First charge) ... 12 years Hard Labour, 1st two years in Irons, for Highway Robbery. (Second charge) ... 6 years on the Roads, to commence from expiration of first sentence. Highway Robbery. (Third charge) ... 12 years on the Roads, 1st two years in Irons, to date from termination of last sentence. Highway Robbery.
> **Date of Conviction:** 18 November 1852.

John Flanigan and his mate Thomas Williams, who is also described in this book, have received comparatively little attention from bushranging historians although their exploits earned each of them a sentence of thirty years imprisonment. Charles White, in his *History of Australian Bushrangers,* gives what is probably the best coverage of the two men. He uses the spelling Flanagan, whereas the newspaper reports of the period used the forms Flannagan and Flanaghan and the prison records spelt it as Flanigan. In any case the bushranger's real name was Owen Gibney, and the various spellings seem almost characteristic of all the confusions about names related to the case in which he was involved.

Flanigan and Williams were ex-convicts from Van Diemen's Land, who crossed to the mainland with many others of their ilk in search of a better living than they could pick up on the island. Some joined the goldrushes, some became itinerant workers, and others took the seemingly easy way to fortune by becoming bushrangers.

By October 1852, bushrangers were becoming a constant menace on all the approaches to Melbourne and were even working as close to the city as the St Kilda Road. On 16 October, a well-organised gang carried out a swift campaign against travellers along the road. Their method was to bail up anyone who seemed to be worth robbing, take him or her into the bush to be tied up with other unfortunates and left under guard of a couple of the gang, and return to the road in search of new victims.

A typical example was that of William Keel and William Robinson, who were driving peacefully along the road when they saw two armed men looking up into the trees as though they were bird-shooting. But when the travellers approached the two men 'presented their muskets and called out "Keep still, or we will blow your brains out." '

The bushrangers robbed Keel and Robinson of £69 and tied them up together with other men and women including Mr and Mrs Bawtree, Mr Larman, Mr Striker, and other 'well-known and wealthy colonists.' But one man, Moody, evaded the bushrangers and the shots they fired after him, and escaped to warn the police. The bushrangers, who had subjected the Bawtrees and others to 'the rudest treatment' and 'the most abominable language,' decided it was time to go.

A few days later, the police arrested two men called Pritchard and John Williams. Pritchard was carrying 'a most splendid and massive gold chain . . . at first supposed to have belonged to Mrs Bawtree, but that has since been ascertained not to be the case.'

On 22 October, the *Argus* reported on a second sighting of the bushrangers, by two unarmed policemen near Bacchus Marsh. The bushrangers were 'armed with double-barrelled guns, and had been robbing people in all directions . . . Twelve armed and mounted men are now on their track, and they will probably be taken. There are about six altogether, of whom four are known. Their names are Carey, Hewlett, Frazer, and Jones . . .'

BUSHRANGERS ON ST. KILDA ROAD

■ *Reports from* The Argus *newspaper of October 1852 are illustrated below. An eyewitness account of 'The St. Kilda Road Incident' is retold here, alongside some frank editorial criticism of the quality of the Victorian Police, and the efficacy of their investigative techniques.*

The Argus.

MELBOURNE : VICTORIA, MONDAY, OCTOBER 18, 1852

18/10/1852

BUSHRANGERS ON THE ST. KILDA ROAD.—On Saturday night information was given at the Police Station, that four mounted and armed bushrangers were committing the most daring depredations on the St. Kilda and Brighton road. About five o'clock in the evening, Mr and Mrs Bawtree were stopped, bailed up, and robbed, and upwards of fifteen other persons were also stopped that evening by the same gang.

19/10/1852

OUTRAGES ON THE BRIGHTON ROAD. So little heed is now taken of the attacks upon person and property, of the more ordinary kind, that it is seldom that we give reports of them, admission to our columns. Mere "sticking up" in the streets, the occasional choking of a passenger into insensibility, robbing him, or knocking him about the head, simple breaking into a store or house, or even ordinary bushranging, have lost the zest of novelty to the newspaper reader, and have become so tiresome from repetition, that they cease to have any particular claims to the attention of the reporter.

The outrage committed on Saturday however, to which we briefly alluded yesterday, was of so unusually audacious a character, even in Victoria, and was so strikingly illustrative of the lawless condition to which we are tamely submitting, in allowing ourselves to be betrayed, that it perhaps deserves rather fuller treatment than ordinary. We have the report personally from some of the actual sufferers.

On Saturday afternoon then, *about half-past three o'clock of a fine bright sunny day* two industrious residents of Brighton,—William Keel and William Robinson,—were driving in a cart along the high road leading past the St Kilda Race-course towards the special survey. Two men were walking before them at a little distance.

On a sudden they found themselves surrounded, guns were placed at each of their heads, and at that of the horse; and they were ordered to descend. The attack was so outrageous, that they thought it was a joke; but as they were addressed in the most abusive language, and told that their brains would be blown out if they delayed, they got out of the cart and submitted to be rifled—the one of £23, the other of about £46. The robbers, whose horses were hung up to trees in the neighbourhood, and who were entirely without disguise, then ordered them to proceed with their cart in o an adjacent wattle scrub; a hempen halter was cut into shreds, and they were tied hand to hand with a strand, and ordered to sit down on the ground; two men with double-barrelled guns keeping guard over them. In a few minutes, the two men whom they had previously seen on the road were brought in, robbed, and also tied and made to sit down. A watch was then kept up and down the road, *and every individual who came up on foot, or horseback, or in a vehicle, for two hours and a half, was stopped, and robbed,* amongst them being Mr and Mrs Bawtree, Mr Larman, of Brighton, Mr Striker, returning from his duties as a juror, a Mr Chambers, in the employment of Mr Powell, ironmonger, of Collins-street, and nearly twenty others. From Mr Bawtree's narrative of what took place, it appears that about half-past four o'clock he and Mrs Bawtree were proceeding from Little Brighton to St Kilda, and were within a mile and a half of the latter place, when two armed bushrangers on foot suddenly came upon them, presenting firearms at them, at the same time ordering them to drive off the road into the bush. After proceeding a little distance, one of the villains became very abusive, using the most blasphemous and violent language, and raising his gun drove the stock into the panel of the gig, threatening to blow their brains out if any resistance were offered. At Mr Bawtree's request that such language and violence should not be used in the presence of his lady, the violent conduct was continued, until they were both ordered to alight from the gig, which was immediately ransacked, and a valuable double-barrelled gun, made by Howe, of Colchester, with powder-flask, taken therefrom. They then searched Mr Bawtree, but obtained neither money nor valuables of any kind. On Mr Bawtree's requesting that his wife should be exempted from a similar indignity, they replied with the grossest language, and therefore Mrs Bawtree was compelled to submit. They were again ordered into their gig, and led to a spot where eight other individuals were tied together. They got out of their vehicle, when Mr Bawtree was tied with a rope to Mr Chambers. A man was placed over the captives, with strict orders to fire upon them, if a hand were stirred. The ringleader then exclaimed, "Put them altogether, so that if you miss miss one you will kill another." In this position they remained for above an hour and a half, during which time seven others were brought and secured in like manner. At sundown the bushrangers drew off the man acting as guard, and shortly afterwards the sound of horses' feet was heard galloping off through the bush, apparently in the direction of South Yarra. They then liberated themselves, and proceeded to their residences.

20/10/1852

DOMESTIC INTELLIGENCE.

THE SUPERINTENDENT OF POLICE.—A charge has been brought against us of misrepresenting the efforts of the superintendent of police in the pursuit of the Brighton bushrangers, in hinting that he confined himself to a daylight ride to St Kilda and back, whereas, in reality, Mr Sturt was out nearly the whole night. We did not intend our statement to be taken literally, and did not suppose that any one would have so read it. It was intended as a hint of the sort of system by which the rampant crime of this community is trifled with, and in reality encouraged. Whatever may have been the efforts of Mr Sturt in this particular case, to his general mismanagement of the police is attributable a very large majority of the outrages which are prevailing. We have no personal feeling against this gentleman, whom we believe to be a well-intentioned man in the main, but it is time to speak out, when, while assured on all sides that "there is no crime," we find a score of people tied together in a scrub, on a main line of road, within five miles of the metropolis. It is time to speak out, we repeat, and in so speaking, we say that the manner in which Mr Sturt has allowed the whole police system of the Colony to crumble away into perfect disorganisation and inefficiency, in trying times like these, is eternally disgraceful to his character, and completely conclusive as to his incompetency for the office he holds. To say that there is no getting together, and keeping together, an efficient police-force, is a piece of contemptible nonsense. If men are properly paid, and properly treated, almost any number, for almost any purpose, can be retained. But while the head is wrong, the members are not likely to be very vigorous, and with Mr Sturt for a superintendent, no wonder that the private constable is not a model of efficiency and zeal. And here, we presume, we shall be met with the old cry — Where are we to look for a better? To which strengthen our ranks by the infusion of fresh blood. We furnish a specimen or two of what we mean, and commend the example to the consideration of those whom it principally concerns.

WANTED, a Superintendent of Police. Apply to the Colonial Secretary.

WANTED, a Colonial Secretary. Apply to the Lieutenant Governor.

WANTED, a Governor. Apply to the people of Victoria.

STAND AND DELIVER

■ *Bushrangers, Victoria Australia 1852. An oil on canvas painted by William Strutt in London in 1887.*
(Courtesy the University of Melbourne Art Collection. Gift of Estate of Sir Russell and Lady Grimwade, 1973)

WILLIAM STRUTT (1825-1915) was born in Devon, England. His father and grandfather were also artists. For health reasons he left England to come to Australia and arrived in Melbourne in July 1850, aged 25 years.

His talents as an artist soon saw him in employment, publishing engravings for the first issue of the 'Illustrated Australian Magazine'.

He designed, engraved or lithographed postage stamps, posters, maps, transparencies or seals and began to learn all about the history of the colony. His friend and patron J.P. Fawkner encouraged him to record important events in the following years.

He sketched many important historical occasions, and received commissions to carry out portraits in oil.

He was living in Brighton, near the St. Kilda Rd. when bushrangers carried out the robbery described on these pages. He would produce lively sketches of the event — 'on the spot' — and later — many years later — would complete the magnificent oil painting 'Bushrangers on the St. Kilda Road'.

William Strutt left Melbourne for the goldfields in February 1852, the hottest part of the year. He would spend a brief time on the Ballarat goldfields where he worked a claim, but failed to find gold in any real quantity.

He soon returned to Melbourne with drawings of the goldfields, and he returned to his old trade and produced lithographs.

He married, and in 1853 he published a book in London about his goldfield experience.

100 AUSTRALIAN BUSHRANGERS 1789-1901

His art recorded historic detail of events of the time — but his heart belonged elsewhere.

He spent a year as a farmer in New Zealand with his wife and daughter, but after the venture failed, he moved back to Melbourne.

He travelled to England, then visited and painted in North Africa and finally, he settled back in England. From 1865 to 1893 he exhibited twenty-three times at the Royal Academy, and twenty-seven times at Suffolk Street London.

At 89, William Strutt, one of Victoria's earliest and most celebrated artists, died at his home in Sussex on 3 January 1915. He left an artist son and three daughters.

It has been said frequently that he was a 'melancholy artist, his work suggests conflict'. It is not so much the violence of the incident that Strutt has painted, but his oil painting reflects his idea of the reactions of the participants.

Bernard Smith in 'Australian Artists' accurately summed up Strutt's painting '... We are presented with a quiet moment at the height of the outrage when the victims are all safely trussed up and the bushrangers are dividing the booty. The prisoners reveal the most varied emotions: fear, defiant disgust, despair, resignation, one handsome young man even seems to be calculating the possibilities of escape. The painting is an admirable social document of the time, revealing the varied types and costumes to be found on the Victorian high road. During the height of the goldrushes, for Strutt... was painstakingly accurate in the rendering of that detail... (Strutt) was not seeking merely to record an incident... he was seeking subjects that would typify Australian Colonial life as a whole'.

William Strutt's 'on the spot' sketches of the bushranging incident, were combined with his interviewing eye-witnesses at the time.

Apparently the two men unnamed in this report were Flanigan and Williams. Their robberies had included the holdup of four diggers at Aitken's Gap.

The Melbourne police, already wise in the ways of bushrangers, began to expect their return to Melbourne to enjoy the spending of their booty. Soon after midnight one night, a party of police met two horsemen in Flinders Lane — 'a suspicious circumstance at such an hour in that locality' — and stopped them both for questioning. Their answers were evasive and the police did not hesitate to 'hurl them from their saddles, and in an instant they were handcuffed and secured.'

A search found £55 in sovereigns and notes, a nugget, a bundle of clothes and a pair of fowls, all in the possession of Thomas Williams. The detective's report said that 'the unlucky rascals had probably anticipated making a comfortable supper, but [the fowls] were destined to feed a more honest man.'

John Flanigan was carrying £47, and each man was armed with a pair of loaded pistols. The money and the weapons gave the magistrate sufficient cause to commit Williams and Flanigan to trial, and the police soon found witnesses to identify them. At the trial, a digger named Anthony Waring testified 'On the 19th October I was at Aitken's Gap; heard a shot, and turning round saw four men galloping towards me: cried "Hallo! Here are the bushrangers!" Williams led the troop, and said, "Keep still, or I'll shoot you." Flannagan was also there. One of the party jumped off his horse and searched all our party. From me he took three sovereigns, when they had concluded the search they took from my bag a pistol, marked on the stock A.W.'

Flanigan had been carrying this pistol when he was arrested, and it was offered in evidence. Edward Waring, presumably Anthony's brother, supported his testimony, and another digger, Saunders, also testified against Williams and Flanigan.

The police were not yet finished with the two men. They brought further witnesses, including men named

Colonial Secretary's Office,
Melbourne, 19th October, 1852.
£200 REWARD.
INFORMATION having been received to the effect that several persons were waylaid and robbed on the road between St. Kilda and Little Brighton on the afternoon of Saturday, the 16th instant, by five armed Bushrangers, His Excellency the Lieutenant-Governor has been pleased to direct that a Reward of £200 be paid for each of the offenders apprehended in any country, and that the Reward be doubled on the apprehension of all.

Further information may be obtained at the office of the Superintendent of Police, Melbourne,

By His Excellency's Command,
W. LONSDALE.

Thomas Newton, Farmer, and McGrath, to testify that Flanigan and Williams had been among the bushrangers on the St Kilda Road on 15 and/or 16 October.

Both men received a thirty-year sentence and Flanigan proved an unruly prisoner. He spent time on the hulks *Sacramento, Lysander,* and *President,* and his record shows an almost endless string of offences: insolence, disobedience, misconduct, threatening language, abusive language, improper behaviour, striking the Chief Warden, having a piece of tin in his cell, being noisy and disobedient, talking on deck, idleness, having tobacco, smoking, having bread, and so on and on. Perhaps he felt that this kind of running warfare against the authorities, who responded by giving him spells of solitary confinement on bread and water ranging from two to thirty days in length, was the only way to preserve his personality under the inhuman conditions of prison life.

In April 1857 he saw his old mate Williams again. Williams had been concerned in the murder of Inspector-general John Price, and Flanigan was transferred to the Melbourne Gaol to act as a witness in the trial of the murderers.

In 1860 he petitioned the Colonial Secretary 'praying for mitigation of his sentence,' and behaved himself for nearly five months. The Colonial Secretary made a decision, noted in Flanigan's file on 15 January 1861, that if he continued to behave himself he would be discharged at the end of ten years imprisonment. This was indeed a substantial mitigation of sentence but Flanigan seemed unable to keep out of trouble and a few more charges were recorded against him between January 1861 and August 1862.

However the authorities decided that such incidents were not bad enough to spoil his chances of release and on 3 December 1862 they gave permission for him to be granted a Ticket of Leave. It was issued on Christmas Eve, 1862, for the district of Melbourne. Apparently Finegan's bushranging days were over because his criminal record concluded on that date.

Also see Thomas Williams

JOHN FOLEY

NO. 60

No. 60 John Foley
Country: New South Wales
Age: 27 years
Religion: Roman Catholic
Former Calling: Stockman
Particulars: Formerly convicted. Mate of Lowry.

NO. 26

Name: John Foley
Born: 1835
Height: 5ft 9ins
Eyes: Grey
Complexion: Fresh

Date/Place Apprehension: 1863 July, Fish River
Offences Committed: Mail Robbery Under Arms in Western District.
How disposed of: 10 years
Particulars: Mate of Lowry, formerly convicted.
Entrance: 19 September 1863.
Where Convicted: Circuit Court, Bathurst.
Convicted: 7 September 1863, Robbing Mudgee Mail.
Sentence: 15 years Labour on Roads, first 2 years in Irons. Forwarded to Parramatta Gaol — 11 November.

NO. 70

No. 70 John Foley
Date of apprehension: August 1865
Place: Parramatta
Particulars: Robbery Under Arms near Penrith
How disposed of: 3 years.
Particulars of former lives: In company with Daws and Freeman, formerly convicted.

John Foley was a bushranging mate of Fred Lowry, whose story is told in this book. Apparently they pulled off various small holdups before they conceived the daring idea of bailing-up the race meeting in Brisbane Valley, on the Fish River, on New Year's Day 1863. They rounded up a crowd of about 100 people but one of them, named Foran, grappled with Lowry and others joined in. Lowry was taken while Foley galloped away, but Lowry later managed to break out of the ramshackle building in which he was secured and rejoin Foley in the bush. Undaunted by their failure they planned and carried out the robbery of the Mudgee Mail Coach on 18 July 1863, of which the details are told in Lowry's story.

Foley then separated from Lowry and remained free until the police troopers McDonald, Lee, and Nicholls, who were on his trail with the aid of a blacktracker, found him at MacKay's Hotel, Campbell's River. They cornered him in his room, and Foley struggled to prevent them from forcing the door open until McDonald managed to get his hand and revolver round the door. He fired, and this was enough to make Foley surrender.

He was brought before the Bathurst Circuit Court on 7 September 1863, at the same time as his brother Francis who was charged with raiding a camp of Chinese at Campbell's River. During the trials, their mother was observed moving in and out of the courtroom and talking to witnesses, obviously in attempts to persuade them to change their evidence. She was cautioned, but persisted until the judge found her in contempt of court and had her locked up.

The official 'Return of Bushrangers' shows that John Foley was sentenced to ten years, whereas the Darlinghurst Gaol records show his sentence as fifteen years. Perhaps there was confusion between the sentences pronounced on John and Francis.

John's brother Timothy endeavoured to prove an alibi for him, but this was so unconvincing that the judge found him also in contempt of court.

The actual sentence was fifteen years, but John Foley was at large again in less than two. In August 1865 he was arrested for robbery under arms near Penrith and sentenced to another three years. Most historians believe that John Foley's bushranging career ended in 1863, but the new evidence recently obtained, and on which further research is necessary, has a different story to tell. He was eventually released in 1873, and like many former bushrangers, he appears to have seen the errors of his ways. Family tradition has it that he settled down, married and led a respectable life.

Also see Fred Lowry

ALEXANDER FORDYCE

Fordyce was a barman at O'Meally's Inn, in the Weddin Ranges which were the bushranging territory of Frank Gardiner, Ben Hall, and their associates. He was forty-two, from Camden in New South Wales, and the records describe him as 'Catholic, labourer, father, a farmer in the Lachlan district.' Exactly how and when he was drawn into the bushranging fraternity is not known, apart from the fact that Frank Gardiner enlisted him for the attack on the Gold Escort which is described in Gardiner's story.

After the robbery, the gang made for Mount Wheogo. They reached there on the morning after the robbery, to split up their fantastic booty and then go their separate ways.

Fordyce was the oldest of the Gardiner gang and it appears that he was far from being a bold and fearless bushranger. Perhaps Gardiner enlisted him only to 'make up the numbers.' In camp after the robbery, Fordyce soothed his nerves with a bottle of gin, and fell asleep. According to Boxall, Gardiner tried to waken him and then noticed that his revolver was still loaded and obviously had not been fired during the attack on the Gold Escort. He flew at Fordyce then, raving 'You bloody coward, you were too much afraid to fire ... I'll cut your rations short for this.'

Presumably 'rations' meant Fordyce's share of the loot. When he returned to his job as barman he took only a share of the banknotes taken from the Gold Escort, while Gardiner retained Fordyce's share of the gold for 'safekeeping.'

Fordyce must have hoped that the dust would die down and that he would eventually profit from the raid, but the police, whom the bushrangers so often affected to despise, soon rounded up most of the gang. Ben Hall, Bill Hall, John Brown, Warrigal Walsh, and Old Paddy O'Meally were released for lack of evidence, but the police made the charges stick against Fordyce, John Bow, and McGuire. They were taken to Sydney, loaded with chains and escorted by twenty troopers.

Fordyce had to hear the dreadful sentence of death passed upon him by Chief Justice Alfred Stephens, but it was commuted to life imprisonment. Accounts vary on the length of time he actually spent in prison, from six years and seven months to eleven years and nine months. After that he was lost from view, until the records show that he died in Liverpool Asylum on 5 January 1899, an old and broken man with his bushranging exploits long behind him.

STEPHEN FOX

Perhaps Fox should be called a pirate rather than a bushranger, because he was one of those who made the successful raid on the ship *Nelson* of which the story is told in this book under the heading of John James. However Stephen Fox and the other members of the gang are usually included in books about Australian bushrangers.

The robbery was certainly one of the most daring in Australian history. The raiders got away with twenty-three boxes containing 8,183 ounces of gold, then valued at about £25,000. Even though it had to be divided among a number of robbers — the exact number has never been determined — it was still an immense sum of money for that period.

But the exuberant robbers did not enjoy their plunder for very long. The authorities mounted a man-hunt which soon roped in Fox and some of the others. On 29 June 1852, in the court at Geelong, they were each sentenced to fifteen years

Born: 1816
Native Place: Bath
Trade: Labourer
Religion: Roman Catholic
Height: 5ft 10ins
Complexion: Fresh
Hair: Sandy
Eyes: Grey
Particular Marks: Pockpitted. E.S.C.R. on right arm, Anchor on left hand (tattoo).
Previous History: Arrived per ship Brothers in 1838. Bond on arrival.
Sentence: 15 years on the Roads of the Colony, first three years in Irons, for Robbery from the Ship Nelson.
Date of Conviction: 29 June 1852. Geelong.

on the roads of the colony with the first three years to be served in irons.

The sentence 'on the roads,' which meant work with the convict gangs making the colonial roads, seems often to have been honoured in the breach rather than the observance. Perhaps the government's plans for roadmaking could not keep up with the number of convicts available.

In Fox's case, he spent his time as a prisoner aboard the dreaded hulks *President, Success,* and *Sacramento*. The dreary hopelessness of such an existence, apart from the appalling physical conditions, is now hard to imagine.

However he behaved himself reasonably well, and received only the occasional spell in solitary for minor misdemeanours. But it is obvious that life aboard the hulks was destroying him physically and mentally. His record shows that in April 1857 he was transferred to the *Success* 'for security, having positively refused to work', and he died in November 1857 at the age of forty-one. The inquest, held on 16 November, records '... verdict returned that deceased died of fever and that all possible care and attention had been shown to him.'
Also see John James

■ *Alexander Fordyce. At forty-two, he was unusually old for a bushranger. He was called the coward of the Gardiner Gang because he did not fire his revolver during the attack on the Gold Escort.*
(Courtesy Public Record Office, Victoria)

■ *The old ship Success was one of several used as 'hulks', or floating prisons, in Hobson's Bay from the 1850s. Many bushrangers, including Stephen Fox, were among the convicts confined aboard these ships.*
(Collection: Queen Victoria Museum and Art Gallery, Launceston)

An 1870s prison photo of Frank Gardiner shortly before his release.
(Courtesy NSW Police, PRD)

FRANK GARDINER

Born in Rosshire, Scotland, five-year-old Francis Christie arrived in Sydney on board the ship *James*, with his parents, one brother and two sisters on November 17, 1834. The family went to live at Boro Creek, near Goulbourn.

The author was the first to locate long-lost official records which confirmed Francis Christie's birthplace — Scotland, not Australia, as authors had written for decades. One such conflicting story is that he was the illegitimate son of an Irishman and an Aboriginal woman, hence his nickname "Darkie", (which was never the case, but which came from the pen of an author many years earlier).

He would be convicted as Francis Clarke, alias Christie, alias Gardiner. He gave himself other names from time to time including Frank Smith, Frank Jones, and Reverend Christie. It seems likely he finally adopted the name of Frank Gardiner after an old settler named James Gardiner, who befriended and employed him in his youth.

Frank, under any of his adopted names, was variously horsethief, cattle thief, petty thief (he and his gang did not hesitate to clean out £100 from sixty people whom they rounded up at Jugiong, which works out to a fairly paltry average), butcher, and bushranger, whose most notable feat was the holdup of the Eugowra Gold Escort. He has been called 'King of the Road' and 'organiser of outlaws,' and despite the fact that his long career of lawbreaking made little distinction between rich and poor (he and a mate did not scorn to rob an unfortunate hawker, James Doyle, twice within ten days in February 1862) he became such a glamorous figure that there was a public outcry for him to be pardoned when he had been captured at last.

There is still some mystery about his background, which he may have compounded by his use of aliases and perhaps by giving false information on the various occasions when he was arrested, but there seems little doubt that his first offences were those of horsestealing. With Jack Newton, he stole two racehorses from Henry O'Brien's Jugiong Station, took them to Victoria, and then teamed up with William Troy, the overseer of Lockhart Morton's Salisbury Plains Station on the Loddon River. They stole a mob of thirty horses and planned to drive them overland to Adelaide or Portland, but Morton quickly sent men in pursuit and wrote to the Melbourne police. Eventually he and some mounted police caught up with the horse thieves and brought them before the court at Geelong, where Frank was sentenced to five years for horsestealing.

He spent a total of about eight months in captivity: in the Hamilton lock-up, in the Geelong watch-house awaiting trial by Mr Justice William a'Beckett, in the Melbourne Gaol, and finally in the hastily-built new stockade at Pentridge, intended to accommodate first offenders and good conduct men. All the lock-ups, gaols, and prisons were overcrowded in those riotous goldrush years, and William Troy had already escaped from the Geelong watch-house by pulling out boards from the wall of his roughly built cell. Frank followed him on 27 March 1851, when he 'absconded from the works.'

He disappeared into the bush, and for the next couple of years led a roaming life until he went back to his old trade of horsestealing. By that time he was up in central New South Wales, where he went into partnership with a man named Ted Prior. They rounded up a mob of horses, kept them in the Abercrombie Ranges for a while, and then drove them down to Yass to sell them. A smart

---

No.216

Born: 1830
Native Place: Rosshire
Trade: Labourer
Height: 5ft 8¼ins
Complexion: Sallow
Hair: Dark brown
Eyes: Hazel
Particular Marks: None
Sentence: Five years Hard Labour on the Roads of the Colony, for Horse Stealing.
Date of Conviction: 22 October 1850, at Geelong.
Previous History: Arrived at Sydney per ship James in 1834. Free. Was never previously convicted. (Details given when arrested as 'Francis Clarke').

■ *Frank Gardiner (left) and unidentified mate. Some recent books claim that the man on the right is John Gilbert, however there is still no conclusive proof of identity, and so it must remain a mystery. Photo taken by G. Pickering, Photograhic Artist, 1861.*
(Courtesy NSW Police, PRD)

■ *(Opposite) An extract from 'Return of Bushrangers' — official documentation concerning offences committed by Gardiner and his gang.*
(Courtesy Archives of NSW)

■ *(Below) Commercial Hotel, Collector, NSW, in the 1860s when Gardiner and his gang roamed.*
(Courtesy La Trobe Collection, State Library of Victoria)

horsedealer recognised some of the horses, and Frank and Ted were soon in the Yass watch-house and then before the Goulburn court. Under the name of Frank Clarke, he was sentenced to fourteen years and sent first to Sydney and then to Cockatoo Island.

His sentence began on 17 March 1854 and he was released on Ticket of Leave, to the district of Carcoar, on 31 December 1859. But rules meant nothing to Frank. He stole a horse and took off for the Kiandra goldfields, where he became a butcher and did good business selling meat to the hungry diggers. He soon realised that he would do even better by stealing cattle instead of buying them, and together with a man named Fogg he prospered until Police Inspector Sir Frederick Pottinger arrested him on suspicion of cattle stealing, in January 1861. He was brought before the magistrate but released on bail, and on 3 May 1861 he 'absconded from the bail and district.'

Now his bushranging career began in earnest. It is likely that he had already practised bushranging on the side, with such old mates as John Gilbert whom he met at Cockatoo Island, John Peisley, and others. Peisley was also a Ticket of Leave holder 'illegally at large.' It seems strange that Gardiner had not been arrested for breaking the conditions of his Ticket of Leave, but perhaps the poor communications of that era, and the pressure of work on the police, and the fact that he was charged as Christie, that he was not recognised by police, had enabled him to get away with it.

Gardiner and his various mates soon ran up a long string of offences. On 16 July 1861, he and John Peisley had a shoot-out with Sergeant Middleton and Trooper Hosie of the Western Patrol at the Fish River. Both the policemen were severely wounded but they managed to capture Frank. Peisley escaped, but soon returned with a mate and got Frank away from the troopers.

It was then a time of running warfare between the bushrangers who infested central New South Wales and the police who tried to keep order on the goldfields and protect the swarms of people flocking into the region.

Gardiner quickly rose to leadership of groups of bushrangers although he usually worked with only one or two of them, as on the occasion when he and another man robbed William Bell, a butcher, of a small sum of money on 1 June 1862, and later on the same day stopped and robbed four Germans on the road.

But Gardiner was looking for the big killing which would enable him to leave the life of an outlaw and retire into comfortable obscurity. He planned to hold up the Gold Escort, and organised about ten of his outlaw mates for the deed. They included Harry Manns, John Bow, Alex Fordyce, Dan Charters, John Gilbert, and Charles Darcy.

To give a greater impact to the raid he had them all dress themselves in red shirts and caps, and blacken their faces. On the morning of Sunday 15 June 1862, the Gold Escort from the Lachlan region trundled along the road between Forbes and Orange and had just reached Coonbong Rock, near Eugowra (later called Escort Rock) when the gang rode out of the bush and attacked the troopers of the escort. In the brief exchange of fire before the police surrendered, Sergeant James Condell was wounded in the ribs and Senior Constable Moran in the groin, while Constable Havilland received a flesh wound in the arm.

The Gold Escort was carrying 2717 ounces of gold and £3700 in cash, the property of the Bank of New South Wales, the Oriental Bank, and the Commercial Banking Company, to a total value of about £14,000. It was an immense haul for those days and the news of the robbery caused a sensation throughout the country.

Frank Gardiner took his share and went to Aphis Creek, Queensland, with Katherine, the wife of a settler John Brown. They opened a store and were so well regarded that local golddiggers even left their gold with him for safety. They might have lived happily ever after, as 'Mr and Mrs Christie,' if Katherine had resisted the temptation to write to her sister Bridget, who was the legal wife of Ben Hall, but living with Jim Taylor. To make matters worse Bridget allowed Jim Taylor to read the letter, and he soon spilt the news when he was on a drunken spree. The police got to hear about it and arrested him on 3 March, 1864, and on 17 May 1864, after less than two years of enjoyment of the Gold Escort proceeds, Frank Gardiner stood in the dock of the Central Criminal Court, Sydney.

The law had no lack of charges to bring against him. He was sentenced to fifteen years, the first two in irons, for shooting with intent to do grievous bodily harm; ten for robbing Alfred Horsington, and seven for robbing Henry Howitt: a total of thirty-two years.

In fact he served only ten years of this sentence. Despite the depredations of the bushrangers there was considerable pressure, during the 1860s and early 1870s, for moderation of the harsh sentences which had been passed upon those who had been captured. Softhearted citizens signed petitions for their release, and Frank Gardiner was the subject of a battle of words between those who condemned him and those who saw him as a glamorous folk hero. Henry Parkes, in a vote-catching ploy, pardoned him in 1874.

But the pardon had a peculiar qualification. He was exiled to China. Naturally this did not suit Frank at all, and he went to America on board the *Charlotte Andrews* instead.

He became a saloon and restaurant owner at 1031 Kearny St, San Francisco. Much folklore has clouded the remainder of his life. Various reports say he married a wealthy widow and had twin sons by her. He was supposed to have lost his saloon because of his drinking habits, and was later shot in a gambling brawl in Colorado.

A supplementary legend claims that his twin sons visited Australia in 1912 under the guise of mining engineers and dug up his share of the Gold Escort treasure from where he had buried it on the summit of Mount Wheogo.

One report in 1904 stated that Frank Gardiner had died from the effects of pneumonia.

There are many tales told of Frank Gardiner. The reader can be assured that the truth would be stranger than any fiction.

HENRY G

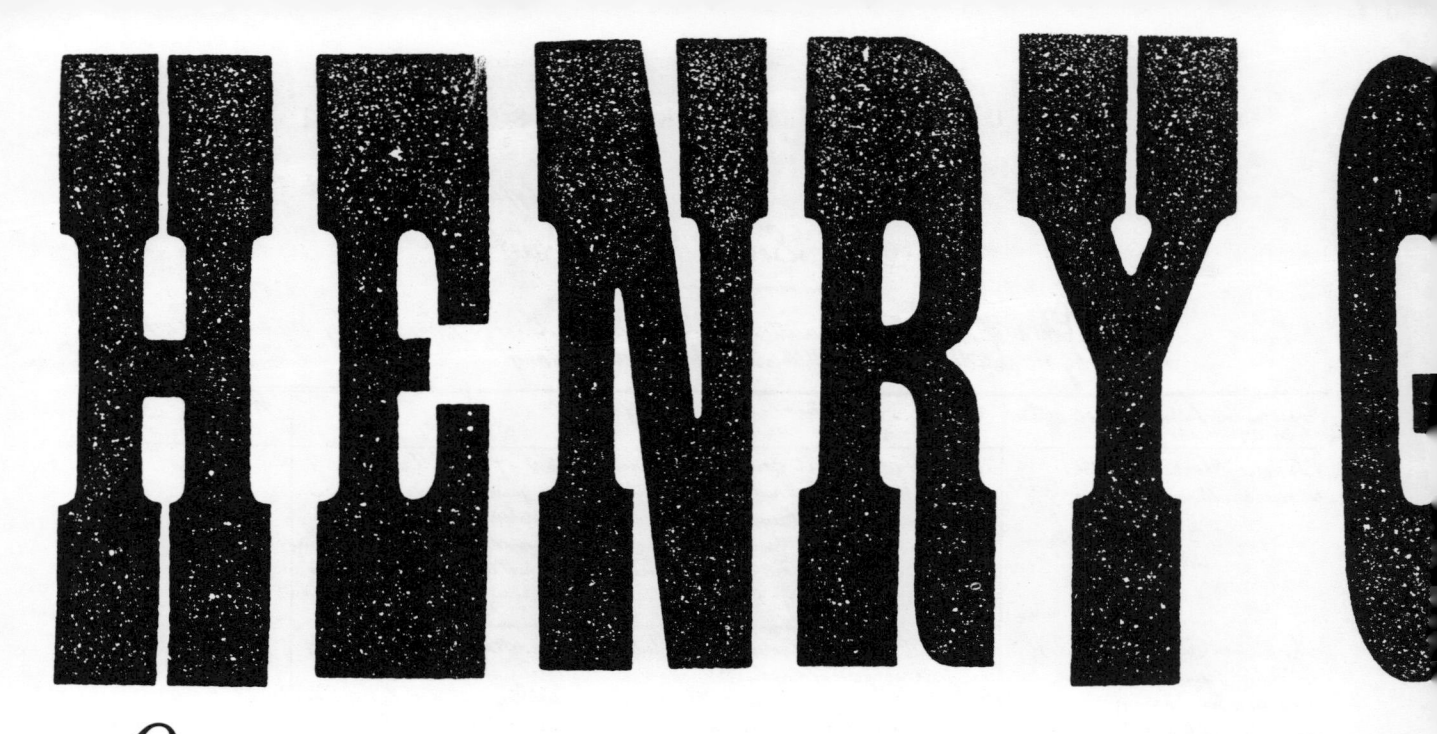

On 16 October 1854, Henry Beresford Garrett together with Henry Marriott, Thomas Quinn, and John Boulton carried out a classic bank robbery.

Thomas Quinn was a stonemason working in Geelong. On 14 October he rode to Ballarat, called on John Boulton and his mate Henry Marriott and played cards with them in their tent, and then walked with them to Garrett's tent at the Big Gravel Pits. It may be presumed that some or all of the men knew each other previously, and that Quinn had made the long ride to Ballarat to discuss the bank robbery. He agreed to join with them on condition that no violence was used, and so they made the robbery with unloaded pistols. They put percussion caps and paper in the chambers of their revolvers, to make them look as though they were loaded with the paper cartridges of that period, and walked from the Big Gravel Pits across Main Street to the Bank of Victoria on Bakery Hill.

Quinn kept watch outside the bank and Marriott stationed himself inside the door, while Garrett and Boulton coolly approached the counter

---

Colonial Secretary's Office,
Melbourne, 18th October, 1854

£1600 REWARD.

WHEREAS the Bank of Victoria at Ballaarat, was, about Two P.M., on Monday, the 16th of October, entered by four armed men, who bound the inmates, and robbed the bank of 233 ounces of gold, and a considerable number of £10 and other notes, the numbers of which are known: Notice is hereby given that a reward of £200 will be given for the apprehension and conviction of each man, which reward will be doubled should all the parties concerned be convicted.

In addition to the above reward, a free pardon, and a passage out of the Colony, will be given to an accomplice, through whose evidence the others shall be convicted.

By His Excellency's Command,
JOHN FOSTER.

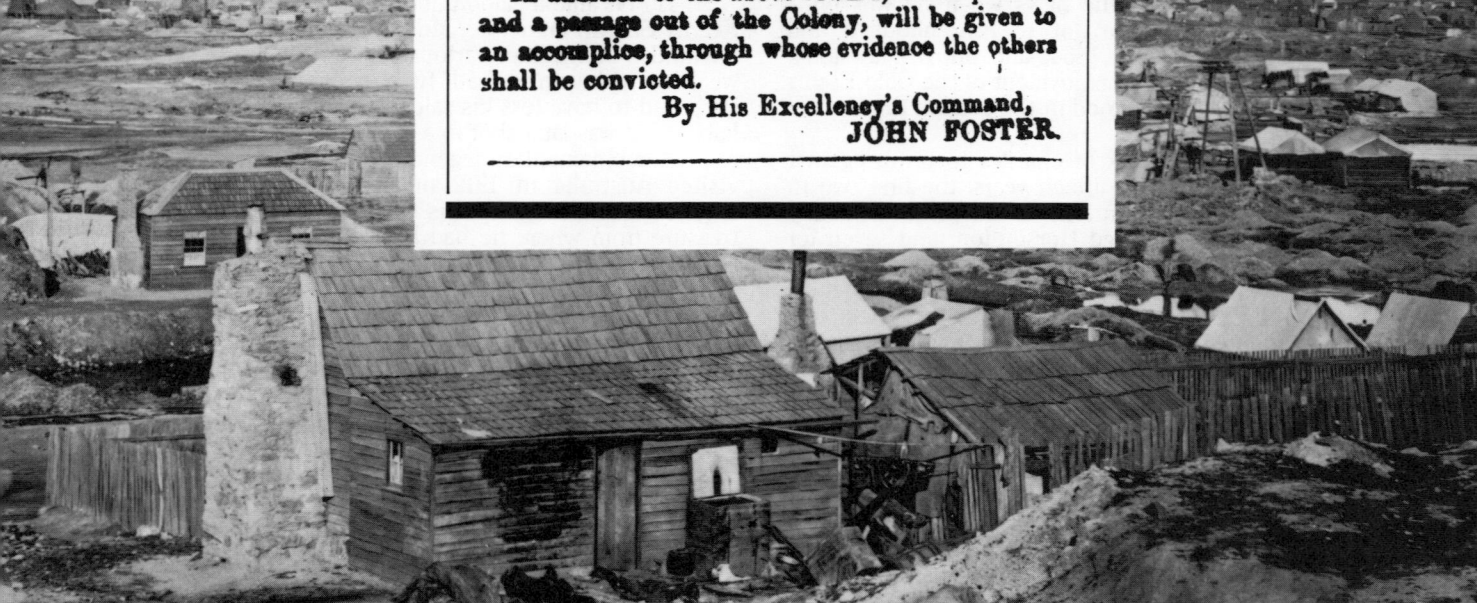

ARRETT

and bailed up the tellers. Everything went swiftly and smoothly and the robbers escaped with about 350 ounces of gold and about £14,300.

Astonishingly, they managed to get clean away with this substantial load of cash and gold, split it up between them, and go their separate ways. Garrett went directly to Melbourne and took ship to England. Marriott calmly proceeded to lodgings in Ballarat and laid low there for a while. Quinn and Boulton went first to Geelong and then to Melbourne, where they sold their share of the gold to the London Chartered Bank in Collins Street. They returned to Geelong and then, in a display either of arrant cheek or blatant stupidity, went back to Ballarat. By way of compounding this foolishness, Boulton went to the very bank which they had robbed and asked for a draft on London for £1,450. When he passed money across the counter to pay for the draft, the sheaf of notes contained some of those which the four men had stolen from the bank.

An astute teller recognised the notes and detained Boulton on some excuse until the police could arrive and take him in charge. With one man in their hands the police quickly tracked down two of the others, including Marriott who was still staying in his lodgings in Lydiard Street in Ballarat. Quinn turned Queen's Evidence and 'dobbed in' his two mates, and disappeared after they had been sentenced to ten years apiece.

By that time, Henry Garrett had arrived safely in London aboard the ship *Dawstone,* and he must have thought he was safe. But the Victoria Police sent

■ *Notice of reward published after Garrett and his mates robbed the Bank of Victoria in Ballarat. The notice states they stole 233 ounces of gold but their haul was found to be a great deal more than that.*

■ *Portion of a large panoramic view of Ballarat in the early 1850s.*
(Courtesy La Trobe Collection, State Library of Victoria)

Detective Henry Webb to England on what must have seemed like the impossible task of tracking him down. Webb used shrewd detective work to trace Garrett to lodgings near Oxford Street, where he was living in style on the proceeds of the robbery.

Various accounts disagree on the exact way that Webb bailed up Garrett in the streets of London. Some say that he used the Australian bush call 'coo-ee,' others that he simply called out 'Garrett!'

Webb escorted him back to Melbourne, where he was sentenced to ten years for his part in the robbery. The *Melbourne Argus* described him as a 'powerfully-built man with an immense quantity of hair on his face: He was released on Ticket of Leave in August 1861, and joined the goldrush to New Zealand.

But he had no intention of joining in the hard work of goldseeking. Early in 1862, he took to the bush between Dunedin and the Otago goldfields, and is credited as the first New Zealand bushranger. It is said he robbed about twenty people near Gabriel's Gully, now known as Lawrence, and he had a lively career until the law caught up with him again. He had returned to Sydney, but was caught and returned to New Zealand, where he was sentenced to a period of eight years gaol.

He joined in an escape attempt with other notorious inmates, including one of his Pentridge mates — Richard Burgess — who would be hanged some years later, for his murderous lifestyle.

Whilst in Dunedin Gaol, Henry Garrett said he had become a devoted convert to religion. He was released on 9 February 1868 — shortly after to be arrested for theft from a Seed Merchant's business.

When his quarters were searched by police they found quantities of poison — including strychnine, chloroform, arsenic, etc. It was later alleged he had intended to murder his enemies by poison, including Mr Justice Greeson, one who had previously sentenced Garrett for bushranging activities.

Richard Burgess would later write an extraordinary autobiography while awaiting trial and execution in Nelson Gaol.

He wrote of Henry Garrett at some length, the full story can be found in the excellent book *"Guilty Wretch That I Am"*. Burgess, in part, states of Henry Garrett '... I never knew you do a manly act towards your fellow yet, but many bad ones. You have no respect for any living being...'

WILLIAM GARROWAY

Born: 1824
Native Place: England
Trade: Labourer
Religion: Protestant
Height: 5ft 7ins
Complexion: Sallow
Hair: Brown
Eyes: Hazel
Particular Marks: 'ME' right arm. Powder marks left cheek.
Previous History: Free per Sarrah to Van Diemen's Land 1836. Bond. Life. Conditional Pardon in 1848. Same name.
Date of Conviction: 26 April 1853. Geelong Circular Court.
Sentence: Ten years on the Roads. First year in irons.

*I*t is interesting to speculate on what the genuine flash bushrangers, men like Frank Gardiner and John Gilbert, must have thought about characters like William Garroway. Presuming that they heard about the activities of such men, then it seems probably that they would have regarded them much as a professional in any trade would look upon some amateur bungler.

William Garroway and his mate Arthur Burrowe, whose story appears earlier in this book, were certainly not much better than rank amateurs in the bushranging business, although they would have been considered dangerous nuisances to the general public.

Burrowes' story, recounts the episode in which the two men held up William Henry Mitchell, and the later robbery of Alexander McLean who tracked them down and brought them to justice.

The two men appeared before the Geelong Circuit Court and received lengthy sentences, which was obviously designed to discourage others from imitating their nefarious activities.

However William Garroway served only five hard years of his original sentence, which had been set at ten years on the roads. He was released on Ticket of Leave, to the district of the Wimmera, on 26 April 1858.

His record shows that a Free Certificate was issued on 10 January 1860, and so it may be presumed that his spell of imprisonment, of which the first year was served in irons, had made him a sadder and wiser man.

Also see Arthur Burrowe

William James Gilbert married Eleanor Wilson in England and after the birth of their daughter Ellen, emigrated in 1830 to settle in Hamilton, Ontario, Canada.

Five sons were born, William, Francis, James, Charles, and John.

John Gilbert was born in 1842, his mother died whilst he was still an infant, and his brother William also died. His father remarried, and two sons Thomas and Nicholas were born. More children would be born in Australia.

On 15 October 1852, the ship *Revenue* arrived in Australia. The Gilbert family part of the second-class passenger list. John Gilbert was ten years old.

Apparently John Gilbert's family settled in the Kyneton-Taradale area of Victoria. His father is buried in the Lauriston Cemetery which is near both these places.

By 1854 young John had left home and went to work at the Kilmore Inn, on the road to the Ovens goldfields, as a stableboy. Diggers and others en route to and from the goldfields stayed at the inn, and young John would have heard many stories of the fortunes to be made by honest or dishonest means. Something in his makeup made him take the latter course and he became associated with a gang of 'hocusers', or conmen and tricksters. Later in life he was described as a flashily-dressed, reckless, and wild-living young man. The foundations of this lifestyle were laid during the time he spent drifting around the goldfields with his hocusing friends, and picking up a living by theft and trickery.

Such activities did not escape the attentions of the police and he was picked up for horsestealing and sent to Cockatoo Island. Some of his numerous biographers believe that his first contact with the bushranger Frank Gardiner was in Kiandra in about 1860, but it seems more likely that he encountered Gardiner at Cockatoo Island,

THE CANADIAN ·JOHN· GILBERT

A sketch by Police Magistrate W. Rose of the incident at Black Springs, when John Gilbert, John Dunn, and Ben Hall attacked the mail coach. Rose was an eye-witness of this classic bushranger's raid, one of the many in which John Gilbert participated with others of the Hall and Gardiner gangs.
(Courtesy Archives of NSW)

where the latter was serving a stretch at the same time as Gilbert.

Neither man had enough sense to learn from this lesson, and by the early 1860s Gilbert was a member of Gardiner's gang. He took part in a number of its most notorious exploits but he was perfectly capable of making bushranging history on his own account, often in company with his mate and fellow robber John O'Meally. They roved the country in the region of Young, Gundagai, and Junee, and in the first nine months of 1863 committed so many offences that they must have been almost continuously on the move. Between February and September 1863 the two bushrangers, occasionally accompanied by a third man described either as 'another' or as Frederick Lowry, held up stores and hotels, bailed up travellers for loot which was occasionally as paltry as the watch and chain they stole off Lewis A. Spencer on the Lambing Flat road, stole horses and racehorses including the mount belonging to Constable David Stewart, and generally made nuisances of themselves. However the local populace, apart from the police and landowners, tended to make heroes of the two men. Gilbert encouraged such feelings when, according to Manning Clark, he distributed free drinks, cigars, and sweetmeats to the mob when he held up Robinson's Hotel in Carcoar in October 1863, and 'kept the company in roars of laughter by giving an account of the police whom he designated as a mob of cowards.'

On 15 November 1864, the bushrangers' contempt for law and order led them to hold up the mail from Gundagai to Yass about four miles from Jugiong. Ben Hall, Gilbert, and John Dunn bailed up the coach, and Gilbert shot and killed Sergeant Edmund Parry in the process.

It was one of the many acts which caused the government to name the members of Ben Hall's gang as outlaws, so that every man's hand might be turned against them. The flash young thief and murderer, John Gilbert, had not much longer to live.

The determined efforts of the police were slowly destroying the murderous groups of bushrangers led by Ben Hall and Frank Gardiner. Gilbert and John Dunn could see that their time was running out after Ben Hall had been killed, and they sought sanctuary in a hut belonging to old John Kelly, a close relation of Dunn. But Kelly betrayed them and led a police party to the hut, no doubt tempted by the reward on the outlaws' heads. Gilbert tried to make a classic last stand while Dunn got away, but the police attack was too vigorous and he too ran out of the hut into the bush. Dunn escaped, to be run down on another day, while Gilbert tried to fight off the police in a gully behind the hut. Constables Bright and Hales fired at him and one of their bullets passed through his chest and through the left ventricle of his heart. His last day alive was Saturday, 13 May 1865.

The police carried his body to Binalong police station, where it was exhibited to the public for some time. The profits of his bushranging career were found in the pockets of his clothing: a gold watch, some bullets and percussion caps, some gold rings, and a few banknotes.

It is said that people walked from as much as thirty miles away to have a look at the body of the notorious bushranger, that his shirt was cut into pieces by souvenir hunters, and that locks of hair were cut from the corpse's head.

On Tuesday, 16 May 1865, the body of John Gilbert was buried on the side of a timbered hill in the Police Paddock, half a mile from the township of Binalong. The local undertaker conducted proceedings, no minister being present. Among the few police witnesses present was Constable Bright.

John Gilbert was 23 years old. (Born 1842).

The final record gives the closing details of an illspent life. No. 69: John Gilbert. Country: New South Wales. Age: 21. Religion: Protestant. Former Calling: Stockman. Particulars: Notorious bushranger, shot dead by Constable Hales.

Also see Benjamin Hall

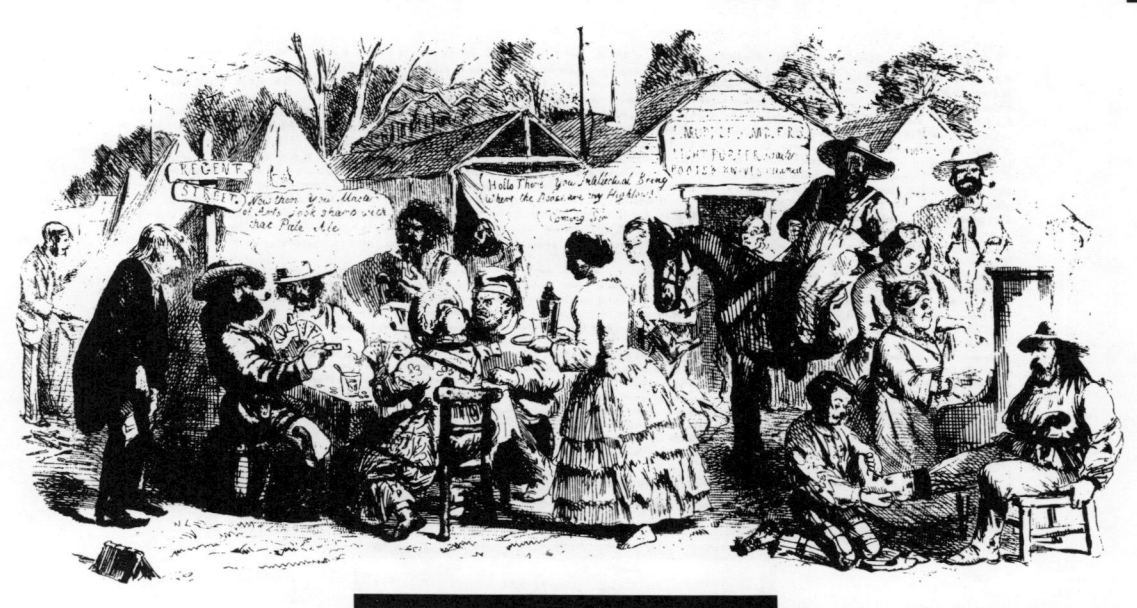

CHRISTOPHER GOODISON

Life on the Goldfields. Topsy-Turvy — or our antipodes. Etching by John Leech.
(Courtesy La Trobe Collection, State Library of Victoria)

Born: 1824
Native Place: Birmingham
Trade: Tinman
Religion: Protestant
Height: 5ft 3ins
Complexion: Fresh
Hair: Brown
Eyes: Blue
Particular Marks: A scar over right eye. A scar between both eyes. 3 moles on right arm.
Previous History: Arrived per ship Egyptian to Van Dieman's Land. Bond. Free on Conviction.
Sentence: 3 years on the Roads of the Colony, for Robbery.
Date of Conviction: 27 April 1852, at Melbourne.

Christopher Goodison and his mate Alfred Stallard must surely have been among the most paltry of the robbers who were classified, at one time or another, as bushrangers. Nobody knows how, when, or why the two men decided to join the criminal population which swarmed on the diggings, but it is obvious that Goodison and Stallard decided not to take the chance of confrontations with other men. Instead, they waited until a digger named William Roberts left his wife alone in their tent at Bendigo Creek, and then approached her with some plausible tale or other. Mrs Roberts must have been a remarkably gullible woman because she accepted a drink of rum which they offered to her, and soon became insensible. Either it was extremely potent rum or it contained one of the soporifics used in those days, such as laudanum.

When Mrs Roberts passed out, the two men stole five ounces of gold from the tent and took off into the bush. William Roberts returned to the tent, heard his wife's sorry tale, and ran to tell the police.

Goodison and Stallard were not even good bushmen. The police had little difficulty in tracing them to a spot near the Loddon River. They chained the two con men to a tree for three days until they were ready to lead them on the long march to justice, which led first to the Camp Reserve at Mount Alexander. Here they were kept chained to a log for ten days, then marched on to Kyneton for incarceration in the lock-up for five days on bread and water. At long last they were put into the coach for Melbourne and on 27 April 1852 they appeared before the well-known Judge Redmond Barry.

He sentenced them to three years 'on the Roads of the Colony,' and ignored their complaints about the harsh treatment meted out by the police.

Goodison must have behaved himself in custody because his record is clean until the final entry, on 29 September 1853. This shows he was discharged on Ticket of Leave after only seventeen months of his sentence. But the *Victoria Police Gazette* of 30 December 1853 shows that he had broken one of the conditions of his Ticket of Leave, the requirement that he should report regularly to a police officer, and so he was posted as 'Illegally at large.'

No doubt the police of that era had more important things on their minds than the apprehension of such a minor lawbreaker, because the records of that period do not list him for any other offence. Perhaps he continued a criminal career under an alias, or perhaps he decided that once was enough and lived honestly thereafter.
Also see Alfred Stallard

STAND AND DELIVER

JAMES GOODWIN

WHEREAS *Matthew Brady, Patrick Bryant, Josiah Bird, William Brown, Michael Cody, Patrick Dunne, James Goodwin, John Gregory, James M'Kenney, James Murphy, Edward Williams,* and *William Tilly* (for whose Apprehension Rewards have been already offered), yet remain at large; and have lately added to their Crimes of Murder, and other personal Outrage and Plunder, by a most wanton and unprovoked Attack upon the Premises and Property of WILLIAM EFFINGHAM LAWRENCE, Esquire, at his Farm near the Lake River, and destroying by Fire his House, with all the Barns and Out-houses, several large Stacks of Wheat, together also with the whole of the Wool produced by the shearing of his Flocks for the last three Years; and when leaving the Farm, threatened to fire and be avenged of all such Persons as followed them, having previously attempted to Murder the Overseer of the Farm by discharging their Guns at him:—AND WHEREAS many evil-disposed Persons connect themselves with the Offenders, by purchasing or procuring a Market for their Plunder, and, so far from giving any Information that may lead to their Apprehension, receive, harbour, and maintain them, thereby committing a Crime punishable by Death, all which Persons are hereby warned not to entertain the slightest hope of Mercy being extended to them in the Event of their Conviction:—NOW, THEREFORE, for the Protection of the Settlers, and inducing them and all other good and peaceable Members of Society, to co-operate promptly and vigorously with the Government in the prosecution of those Measures, which it is constantly desirous of adopting for the Welfare of the Inhabitants of this Island, and in particular at this important Time—
I DO HEREBY PROCLAIM, that, instead of the Rewards already offered, the Persons who may apprehend and lodge in any of His Majesty's Gaols in this Island, the Twelve Offenders before named, or any of them, shall immediately receive from the Government as follows, that is to say:—For every such Offender, either the Sum of One Hundred Guineas, or, (at their election) Three Hundred Acres of Land, free from all Restrictions:—And that if the Offenders shall be apprehended by Prisoners, or Prisoners shall be of the Party by whom those Offenders may be apprehended, such Prisoners shall receive a Free Pardon, in addition to their Share of the before-mentioned Reward:—AND I DO HEREBY FURTHER PROCLAIM, that any Person giving such Information as may lead to the Apprehension of the said Offenders, shall immediately afterwards receive from the Government either the Sum of One Hundred Guineas, or, (at his election) Three Hundred Acres of Land, free from all Restriction:—And that if the Information be given by a Prisoner, he shall receive a Free Pardon and be provided with a free Passage to England, in addition to the last-mentioned Reward:—AND I DO HEREBY FURTHER PROCLAIM, that the Chief Constable of the District in which the Offenders may be apprehended, shall immediately afterwards, receive a Grant of One Hundred Acres of Land, free from all Restrictions, provided it can be certified by the Magistrates of such District, that he then, and at all Times, zealously exerted himself to detect and apprehend the said Offenders:—And, for the Purpose of aiding and assisting in clearing the Island of this most hardened Banditti, the Settlers are hereby most earnestly entreated forthwith to arm themselves, and associate in Parties, under the Advice and Direction of the Magistrates of their Districts, with whom all the Military Parties have been placed in Communication; or, if there shall not be any Magistrate residing in the District, then of their Chief District Constable:—LASTLY, I do hereby strictly command the Chief and Petty Constables throughout the Island, *and particularly Prisoners holding Tickets of Leave,* to be aiding and assisting the Magistrates, to the utmost of their Power, by all possible Means, not only in the apprehension of the Offenders before referred to, but also in discovering and communicating, as quickly as possible, the Names and Residences of those who receive, harbour, or maintain the said Offenders, or any of them.

Given under my Hand and Seal at Government House, the First Day of March, in the Year of Our Lord One thousand eight hundred and twenty-six.

Age: 20 (1826)
Native Place: Glasgow
Trade: Weaver
Height: 5ft 5¼ins
Hair: Brown
Eyes: Dark Grey
Particular Marks: 'J.G.', anchor and thistle on right hand.
Previous History: Tried Stirling 19 September 1823, for Housebreaking and sentenced for seven years Transportation. Goal report — very bad. Hulk report — orderly. Single. He stated his offence as Housebreaking — once in custody for theft. Arrived in Hobart per Lady East on 9 April 1825. He absconded from the service of a Mr. Peevor on 24/12/1825; and a Reward of £2 was offered for his capture.

There can be no doubt that the convicts sent to Van Diemen's Land in the earlier days of that penal settlement had to suffer appalling conditions in the prison ships and when they were first put ashore, but it is equally true that the authorities were eager to get them off their hands and even to give them a chance to reform.

Many were assigned as servants to the free settlers, and they very often settled down in reasonable contentment and eventually achieved freedom to make their own way in the colony.

In other cases, however, the convict had already been so hardened by his criminal career that there was little likelihood of reform, and sometimes the master to whom he was assigned treated him so badly that he took to the bush rather than exist under such conditions.

James Goodwin, the young weaver who was sentenced to seven years transportation for housebreaking, received a bad report for his conduct while in prison but he was assigned to the service of a Mr Peevor quite soon after his arrival in Hobart.

Whether Peevor treated him badly, or whether he was simply unable to accept the hard work and discipline of working as an assigned servant, cannot now be known, but on Christmas Eve 1825 he absconded from Peevor's service and joined up with Matthew Brady the 'gentleman bushranger' whose story is told elsewhere in this book.

For young James Goodwin, a bushranging career was to be a short life but perhaps not a merry one. Matthew Brady's comments on the life of a bushranger make one feel that it must have resembled that of a hunted animal.

Goodwin was caught with the rest of the Brady gang and brought to trial on 25 April 1826. The charge was 'Maliciously setting fire to the dwelling house of William Effingham Laurence,' for which he was found guilty and sentenced to death.

Somewhat redundantly, he was also sentenced to death on a second charge, that of 'Stealing three mares value £200 and one gelding valued at £50; the property of William Effingham Laurence.'

In these days, when a brutal murderer may get away with no more than a few years in prison, the harshness of the law 150 years ago is almost unbelievable. The six men of Brady's gang were hanged for burning down Laurence's house and stealing his four horses.

James Goodwin was hanged on 5 May 1826. He was twenty years old.
Also see Matthew Brady

100 AUSTRALIAN BUSHRANGERS 1789-1901

JIMMY GOVERNER

> *No. 8194*
> <u>Native Place:</u> Talbragar
> <u>Arrived:</u> Born in Colony
> <u>Trade:</u> Horsebreaker
> <u>Religion:</u> Church of England.
> <u>Education:</u> Read and Write
> <u>Height:</u> 5ft 7½ins
> <u>Weight:</u> 132lbs.
> <u>Hair:</u> Black
> <u>Eyes:</u> Black
>
> *No. 4*
> <u>Address:</u> Breelong
> <u>Committed:</u> (?) 30 October 1900.
> <u>Offence:</u> Murder
> <u>Sentence:</u> Trial 19/11/1900
> Death 23/11/1900
> <u>Where Born:</u> Talbragar
> <u>Religion:</u> Church of England
> <u>Trade:</u> Horsebreaker
> <u>Age:</u> 25
> <u>Height:</u> 5ft 8ins
> <u>Hair:</u> Black
> <u>Eyes:</u> Black
> <u>Education:</u> Read and Write
> <u>Remarks:</u> (?) 1 month Hard Labour in 1893 or 94
> <u>Disposal:</u> Executed 18/01/1901.
> Married, wife's address unknown.

Jimmy Governor was a part-Aboriginal who seemed to be fairly well integrated into the white society of the Gulgong/Breelong/Cassilis area of New South Wales. He could read and write, he worked as a tracker for the police at Cassilis and was an expert horsebreaker, and he felt himself well enough accepted to be able to court and marry a sixteen-year-old white girl, Ethel Mary Jane Page. Jimmy was twenty-three.

But the young couple had broken a rigid rule, and the 'mixed marriage' brought immediate hatred and contempt from the white women in the district. Obviously the men did not feel so violently about the matter because John Mawbey, a Breelong pastoralist, gave Jimmy a job on his West Breelong property. Jimmy and Ethel moved into a rough earthen-floored shack on the property.

In the usual style of that period, Jimmy was working for a small wage plus rations. One day, Ethel went to the homestead to ask for the flour ration. She was met by Mrs Mawbey and by Helen Kerz, the district schoolteacher whose school was at Breelong. The two women abused Ethel, using such words as 'scum,' for having married a black man, and turned her away empty-handed.

When she told Jimmy about this, he went first to see Mr Mawbey, who was staying with a gang of men at the old Breelong homestead some distance from the main homestead. They were camped there in readiness to start work on bagging the wheat harvest.

Mawbey promised that he would provide the necessary rations, but Jimmy was still angry about the insults to Ethel. He brooded over the matter for a while, and then took his mate Jacky Underwood with him to the main homestead. They were armed with axes and a rifle.

On that night the homestead was occupied by Mrs Sarah Mawbey, Helen Kerz, the Mawbey children Grace, Hilda, Percy, Bert, Cecil, and Garnet, their cousin George, and a friend named Elsie Clarke. When Jimmy and Jacky hammered at the door it was opened by Mrs Mawbey and Helen Kerz, with the older girls standing behind them in their nightdresses.

Jimmy demanded an apology for Mrs Mawbey's treatment of Ethel, but she and Hilda were not afraid of the two armed men. Mrs Mawbey ordered them off the property, while Helen Kerz added such words as 'You black rubbish! You should be shot for marrying a white woman!'

Jimmy and Jacky exploded. They attacked the women and children with savage blows of their axes. Helen, Grace, and young Bert managed to escape from the house but Helen and Grace did not get far before Jimmy caught up with them and slaughtered them with his axe. Inside the house, the two attackers laid about them in a blood frenzy before hurrying off into the darkness.

Bert Mawbey, only eight years old, found his father and brought him and the other men back to the homestead. They found Cecil and Garnet, who had been sleeping on the floor of the kitchen which was separated from the main house, still alive. Their cousin George, who had hidden under a bed, had also survived. Cecil and Garnet, now still living, can remember their father

81

No. 8194 Name Jimmy Governor
Date when Portrait was taken, 22 — 11 — 1900

Native place Talbragar
Year of birth 1875
Arrived in Colony { Ship / Year }
Trade or occupation previous to conviction Horsebreaker
Religion C of E
Education, degree of R.W.
Height 5 feet 7½ inches
Weight { On committal 132 / On discharge }
Colour of hair Black
Colour of eyes Black
Marks or special features:—

(No. of previous Portrait   ).

PREVIOUS CONVICTIONS.

Where and When.	Offence.	Sentence.
Denison Town PC 16·2·95	Stealing	1 month H.L.
Lyd. G.D. 22·11·1900	Murder	Death Executed 18/1/01

weeping as he looked at the carnage. His wife, Helen Kerz, Grace, Percy, and Elsie Clarke all lay in pools of blood, either dead or dying. Percy's head was almost severed from his body.

The horrified white community immediately rose up in arms and took off in pursuit of the murderers. They had now been joined by Jimmy's brother Joe Governor, and it is said that Jimmy claimed they would be bushrangers, 'just like Ned Kelly.'

For the next sixty-eight days they covered about 2500 square miles of territory, in bushranging rampages which certainly struck as much terror into the settlers as any of the bushrangers of the past. The vital difference between them and the Kelly Gang is that many people were sympathetic towards the Kellys, whereas every man's hand was against the Governors.

The death-toll at the Mawbey homestead had been Sarah, Grace, Hilda, and Percy Mawbey and Helen Kerz. The Governor gang soon added others to this list: Elizabeth O'Brien and her baby at Poggi, Kiernan Fitzpatrick at Wollar, and Alex McKay at Ulan. Mary McKay and Catherine Bennett were wounded. It is also said that Jimmy raped a fifteen-year-old girl.

Two hundred police and 2000 civilians were pursuing the Governors and the end was only a matter of time. One of the most determined pursuers was Bert Byers, the fiance of Helen Kerz, with his mate Bob Woods. These two men became relentless trackers of the 'black outlaws,' who committed about eighty crimes ranging from robbery under arms to murder. A reward of £1000 for their capture made the pursuers even more anxious to catch them.

Jacky Underwood was the first to be caught. He seems to have been a rather simple-minded character, perhaps led astray by Jimmy. When he was hanged on 14 January 1901 he asked whether he would be in heaven in time for dinner.

Bert Byers and Bob Woods spotted Jimmy and Joe on 13 October 1900 and fired at them. A bullet tore a terrible wound across Jimmy's mouth, but he and Joe managed to escape again although they were separated. Jimmy was caught on 27 October but Joe remained at large until the last day of the month. He was spotted by two graziers near Falbrook Creek, and ran into the bush when they called on him to surrender. They fired five shots, one of which pierced his skull, killing him instantly.

There is a strange sad document in the archives of New South Wales, entitled The Diary of Officer doing duty over Jimmy Governor. Probably unique in Australia, it is an almost minute-by-minute account of Jimmy's last days, from 6 November 1900 to 18 January 1901. His mood fluctuated between hope and despair; between anger and resignation; between acceptance of the chaplain's attempts to console him and violent rejection. The entry for Christmas Day 1900 reads: 'Not very good, has been in very bad humour all this morning. Complained about the Chaplain trying to drive him, instead of leading him. Refused to see the Chaplain, told him to clear out of his cell. Sullen and very irritable. Would not eat his meals today.'

On 18 January 1901, Jimmy Governor ate breakfast and prayed with the chaplain for the last time. At nine a.m. the executioner, Robert 'Nosey Bob' Howard, who had hanged Jacky Underwood at Dubbo a few days earlier, positioned him on the scaffold, adjusted the noose, and pulled the white hood over his face. Jimmy muttered something unintelligible and Howard pulled the lever.

Ethel Governor, who had been the unwitting cause of so many ghastly deaths, had co-operated with the police throughout the pursuit of the Governors and given evidence against Jimmy. She soon married again, had ten children by her second husband, and died in Newington State Hospital in 1945.

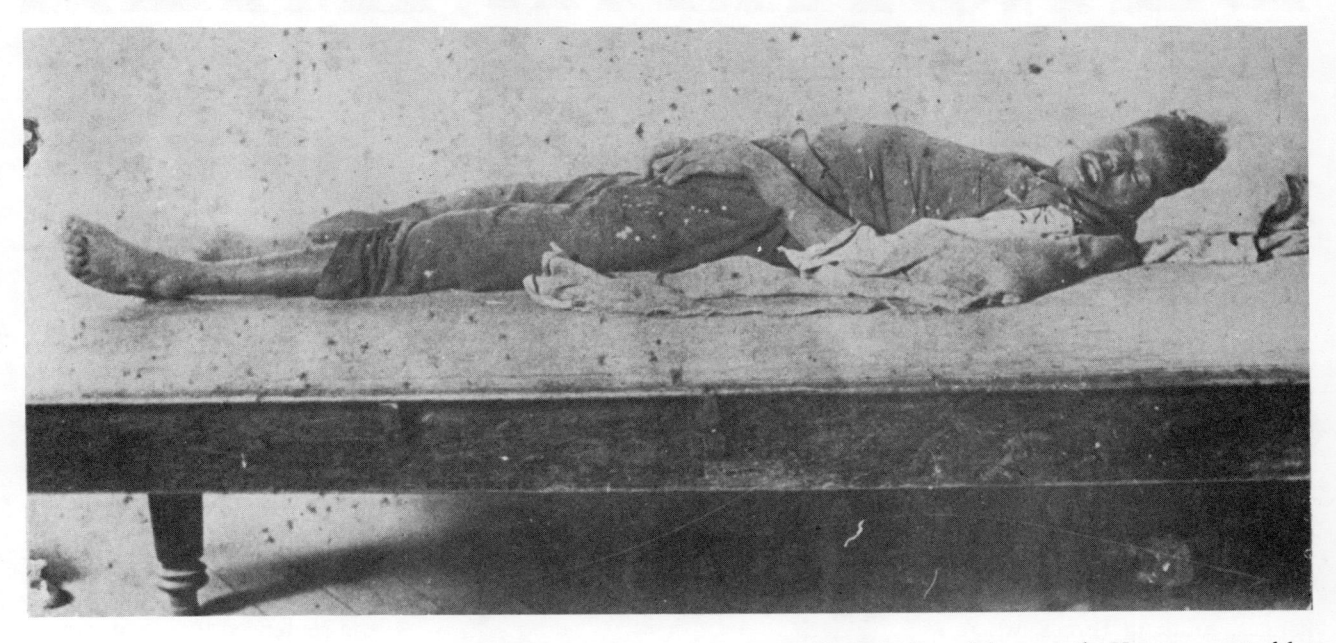

■ *The corpse of Joe Governor, shot by two graziers in October 1900.*
(Courtesy Archives of NSW)

STAND AND DELIVER

BENJAMIN HALL

Ben Hall is believed to have been born at Breeza, on Liverpool Plains, NSW in 1837; however no official recording of the event has been located.

His bushranging career lasted for almost exactly three years, from April 1862 to May 1865, and like most bushrangers he died young. He was only twenty-eight when he died in the final shoot-out with the police, near Billabong Creek a few miles north of Forbes, on 6 May 1865.

His parents were both ex-convicts who had been transported to Australia.

By the time he was nineteen he was in the Wheogo Ranges, south of Forbes, where he married Bridget Walsh. Together with his brother-in-law John Maguire they took up Sandy Creek station, where the son of Ben and Bridget, also called Ben, was born.

By the early 1860s, the whole area south of Forbes was bushranger territory. Frank Gardiner and his associates roamed the Weddin Ranges and were building up for their most daring robbery, that of the Gold Escort. Sir Frederick Pottinger had been placed in charge of the Western Division of the New South Wales Police, with a mandate to stamp out this bushranger infestation.

It is uncertain whether Ben Hall was associated with Gardiner and the others in their early depredations, but he seems somehow to have attracted the attention of the police. In April 1862 they took Ben Hall to Forbes as a suspected accomplice of Gardiner after wagons of a William Bacon had been held up near the township. After some deliberation the jury acquitted Hall, and he was found 'not guilty'.

Soon after he joined Frank Gardiner and became leader of the gang when Gardiner went to Queensland after the Gold Escort robbery on Sunday, 15 June 1862. John Gilbert became his second-in-command as he had been Gardiner's.

In the *Return of Bushrangers* documents which survive in the official files there is an enormous list of offences attributed to Ben Hall and his mates, although

■ *Ben Hall — a damaged portrait of the flashily-dressed young squatter. One of his victims described him as a 'robust-looking man, with a fine frank-looking face.'*
(Courtesy NSW Police PRD)

Ben is surprisingly omitted from the names of those who robbed the Gold Escort.

He is recorded first, on February 1863, as having stolen a rifle, carbine, ammunition, a pair of saddle bags, and bridle from the Pinnacle Police Station, in company with Patrick and John Daley, 'during the absence of the police on duty'. After that, the list comprises fifty-one offences committed either alone or in company with such men as John O'Meally, James Gordon, John Gilbert, James Dunleavy, John Vane, and John Dunn. James Gordon, alias Mount, was a Ticket of Leave man in his forties who was finally caught and sentenced to a long term of imprisonment.

During the heyday of the Ben Hall gang they ranged far and wide around the region of which Forbes is the approximate centre. A good many of their thefts were of horses, always of the best quality, which enabled them to keep moving fast and to outdistance the police on their government nags. Nobody ever knew when or where they would appear, and they seemed to have an exact knowledge of valuable consignments being transported by road. Such knowledge, of course, was given to them by the 'bush telegraph'. Plenty of men and women in the district had no cause to love the police, either because they had come into collision with them or because they had inherited an antagonism towards authority from their convict forebears. A section of the community saw Ben Hall and his mates as a demonstration of the ordinary man's rebellion against authority and were only too glad to pass on valuable information.

In classic bushranger style the Ben Hall gang bailed up the mail coaches again and again, and robbed the passengers and the mailbags: at Crocker's Inn, at Smelly's Creek, on the road from Binalong to Yass, three times near Jugiong, on the Breadalbane Plains, twice near Tawrang, and at Geary's Gap. These hold-ups brought them into frequent conflict with the police, as did their unsuccessful attempt to hold up the Araluen Gold Escort on 13 March 1865. The police fought them

84

off on that occasion, although two troopers were wounded.

Contrary to earlier writings, Ben Hall and his gang were not the 'Robin Hood rob-the-rich and give-to-the-poor' type. Many of the robberies were against ordinary working class people. As more and more research is done on official reports, the facts show that the hero-worship of bushrangers came from an era when many writers were against authority. Australians love to be anti-authority. In some cases justifiably so.

He began his bushranging career as a fairly minor criminal, but the range and scope of his activities and the vandalism which he added to his ordinary robberies, such as the burning down of stores and even the burning of a storekeeper's account books when the gang robbed John Pierce's store at Canowindra on 22 June 1864, show that he was impelled by a kind of lust for revenge against society. He may have seemed like a glamorous free spirit to some of his contemporaries, who perhaps would have liked to join him in the bush but lacked the courage to

■ *Sticking up the Mudgee Mail.*
A fictionalised illustration done many years after the event.
(Courtesy La Trobe Collection, State Library of Victoria)

The gang did not escape unscathed during these and many other raids, whether on stations, stores, woolsheds, carriers, homesteads, or parties of travellers. When Hall and four of his mates tried to raid Mr Commissioner Keightley's house at Dunn's Plains, on 24 October 1863, Keightley fought back with a double-barrelled shotgun and killed Burke with a charge of shot in the belly. In an affray at Goimbla Station on Eugowra Creek, on 19 November 1863, Henry and William Campbell withstood a siege by Hall, John Gilbert, and John O'Meally. William Campbell was wounded, but Henry killed O'Meally and the others rode off after setting fire to the outbuildings. Hall and Dunleavy each took bullets in the arm when three troopers caught them stealing horses on 18 August 1864, but the bushrangers got away. The police, including Constable Nelson who was murdered during the raid on Collector and several who were wounded in various skirmishes with the bushrangers, also suffered during the three-year rampage of Ben Hall and his gang. The list of crimes they committed is too long to fully list here.

do so, but those whom he robbed would have felt very differently about him. His attitude towards the community was displayed on 1 April 1864. He single-handedly entered the homestead of Frederick Chisholm at Bland River, tied up Chisholm and two servants, threatened Chisholm 'for having ridden with the police from Junee', and left again after stealing 'a gold watch and other property'.

The end, for such a man, was inevitable. On 29 April 1865, a police party led by Sub-Inspector James Davidson, with the aid of two black trackers (Billy Dargin and Charley) left Forbes. Information had been received from an informer, believed to have had close associations with the gang.

On the night of 4 May the police party, acting on information received, found their man in the bush near Billabong Creek.

A cold apprehensive night was spent in the bush, and on the morning of 5 May 1865, Ben Hall would die in a hail of bullets.

Some reports say he had at least thirty bullets smash into him. His last words were reported to have been 'I am wounded — shoot me dead'.

Ben Hall was buried in Forbes Cemetery on Sunday 7 May 1865.
Also see Frank Gardiner, John Gilbert

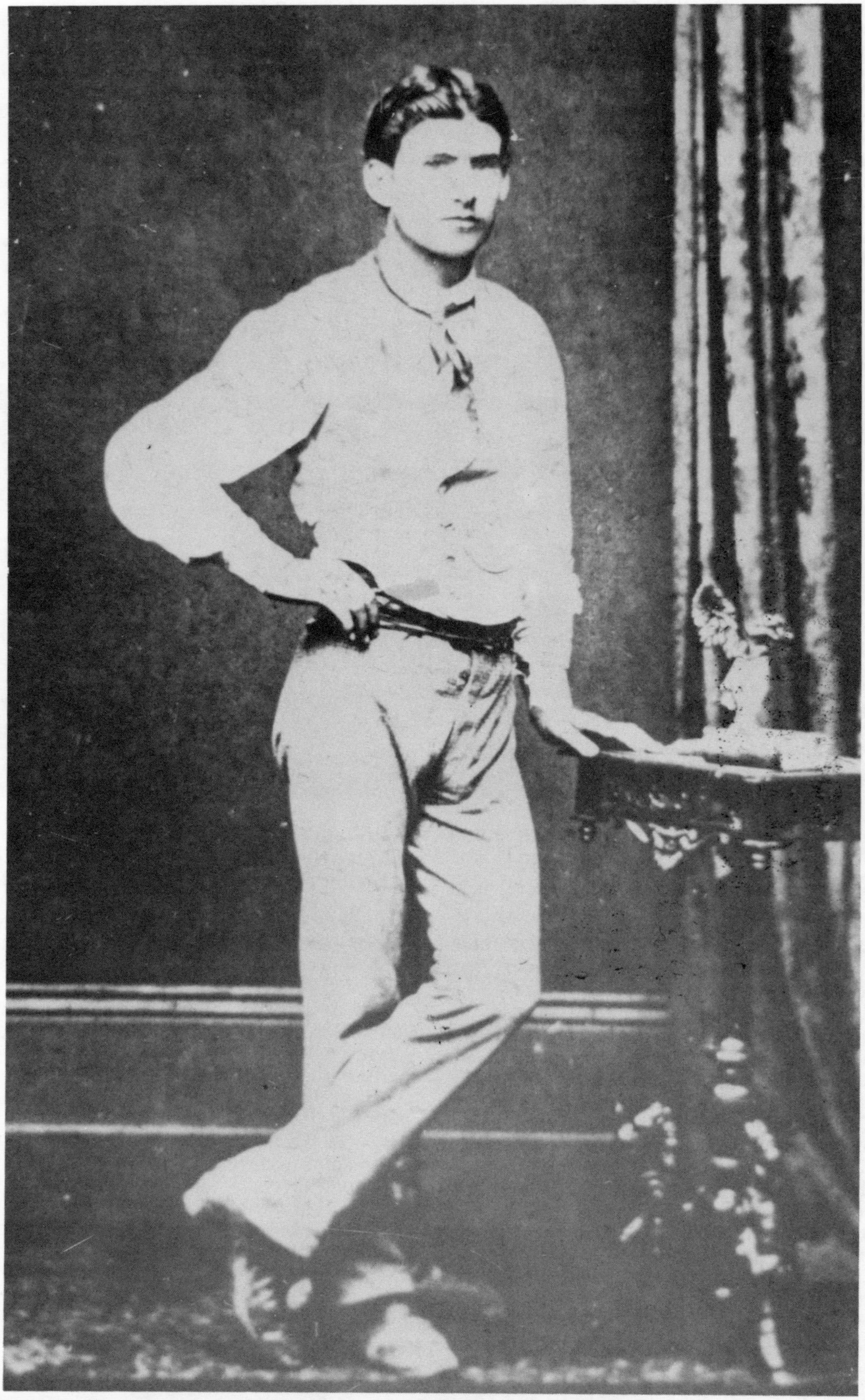

STEPHEN HART

> Born: (probably 1860)
> Native Place: Victoria
> Trade: Labourer
> Religion: Roman Catholic
> Education: Read and Write
> Height: 5ft 6ins
> Complexion: Fresh
> Hair: Brown
> Eyes: Hazel
> Particular Marks: None recorded.
> Previous History: None recorded.
> Sentence: (First charge) — 4 months Hard Labour.
> (Second charge) — 4 months Hard Labour concurrent.
> (Third charge) — 4 months Hard Labour concurrent. All charges are for Unlawfully using a Horse.
> Date of Conviction: 23 July 1877, 30 July 1877, Wangaratta Petty Sessions.

Stephen Hart was yet another of the devil-may-care young bushmen who was attracted by the fatal glamour of the Kelly Gang. He was born at Beechworth in 1859, but after a brief period of schooling, spent most of his young life working on his parents' 230-acre selection near the Three Mile Creek and Wangaratta Racecourse. He grew up to be an expert bushman and horseman. He is described as a short, lightly built youth. His family were described as good farmers and popular with their class.

Max Brown in *Australian Son* says that he won local fame as the only man who could jump his horse over the high railway gates at Wangaratta, and that he became associated with a group of local larrikins who called themselves the Greta Mob. This led to trouble with the police, and he ended up serving twelve months in Beechworth Gaol.

The records show that Steve Hart had been pulled in by the police on three charges of 'unlawfully using a horse'. They brought him before the Wangaratta Petty Sessions on 23 and 30 July 1877, and he received three sentences of four months hard labour, to be served concurrently. He was received at Beechworth Gaol on 30 July 1877, and despite his resentment against the police and contempt for the law he must have behaved himself in prison. His record is clean and he was released on 7 June 1878 to 'Freedom by Remission'.

J.J. Kenneally, in *The Inner History of the Kelly Gang* says that he joined the Kellys in their gold-seeking venture on Stringybark and Kelly's Creeks, and that 'during the period of his outlawry (he) frequently rode about in feminine attire. So successful was this disguise that he was taken to be one of the Kelly sisters, and the police attributed many of his daring exploits to Kate Kelly'.

There can be no doubt of his loyalty, daring, and resourcefulness, even though there are varying accounts of the way in which he joined the Kelly Gang. He played an active part in the robbery of the National Bank at Euroa and in holding up the township of Jerilderie, and like the rest of the gang he eventually had a price of £2000 on his head.

The end came for Steve Hart, as it did for most of the Gang, during the seige of the Glenrowan Inn on Sunday 27 June 1880. (The events of the seige are told in the Kelly Family story.

After the inn had been burnt down by the police, the bodies of Dan Kelly and Steve Hart were dragged out of the smouldering ruins and laid on sheets of bark. The charred remains were never positively identified as those of Dan and Steve, and it was impossible to find fatal bullet wounds on the bodies. These facts have led to a variety of legends, including those that they either committed suicide by poisoning themselves or that they shot each other simultaneously. The poison story is rather hard to believe, but it is certainly possible that they shot themselves to escape inevitable death by hanging.

Ned Kelly's sister Margaret (Skillion), summed up what most of the family would have thought, saying 'Thank God they are burned. I would rather see them burned than shot by police'.

The charred bodies of Dan and Steve were taken by the relatives, to Mrs Skillions selection. An undertaker was employed to provide coffins. Each had lettering on the lids, one stating 'Stephen Hart, died 28th June 1880, aged 21 years.

Also see the Kelly family

STAND AND DELIVER
MICHAEL HOWE

Australian bushrangers were in a sense the descendants of the highwaymen of England: men such as Jack Shepherd and Dick Turpin who cried 'Stand and deliver!' instead of 'Bail up!' Michael Howe, known as 'the last and worst of the bushrangers of Van Diemen's Land,' in fact learned his trade in 'the Old Dart.' He was a Yorkshireman, born in Pontefract as the son of Thomas and Elizabeth Howe. He went to sea in a merchant ship sailing out of Hull and, according to the *Australian Dictionary of Biography,* deserted to join the Royal Navy. In about 1806 he joined the army, but it seems that he did not enjoy service life because he deserted yet again. On 31 July 1811 he appeared before the York Assizes on a charge of highway robbery. The judge sentenced him to seven years transportation and he arrived in Tasmania in October 1812 aboard the ship *Indefatigable.*

The Tasmanian penal settlements had been established with the worst convicts from the mainland, many serving extra sentences for crimes committed while a prisoner. Some of these hardbitten men had 'bolted' to form the ruthless gangs which terrorised the island early last century.

Michael Howe soon heard about these bushrangers, and their lifestyle appealed to him considerably more than working as an assigned servant for a merchant and stockraiser named John Ingle. He soon 'bolted' into the bush and linked up with the gang led by the notorious John Whitehead, whose story is told later in this book. Whitehead also had been sentenced to transportation by the York Assizes, a few months earlier than Howe, so there is a possibility that they had met in England.

Howe, Whitehead, and their mates were among those bushrangers who caused so much trouble in the settled areas that Governor Lachlan Macquarie tried to solve the problem by offering a free pardon to all who surrendered. Whitehead and Howe accepted the offer, made in May 1814, but the call of an outlaw's life was too strong for them and they were soon back in the bush again. Macquarie decided that his amnesty was useless in an attempt to reform such hardened criminals and he ordered Lieutenant-Governor Thomas Davey to offer rewards for their capture and mount a stern pursuit. Before the bushrangers were captured, Davey had had to bring the island under martial law.

In October 1815, Whitehead led his gang in an attack on the property of Police Magistrate Humphrey, who had been especially vigorous against the bushrangers. Humphrey was away, but the bushrangers tied up his servants, looted his house, and then set fire to the house and the farm buildings.

Their next stop was at the farm of a Mr McCarthy, which they intended to treat in the same way. They announced their arrival with a volley of shots, but this fire was returned by a detachment of the 48th Regiment waiting in ambush. Whitehead was wounded and he begged Howe to finish him off and cut off his head, so that he would neither be captured alive nor recognised as a corpse.

Howe obeyed this gruesome instruction and even held up the dead bushranger's head, for the soldiers to see, before running off into the bush. The soldiers later found the severed head, and they took Whitehead's body back to Hobart to be displayed on the gibbet on Hunter's Island.

Howe was now the leader of the gang, which he commanded with the kind of discipline against which he had rebelled in the armed forces. He laid down rules of conduct which must be obeyed, administered oaths of loyalty and exacted promises of obedience, and handed out punishments to any who infringed his code of conduct.

The gang followed him on raids to many parts of the settled areas and their depredations were reported from as far afield as Launceston in the north to Bagdad on the east coast. The authorities in Hobart were infuriated by Howe's habit of writing letters to them, but at last it became apparent that Howe was tiring of a bushranger's life. In a letter to Lieutenant-Governor Sorell, addressed 'from the Governor of the Ranges to the Governor of the Town,' he offered to betray all his mates and give himself up if he were granted a free pardon.

Sorell accepted the offer and sent Captain Nairne into the bush to meet with Howe and bring him back to Hobart. Sorell also advised Macquarie of this move, but received a reply from Sydney to the effect that his acceptance of the bushranger's offer was illegal. Consequently Howe found himself in captivity in Hobart without much likelihood of the pardon.

His response to this was to break his parole and head back to the bush, in July 1817. Sorell promptly proclaimed him an outlaw and posted a reward of £100 for the capture of Michael Howe, dead or alive. Any convict who caught him was to receive a free pardon.

Two Ticket of Leave men, William Drew and George Watts, thought they had won the reward when they came across Howe sleeping in the bush, and managed to

Main Street at Port Arthur, the penal settlement of Van Diemen's Land.
(Courtesy Archives of Tasmania)

subdue him and tie him up. But their triumph was shortlived. Howe worked free of his bonds and tried to get away. In the fight that followed he grabbed a knife and stabbed Watts to death, and then seized Watts' gun and shot Drew. The latter managed to stagger through the bush to a nearby farm but he died of his wound.

Despite Howe's desertion of his gang, and his offer to betray them, it seems that his force of character was sufficient to make them accept him once more as their leader. He led them on further raids but the soldiers were hot on his trail and they had a number of brushes with the bushrangers. After one of these skirmishes Michael Howe shot his Aboriginal girl, Black Mary, because she could not keep up with him. She was only wounded but she never forgave him and helped the soldiers in their pursuit.

At last a young private, William Pugh of the 48th Regiment, suggested a plan to capture Howe and his commanding officer gave him permission to try. The plan involved a 'double agent,' a kangaroo shooter named Warburton, who had a hut in the rugged bushland of the Shannon region. He was on good terms with the soldiers but was also known to be friendly with Howe.

No doubt a promised share in the reward had persuaded Warburton to betray Howe, and bring him to his hut where Pugh waited with a local stockman, Thomas Worrall, who had joined in the hunt. Howe was a strange sight, clad only in kangaroo skins, wearing a thick black beard, and with a haversack and powder horn across his shoulders.

Howe was too quick for Pugh and Worrall. They exchanged shots without doing any harm, and then Howe turned and ran back into the bush. He would have escaped if he had not slipped back down a steep bank, so that Worrall could catch up with him.

For a moment the two hesitated: the blackbearded Howe staring at greybearded Worrall. In true bushranger style, Howe was game to the last. He shouted 'Black beard against grey beard for a million!' and fired his pistol at Worrall but missed again. Worrall fired back and Howe staggered but recovered himself, drawing his clasp knife and making another attempt to get away just as Pugh ran up and clubbed him with the butt of his empty musket. Howe fell and Pugh did not give him a chance to rise again, but 'battered his brains out' with the musket-butt.

It was an ignominious end for the 'last and worst' of the Tasmanian bushrangers, but Howe died as he had lived: without mercy given or received. It is believed that Howe had killed at least four white men and an unknown number of blacks.

HENRY HUNTER

*H*enry Hunter, alias James Russell, alias Dixon, alias The Frenchman, was one of the few bushrangers to follow his nefarious profession in Queensland.

Not much more is known of him than may be traced in the State Archives of Queensland and in P. H. McCarthy's book *The Wild Scotsman,* a biography of the bushranger James McPherson, which contains some details of Hunter's career.

This book describes him as a slender man of slight build, about five feet ten or eleven inches tall, with a dark complexion, long thin features, high cheekbones, dark brown to black hair, grey eyes, a long nose and a small brown chinbeard. Perhaps the dark complexion and aquiline features earned him the nickname of Frenchman.

He was said to wear 'the typical dress of a man of the road': a tweed coat, light brown Crimean shirt, moleskin trousers tucked into Wellington boots, and a cabbage-tree hat with black band.

He first stepped onto the bushranging stage at the age of twenty-one, in January 1866, when he carried out what seems to have been a singularly futile robbery. Armed with two pistols he bailed up the mailman, Willie Madden, on the road to Springsure. He commandeered the mailbags but did nothing but sort through them and take three or four newspapers and a few postage stamps.

On Madden's return trip the Frenchman held him up yet again, but on this occasion took nothing from the bags. In early February there was a repeat performance. Once more the bushranger rifled the mailbags, and for some reason threw some of the letters into a fire. He told Madden that it was too late to sort through the remainder and rode away with two mailbags over his saddle-bow.

Poor Willie Madden must have thought that three times was sufficient, but the Frenchman appeared a fourth time: on 14 March 1866. He took £50 gold sovereigns and notes from the bags, but discarded £1100 worth of cheques.

Soon, on 3 April 1866, the Frenchman bailed up another mailman, William Duncombe. Duncombe was riding along the road near Gainsford in company with Constable William Mahoney, who was dressed in plain clothes. The Frenchman held them both up and told them to sit by the roadside while he ransacked the mailbags.

Mahoney asked if he could take his pipe out of his swag, but when the Frenchman agreed Mahoney produced a revolver and fired at him, calling on him to surrender. The bushranger fired back and escaped into the bush.

In April, the Frenchman was sighted a long way south of his first appearance. He was seen at Wallan, north of Condamine, and a party promptly set out to capture him.

They cornered him in a hut, from which he answered a call to surrender with shots from his carbine. A noisy but harmless shoot-out followed, and ended when the bushranger had only two cartridges left and he saw reinforcements arriving. He walked out, threw down his carbine, and gave himself up.

He was taken to the lock-up at Condamine and then on to Brisbane. There seems to have been some uncertainty as to where he should stand trial, because he appeared before several courts until he was charged in the Rockhampton court on 16 September 1866. The charge was that he had assaulted William Duncombe and stolen five mail bags and 100 letters. The jury took only eight minutes to reach a verdict and the judge handed down the sentence of twenty-two years penal servitude.

JOHN JAMES

*M*any different stories have been told about the robbery of the ship *Nelson* when she was lying off Port Melbourne on 2 April 1852. She had arrived at Geelong from London in March that year, discharged her cargo and passengers, and sailed up to Hobson's Bay to load cargo for home. It included twenty-three boxes containing more than 8000 ounces of gold valued at about £25,000, which was an immense sum of money for that period.

There can have been little or no attempt at secrecy and it may be presumed that the news of this valuable cargo soon spread around the waterfront and up into Melbourne, where it was heard by the bushranging trio John James (alias Johnston), James Duncan and James Morgan. They had been working in the Keilor Plains and Black Forest areas, where many diggers en route to and from the northern goldfields were bailed up for their gold or other possessions.

Perhaps the three men were spending some of their loot on a 'holiday' in Melbourne when they heard the news, and it seems likely that they soon enlisted some accomplices. Various people have given various estimates of the size of the gang. Thomas McCombie, who was in Melbourne at the time of the robbery, says that it consisted only of four men. 'Old Chum,' writing in the *Melbourne Truth* on 16 July 1910, agrees with him. But the *Argus* of 8 October 1852 also mentions William Barnes and Edward Wilson as 'two of the *Nelson* robbers,' and the prison record of Stephen Fox, as well as those of James, Duncan, Morgan, and John Roberts, states that he also was charged with the robbery. It seems probable that seven men were involved. Other statements, that fourteen or twenty-two robbers boarded the *Nelson*, may be excessive. No doubt the stories that circulated at the time were well embroidered, so that they have added to the mystery surrounding the whole affair.

According to one report, the ship with her golden treasure lay at anchor completely unguarded. The only people aboard at two a.m. on 2 April 1852 were Mr Draper the mate, three seamen, three passengers, the cook, and Mr Davis the second mate, three seamen, three passengers, the cook, and Mr Davis the second mate of the Royal George, lying at anchor nearby, who was paying a visit to the *Nelson*.

They were all asleep in their cabins, when they were 'roused by loud calls' from the deck, and as each of them emerged to see what all the row was about he was seized and lashed to the bulwarks. When they had all been secured, the leader of the robbers untied Draper and ordered him to show where the gold was hidden.

Draper refused, whereupon the robber shot him in the side and threatened to kill him if he refused again, while another robber prodded Draper with a sword. Draper gave in and led them to the lazaret (storeroom) where the gold was stowed, and they soon broke the door down and carried the boxes out on deck.

Two boats belonging to Mr Liardet, who had a hotel on the shore close to the *Nelson's* anchorage, had been stolen by the robbers and were lying alongside.

The robbers lowered the gold into these, herded the ship's people into the lazaret and secured them by nailing the broken door back across the doorway, and made their escape. The prisoners seem to have been very confused about the number of their assailants, and apparently could not identify them because they were masked with black crepe.

The ship's people were released soon after daybreak when the stevedore came out with his men to continue loading the ship, and the police were informed. The government quickly offered a reward of £250 for the capture and conviction of the thieves, and Messrs Jackson, Rae, & Co., the consigners of the gold, offered another £500.

James, Morgan, and Duncan were captured so quickly that the reward must surely have tempted some accomplice, or some other person, to betray them. James was convicted on 28 May 1852 and sentenced to fifteen years on the roads, the first three years to be served in irons. He was received on board the hulk *President* on 18 December 1852 and remained in irons until 30 December 1856.

His prison record is comparatively clean, but it is remarkable to read the entry of 2 June 1858 stating: 'Letter from the Under Secretary transmitting a free pardon granted by His Excellency the Governor.' He was released on 4 June to 'Freedom by remission,' after only six years of his long sentence.

The free pardon only adds to the mystery surrounding the *Nelson* robbery, on which there are still so many theories. 'Old Chum' believed that the robbers sold the gold to a Melbourne publican soon after they brought it ashore, and that he bought it for thirty shillings an ounce. After that he stored it in his cellars until he took it to England, where he stayed for several years before returning to Melbourne.

'Old Chum' claimed that one of the robbers told this story to his defence counsel, and he wrote also that the robbers did not get away with as much gold as everyone believes. He based this statement, and his theory that only four robbers were involved, on the fact that James Duncan had a bank account of £1,200 when he was arrested. This, said 'Old Chum,' could have been a one-fourth share of £4,912, which would have been the amount the robbers received if they sold 3257 ounces of gold at thirty shillings an ounce. He said the records showed that this amount of gold was shipped at Geelong, whereas there were no records of any gold being loaded in Melbourne.

If such records existed they have long since disappeared, but 'Old Chum's' theory does not allow for Stephen Fox, whose prison record involves him in the robbery, or for William Barnes and Edward Wilson who seem likely to have been involved.

Another weakness in 'Old Chum's' theory is that the £1200 in James Duncan's account was there a long time after the *Nelson* robbery, at the time, in fact, when he was arrested for burgling a jeweller's shop in Bourke Street, near the Theatre Royal. (See his story earlier in this book).

However it is interesting to consider all the theories and statements concerning Australia's 'crime of the nineteenth century,' especially since it is almost certain that nobody will ever know the truth.

Also see James Duncan, James Morgan.

Born: 1819
Native Place: London
Trade: Labourer
Religion: Roman Catholic
Height: 5ft 10¼ins
Complexion: Pale
Hair: Brown
Eyes: Grey
Particular Marks: None
Previous History: Arrived per ship Theresa. Bond on Arrival. Per Constant 1843, 15 years. Tortoise to Van Diemen's Land 1842, 15 years by name 'Chas Henry Johnson'.
Sentence: 15 years on the Roads of the Colony, the first 3 In Irons, for Robbery of the Ship Nelson.
Date of Conviction: 28 May 1852.

THOMAS JEFFRIES

Thomas Jeffries, sometimes incorrectly referred to as Mark Jeffries although the records show his name as 'Thomas Jeffery or Jeffries,' was one of the 'twice transported' convicts who were sent first to New South Wales and later sent on to the Tasmanian penal colonies as punishment for offences committed as a convict. In Jeffries' case, the reason why he was transported to Tasmania is unknown. The records show only that he arrived at Port Dalrymple on 22 April 1822, aboard the brig *Harvies* from Sydney.

Apparently he behaved himself well enough to be treated as a 'trusty,' and employed as a Watch House guard, but he could not resist temptation and was soon fined ten shillings for being drunk and disorderly and twenty shillings for 'taking a female prisoner out of the Watch House.' After that he went completely to the bad and received fifty lashes for absconding, and twelve months at Macquarie Harbour for threatening to stab a Constable Lawson on 21 June 1824.

In 1825 he escaped from Macquarie Harbour in company with two other convicts, Hopkins and Russell. Their stolen food supplies ran out as they tramped through the bush, but Jeffries and Hopkins soon found a

Thomas Jefferies Hanged for Murder 1826

arrived from Sydney New South Wales, at Port Dalrymple 22nd April 1822

When	Whence	Trade or Calling	Remarks
Nottingham		Life	Palmer

Thomas Jeffries — copy of his convict Indent, spelling his name Jeffery, whereas other offical documentation spells it Jeffries.

solution to this problem. Jeffries shot Russell, and the two horrible companions cut up the corpse and lived on it for four days.

This ghastly provender sustained them for long enough to reach the settled areas and begin a bloody career of bushranging. One of their most notorious exploits was a raid on the homestead of a Mr Tibbs. They shot Tibbs and a stockman and forced Mrs Tibbs, who had a five months old baby at her breast, to accompany them into the bush. When she found difficulty in keeping up with them, Jeffries grabbed the baby from her arms, swung it by the legs, and smashed its head against a tree-trunk.

Other crimes included the robbery and murder of a Mr Baker at Georgetown, but the two bushrangers did not escape justice for very long. John Batman, the captor of Matthew Brady, tracked Jeffries down and took him to Hobart, where the news of his cannibalism and murders spread quickly. The public tried to pull him from the cart in which he was being taken to prison, but although his escort fought off this attempt to lynch him he did not escape legal execution.

He was taken to the gallows with four other bushrangers: Bryant, Perry, Thompson, and Matthew Brady, who complained bitterly at having to share the scaffold with a cannibal. *The Hobart Town Gazette* of 6 May 1826 related 'Having mounted the scaffold with trembling steps, Jeffries requested Mr Bedford to state to the spectators that he died justly, and that strong drink had been the primary cause of his errors. At the conclusion of the final prayer, which closed with the word "death," the Sheriff and Clergymen hastened down the steps, the executioner withdrew the bolt, the platform fell, and the miserable men dropped to eternity.'

Signed/ F. Goulburn
Col. Secretary

HENRY JOHNSTON

Henry Johnston was one of the Eureka Gang, whose story is told in this book in the biographies of John Finegan and John Donovan.

When the gang was rounded up and brought before the court at Geelong, Henry Johnston received the comparatively light sentence of six years on the roads. He was received at the Main Depot, Pentridge, on 6 November 1852, and soon showed that he would serve his sentence in the hard way. In January 1853 he was put in solitary confinement for three months as a punishment for disobedience. Almost as soon as he was released he was in trouble again, once more for disobedience, but was punished only by three days in cells on half-rations. This incident was followed by a series of offences and punishments: for smoking, misconduct, refusing to work, insolent language, refusing to answer a question, and so on. The punishments ranged from four days in cells to twenty days solitary.

Understandably, the authorities refused his requests for a Ticket of Leave, submitted in October 1854 and January 1855, but they relented in May 1857. A letter from the Chief Secretary authorised him to be released 'later that year,' and he stepped out of prison with a Ticket of Leave on 23 October 1857.

But Pentridge had not seen the last of Henry Johnston. On 29 August 1859 he was brought before the court at Sandhurst (Bendigo) on a charge of Robbery from the Person, and sentenced to five years on the roads.

Most of his record for this second sentence has been stained by dampness and is practically indecipherable, but it is possible to read that in September 1859 his conduct was 'Good.' On 17 May 1860 he was reprimanded for misconduct, and on 6 August he was charged with 'Not falling in.' The punishment for this offence is no longer legible.

The last decipherable record of Henry Johnston's life was made on 11 February 1861. For talking in the ranks, he was given three days solitary confinement.

After that, no one now knows what happened to this erstwhile member of the Eureka Gang.

Also see John Finegan

Born: 1826
Native Place: Dublin
Trade: Labourer
Religion: Protestant
Height: 5ft 9ins
Complexion: Pale
Hair: Brown
Eyes: Blue
Particular Marks: Scars right side of head, right side of forhead and left, on left eyebrow and cheekbone. Bridge of nose broken. Scars on right and left arms, slightly pockpitted on arm.
Previous History: Arrived per ship City of Manchester 1851. Free. Marion to Van Diemen's Land 1845. 7 years. Same name.
Sentence: Six years on the Roads for Highway Robbery.
Date of Conviction: 23 October, 1852 at Geelong.

GEORGE JONES

George Jones, whose real name may have been George Davis, appears to have started his lengthy bushranging career as a highwayman on the roads of Surrey in England.

He was tried there on 30 March 1829, with two other men, and a merciful judge and jury must have been reluctant to impose the death sentence which the crime of highway robbery could have brought, but the judge committed George Jones to the sentence of transportation for life, and he arrived in Sydney on 30 March 1830.

He seems to have behaved himself for the first couple of years, but after that his convict record is thick with offences and punishments. On 28 June 1833 he was given twenty-five lashes for 'stealing ropes' (?) and after that he received a total of 200 lashes for offences ranging from disobedience to attempting to escape. Twelve months in irons, plus this horrifying series of floggings, did not serve to subdue him, and on 4 April 1842 he was again tried in Sydney for highway robbery and sentenced to 'Life in a Penal Settlement.'

This meant transportation to Tasmania, although there is no record as to the date of his arrival. Probably he was sent to Hobart aboard the *Marion Watson* soon after his sentencing, and he was quickly in trouble again. Seventy-five lashes for absconding, and three days solitary confinement for misconduct, served only to harden his resolution, and he escaped from Port Arthur with Martin Cash and Lawrence Kavanagh on 26 December 1842.

Age: 27 (in 1830?)
Native Place: London
Trade: Labourer and Quarryman
Religion: Church of England
Education: Read and Write
Height: 5ft 7ins
Previous History/Remarks: Father — Griffiths Davis in London. My name is George Davis. Per Dunveyan Castle. Arrived Sydney 30 March 1830, and sentenced to Life for Highway Robbery. (Two other men had taken part in Highway Robbery with Jones.)

Apparently George Jones did not take part in Martin Cash's strange ventures into Hobart accompanied by Kavanagh, when the notorious bushranger decided to take revenge upon his unfaithful girlfriend. Cash and Kavanagh were captured, and Jones was left alone in the bush.

He soon found most congenial company in the form of two other bushrangers: James Platt and the escaped convict Moore. But George Jones had nothing like the style and flair of Martin Cash. 'Cash & Company' had concentrated their efforts upon the wealthier settlers, but Jones and his gang robbed the huts and homesteads of poor people and quickly earned themselves a reputation for ruthlessness. This became even worse when Jones displayed a streak of cruelty which led him to torture Harriet Devereaux. He believed that she had more money than they had been able to take from her, and so the bushranging trio tied her to a bench so that Jones could burn her legs with a red-hot spade.

They had shooting affrays with various settlers who protected their property by fighting back, but managed to continue their bushranging career for a few months after Martin Cash was captured. The police and troopers were hot on their trail and eventually caught up with them, by surrounding a hut in which they had taken refuge. There was a brief exchange of shots until the troopers set fire to the hut and called to the bushrangers to throw down their arms and surrender. Jones came out but he was still carrying his weapon, and one of the pursuers fired at him with a shotgun. Jones received a charge of buckshot full in the face.

The police quickly overcame the blinded and mutilated bushranger, who was taken back to Hobart and looked after until he was well enough to stand trial.

In those days when the Van Diemen's Land administration was determined to stamp out bushranging the result was a foregone conclusion, and George Jones went to the gallows on 30 April 1844.

Also see
Martin Cash, Lawrence Kavanagh

LAWRENCE KAVANAGH

As the name indicates, Lawrence Kavanagh was an Irishman. The record shows that he was a man of indomitable spirit who could not be subdued by the brutalities of the convict system, and it seems a pity that a man of such courage and resolution should have chosen a career of crime. In different circumstances he might have earned a worthwhile reputation.

On 24 August 1828 he was tried in Dublin for burglary and sentenced to transportation for life. He arrived in Sydney in 1829 aboard the *Ferguson* and quickly showed that he did not intend to accept the life of a convict. During the next couple of years he committed so many offences, including an attempt at highway robbery, that he was sent to Norfolk Island for fourteen years.

The principal purpose of the penal settlement on Norfolk Island was to break the spirit of men like Lawrence Kavanagh, but it failed in his case as it did with so many others. On 13 February 1833 he received forty lashes for insolence and disobedience, and in January 1834 he received 150 lashes for 'attempting to run away.'

But it was virtually impossible to escape from Norfolk Island, and he remained there for nine years until he was returned to Sydney. Arrival on the mainland must have revived his hopes of freedom, because he received thirty-six lashes on 19 January 1842 for 'Cutting his irons.' His next escape attempt was successful but his spell of freedom lasted only seventeen days. The Colonial Secretary, Captain Hunter, and Dr Dobbie, recognised him at South Head, in company with Thomas Brown and Joseph Johnson who had escaped with him. The three men fired two shots at Hunter and Dobbie but the two officials got away and raised the alarm, and Kavanagh and his mates were soon tracked down and charged with attempted murder.

The Sydney Supreme Court sentenced Kavanagh to life imprisonment on 12 April 1842 and he was sent to Hobart Town, where he arrived on 8 June 1842 in the *Marion Watson*. The Tasmanian authorities sent him to Port Arthur, probably in company with George Jones.

Jones and Kavanagh met Martin Cash in Port Arthur and soon hatched the escape plot which took them to freedom in the afternoon of 26 December 1842.

The trio which became known as 'Cash & Company' began their bushranging rampage in the valley of the Derwent and in other areas including Pittwater, Bagdad, and New Norfolk. They robbed homesteads, inns, and travellers, and might have continued a profitable career if Cash had not decided to visit Hobart to revenge himself on his girlfriend. Kavanagh went along with him, and was wounded in the shoot-out after Cash was recognised.

Some accounts say that Kavanagh was wounded by one of the pursuers, and others that he fell

STAND AND DELIVER

Murder's Mound, burial ground, Norfolk Island.
(Collection: Queen Victoria Museum and Art Gallery, Launceston)

> *Born:* Not recorded
> *Native Place:* Waterford, Ireland/Wicklow, Ireland
> *Trade:* Stonemason and Quarryman
> *Religion:* Roman Catholic
> *Education:* Read
> *Age:* Not recorded
> *Height:* 5ft 10½ins
> *Complexion:* Pale
> *Hair:* Brown to Grey
> *Eyes:* Light brown/light grey
> *Nose:* Long and sharp
> *Head:* Lone eye
> *Whiskers:* Brown
> *Visage:* Long
> *Forehead:* High
> *Eyebrows:* Brown
> *Mouth:* Medium
> *Chin:* Medium
> *Particular Marks:* 'A.D.' above elbow joint left arm. Two stars in palm of left hand, one in wrist. Lost little finger right hand.
> *Previous History:* Tried Dublin 24 August 1828, for House Robbery, sentenced to Transportation for Life. Arrived per Ferguson to Sydney 1829. He had various offences recorded against him at Sydney, and in 1833 he was sentenced to Norfolk Island for 14 years for Assault and Intent to rob Campbell Town Q.S. (Highway Robbery).
> 13/02/1833 40 lashes, for Insolence and disobedience. Remained on Norfolk for 9 years, before being returned to Sydney, where he managed to escape. Two notes on his Norfolk record state:
> 14/04/1834 7 days cell Rioting in gaol.
> 26/01/?? 150 lashes attempting to run away.

Some accounts say that Kavanagh was wounded by one of the pursuers, and others that he fell while running away over a rocky stretch of road, causing his weapon to discharge and send a bullet through his arm from elbow to wrist. However that may be he managed to evade the pursuers and escape into the bush with Martin Cash.

Apparently this wound was the last straw for the Irish bushranger. He determined to give himself up, and nothing that Cash or Jones said could dissuade him. His wound was troublesome, and perhaps after six-and-a-half months in the bush he was tired of running. He surrendered himself to Magistrate John Clark at Cluny on Sunday 9 July 1843. Clark arranged medical treatment for his wound and had him secured in the lock-up at Bothwell, where he stayed until he was brought to trial. In the meantime, his bushranging companion Martin Cash had been captured during another attempt to track down his faithless girlfriend. The two bushrangers were brought to trial at the Hobart Town Criminal Sessions on 4 September, with the charge against Kavanagh that of holding up the Launceston coach at Epping Forest on 3 July 1843.

He pleaded not guilty and conducted his own defence but failed to convince the jury of his innocence. Together with Cash, who was charged with murder, he was sentenced to death by hanging and the date for execution of the sentence was set as Monday 18 September.

Only an hour before the two men were to begin the last walk, execution was postponed for fourteen days and the sentence was eventually remitted to a term of imprisonment.

Kavanagh was taken to the Prisoners' Barracks in Campbell Street to await transportation to Norfolk Island.

On 6 December 1844, His Excellency, the Colonial Secretary wrote: 'Kavanagh, with good conduct, may look forward to my recommendation to have his period shortened, heinous as his offences have been, but at present it is quite out of the question my doing so.'

But Lawrence Kavanagh was to turn down this last chance. In October 1846 he joined with Jacky Jacky (William Westwood) and others in a violent prison mutiny. They smashed in the head of the cookhouse overseer, clubbed a man named Ingram, axed two other men, and carried out various acts of mayhem.

Justice was swift on Norfolk Island. Lawrence Kavanagh, with thirteen others, died on the gallows on 12 October 1846. Shortly before the execution he asked to see his old mate, Martin Cash, and they exchanged their last farewells before they parted: Lawrence Kavanagh to his death on the scaffold, whilst his companion in crime, Martin Cash would eventually end his days free from the constraints of prison life.

Also see Martin Cash, George Jones

100 AUSTRALIAN BUSHRANGERS 1789-1901

ANDREW KELLY

> *Born:* Not recorded
> *Native Place:* Sunderland (?)
> *Trade:* Labourer
> *Religion:* Church of England
> *Education:* Read and Write a little
> *Height:* 5ft 3ins
> *Age:* 19
> *Complexion:* Ruddy
> *Head:* Small, round
> *Hair:* Brown
> *Whiskers:* None
> *Visage:* Full
> *Forehead:* Low
> *Eyebrows:* Brown
> *Eyes:* Hazel
> *Nose:* Large
> *Mouth:* Small
> *Chin:* Small
> *Particular Marks:* Some of face freckled.
> *Previous History:* Transported for stealing 13 shirts valued at 52/-. To Van Diemen's Land per *Elphinstone*. Tried Durham, 7 years for stealing money, was free by servitude. Single.

A stained and faded page of the convict records, only recently discovered, shows that Andrew Kelly began his criminal career at a very early age. It states that he 'commenced stealing at 9 years of age.' Some of the record is indecipherable, but it appears that he was in trouble in England for stealing three shillings from a woman in Sutherland, for stealing a pair of trousers, and for other offences of stealing money. Eventually he was transported to Van Diemen's Land in the *Elphinstone*.

He arrived at some time in the late 1840s and soon showed himself to be a difficult and troublesome prisoner. The blotched and faded handwriting on his record, on which numerous words are impossible to read, states: 'Tried Hobart Town Supreme Court 6th December 1849 for assaulting, being armed with an axe, one Bartholomew Reardon, putting him in bodily fear . . . 2/- of the . . . property of said B.R. Guilty . . . To be transported for Life and to be kept at Norfolk Island 6 years then to be reported to Lieut. Gov. 21 Dec. 1849.'

Kelly was one of the many hardened prisoners who were sent to Australia's own Devil's Island, where he quickly became a violent man in a violent environment. He was in trouble over and over again and his record shows a long string of offences and punishments such as '28 March 1850: Disobedience. 1 mth Hard Labour. 9 July 1850: Disobedience. 1 mth Hard Labour. 30 July 1850: Disobedience. 14 days Hard Labour. (Same date) Insolence. 1 mth Hard Labour. 8 Oct. 1850: Absent. 4 mths Hard Labour. 22 Oct. 1850: Fighting. 50 lashes. (Same date) Fighting. 2 mths Hard Labour. 3 Dec. 1850: Striking (?) 4 mths Hard Labour. 25 April 1851: Disobedience & Indecent conduct. 6 months Hard Labour, and (?) placed in separate treatment. 20 Oct. 1851: Fighting. 3 mths Hard Labour (repeated). 19 April 1852: Assaulting a fellow prisoner with an axe . . . 9 mths Hard Labour. 2 years added to probation.'

The actual date on which he was returned to Van Diemen's Land cannot be traced on the record, but it would have been some time in 1852.

He was sent to Port Arthur in company with fellow-prisoners from Norfolk Island, including James Dalton.

Kelly and Dalton, with other prisoners, carried out a daring escape from Port Arthur. This story, together with that of the bushranging career of Kelly and Dalton, is told in James Dalton's biography in this book.

The James Dalton story also covers their escape from Van Diemen's Land to Victoria, and their capture in Melbourne. The Victoria police returned them to Launceston to stand trial.

On 23 February 1853 the magistrates committed them for trial on a charge of 'Having at Bona Vista in the Island of Van Diemen's Land feloniously killed and murdered Thomas Buckmaster on 6th January.' They were tried in the Launceston Supreme Court on 7 April 1853, condemned to death, and executed at Launceston on 26 April 1853. A crowd of about 2000 people watched them die.

One of the comments on Andrew Kelly's convict record is that, as a labourer, he was 'Considerably good, could earn his livelihood.' Unfortunately he chose to 'earn his livelihood' as a bushranger, with the inevitable result.

Also see James Dalton

MUR
Of Police, nea

£20
R E W

For Capture of offen
others, increased
offen

THE FOUR OFFENDE

By Order

DER

Mansfield.

O⋎⋎
ARD.

ers K llys, and tvvc
£500 for each
er.

S ARE OUTLAWED

nly Ellis,

372 S. C. POLICE

THE KELLY FAMILY

Countless thousands of words have been written about the Kelly family and the Kelly gang. The number of books about them seems to be endless, because a new one appears every year or so. It seems likely that writers, researchers, and academics have devoted more time to the Kellys than to any other group of Australian historical figures. It may seem strange that so much effort should have gone into recording the life and times of a family of lawbreakers, but the reason may be that opinions about the Kellys are are still as deeply divided as they were when the Kelly gang was riding the ranges.

One school of thought looks upon the Kellys as folk heroes, symbolic of the men and women who stood up for the rights of the individual against the oppression of authority. Another sees them simply as ruthless criminals, and Ned Kelly as a psychopathic murderer. The truth, perhaps, lies somewhere in between, and the search for this truth has fascinated countless people since Ned Kelly died on the gallows of Melbourne Gaol on 11 November 1880.

Various reports have been put forward about Ned Kelly's last moments on the cold gallows. Reports vary considerably, from describing the scene as Ned's 'jaunty air' was gone, and that his face was 'livid' and his eyes had a 'frightened' look. Another said that 'he seemed calm and collected'. Witnesses including Mr Glenny J.P., Warder Henry White, and even the executioner Elijah Upjohn, spoke of the courage and calmness with which Ned faced death. His last words are believed to have been '... Ah well, I suppose it has (or had to) come to this.... such is life.'

The members of the Australian branch of the Kelly family were

■ *Mrs. Kelly and unidentified relative.*
(Courtesy La Trobe Collection, State Library of Victoria)

pureblood Irish. Their father, John Kelly, who was usually known as 'Red', was transported from Ireland to Van Diemen's Land in 1841. Their mother, Ellen Quinn, also was Irish. There was a connection with another Irish family, bearing the Welsh name of Lloyd, which arrived in Australia in the same era and was grouped with the Kellys during their period of notoriety. Thomas and John Lloyd were Ned Kelly's uncles, and their sons, also named Thomas and John, were his cousins.

The Lloyds were comparatively minor criminals, although they all appeared before the courts in the Donnybrook-Kilmore-Beechworth-Benalla areas of Victoria, at various times between 5 October 1860 and January 1879, on charges including drunk and disorderly, cattle stealing, larceny, indecent assault, maliciously killing a horse, and manslaughter. Thomas Lloyd junior faced the Beechworth court on the last-named charge, but was discharged. All of them were charged, during 1879, with being 'Kelly sympathisers,' but there was no evidence ever brought against the sympathisers, but by an outrageous ploy, they were remanded, week by week, for three months.

The menfolk of the Quinn families, who lived in the same region, were closely related to Ned Kelly's mother and they also were in frequent trouble with the police. Their names appear on the police records at least twenty times, from 1856 to 1880, although there were more charges to follow.

On 2 December 1856 James (Jimmy) Quinn junior was charged with cattle stealing but discharged for lack of evidence. His record runs until 1879, when he faced three charges of horsestealing, which brought him no more than one fine of £5 or six weeks in gaol, and a number of charges of assault. He was an extremely violent man, who couldn't keep out of fights and trouble in general. Charges ranged from 'Violent assault' and 'Assaulting police' to four charges of causing bodily harm.

He was discharged on some counts, fined on others, and gaoled on five. His prison sentences totalled nearly nine years but he does not seem to have served full time on most of them. He would be in trouble for most of his life, and he has been described as 'mad as a meat axe'.

Edward Kelly
Both Illustrations on this page are from Illustrated Australian News, *3 October, 1878.*
(Courtesy La Trobe Collection, State Library of Victoria)

John (Jack) Quinn was Jimmy's brother, and he faced one charge of horse stealing, one of cattle stealing, and one of robbery under arms during the period 1860-61. He was discharged on all of these, but whether this means that the police did not prepare their cases properly, or whether they were simply trying to 'set him up', it is now difficult to say. Patrick Quinn, a member of another branch of the Quinn family and the son-in-law of James Quinn senior, was charged only once. In October 1870, he was gaoled for four years for having caused 'Grievous bodily harm.'

Young Ned Kelly, and his brothers Dan and James, grew up in this atmosphere of petty crime and frequent violence, and in what seems to have been an atmosphere of resentment against authority inspired by the fact that the Lloyd-Quinn-Kelly community were Irish in origin and Roman Catholic by religion. They had inherited a hatred of 'English oppressors' which had been exacerbated by transportation as convicts, and they would have seen the principal landowners, and the authorities, as representing the hated English.

The date of Ned Kelly's birth is uncertain. Professor John Molony, in

Edward (Ned)
Born: 1856
Native Place: Victoria
Trade: Labourer
Religion: Roman Catholic
Education: Read and write
Height: 5ft 10ins
Weight: 11st 4lbs
Complexion: Sallow
Hair: Dark brown
Eyes: Hazel
Nose: Medium
Mouth: Medium
Chin: Medium
Eyebrows: Dark brown
Visage: Broad
Forehead: Low
Particular Marks: Scar top of head, two scars crown of ditto, scar front of head, eyebrows meeting, two natural marks between shoulder blade, two freckles lower left arm, scar ball of left thumb, scar back of right hand, three scars left thumb.
Previous History: Single, Mother Ellen Kelly living at Greta, Devil's River; Uncle James Kelly a prisoner at Pentridge and another, James Quinn, now at Beechworth awaiting trial, and John Lloyd an Uncle a prisoner at Pentridge. Three convictions same day at Wangaratta Police Court: 3 months, 3 months, and 12 months in default of bail — bail found.
Sentence: Three years Hard Labour, for Receiving a stolen horse.
Date of Conviction: 2 August 1871, Beechworth General Sessions

Daniel
Born: 1861
Native Place: Victoria
Trade: Labourer
Religion: Roman Catholic
Education: Read and write
Height: 5ft 5ins
Complexion: Fair
Hair: Dark brown
Eyes: Blue
Particular Marks: Scar left cheek, mark of burn left elbow.
Previous History: Brother Edward 10926, James 10861.
Sentence: Three months imprisonment for Wilful Damage.
Date of Conviction: 19 October 1877, Benalla Petty Sessions.

his book *I am Ned Kelly* believes Ned was born in January 1855. Dr. John McQuilton in his book *The Kelly Outbreak*, gives it as 'late November or early December 1854'. Noted Kelly expert, Ian Jones, from his own research, believes it to be December 1854. Frank Clune, in *Ned Kelly's Last Stand*, says it was June 1855. Other people have given other dates, but Ned's own prison record, entered when he was convicted to three years hard labour at Beechworth General Sessions on 2 August 1871 for receiving a stolen horse, gives his birthdate as 1856.

Ned would have given the details to his captors, but his own

Daniel Kelly

detailing differs also. Other documents give alternative dates. In absence of his official birth certificate, it remains as one of the unsolved mysteries of the Kelly story. His brother James was born in 1860 and Dan in 1861, which means that all were very young men when the Kelly Gang was on the rampage.

When young Ned was growing up in the Beveridge-Wallan Wallan-Avenel districts, and later at Eleven Mile Creek, near Benalla, his uncle James Kelly was in plenty of trouble. He was arrested twice for cattle stealing in 1862, but was discharged for lack of evidence, and again in 1863. On that occasion the court at Kilmore gave him three years, and he was not long freed from this sentence before he appeared at Wangaratta on a charge of arson. He

■ *James Kelly — a prison record photo.*
(Courtesy Public Record Office, Victoria)

had set fire to a house occupied by his sister-in-law, her sister and their families, when they refused to let him in because he was roaring drunk. It gained him a sentence of fifteen years.

Ned's father, Red Kelly, was sentenced to six months at Avenel, in May 1865, for unlawful possession of a hide. He died on 27 December 1866, and it prompted Mrs Kelly to pack up and move her young family to the north-east of Victoria.

What with these charges against his father and his uncle James, and the fact that his cousin James Quinn junior was constantly in and out of trouble with the police, young Ned would have reached his teens with a fairly firm conviction that the police were his enemies. Life was hard at Eleven Mile Creek, where the family holding returned barely enough for subsistence, and a career in lawbreaking may well have seemed the most natural way for a youngster to make a living.

Towards the late 1860s, the most notable bushranger in the north-east region was another Irishman, Harry Power. (His story is told later in this book). Power ranged far and wide through that part of Victoria and would certainly have been assisted by the Lloyds,

James

Born: 1860
Native Place: Wallan Wallan, Victoria
Trade: Not recorded
Religion: Roman Catholic
Education: Read a little
Height: 5ft 4ins
Weight: 8st 13lbs
Complexion: Fresh
Hair: Dark brown
Eyes: Hazel
Nose: Small
Mouth: Medium
Chin: Small
Eyebrows: Dark brown
Visage: Square
Forehead: Low
Particular Marks: Scar front of head, ditto top of ditto, ditto left eyebrow, ditto outside left eye, freckle right side of neck, scar inside left wrist, several scars left thumb and forefinger, scar outside right leg, ditto top of right foot, ditto near fourth toe left foot.
Previous History: Father dead, Mother Ellen Kelly one brother and five sisters living at Greta near Benalla. No. P.C. (previous convictions). Brothers: Edward 10926, Daniel 14991.
Sentence: (1st charge) Two-and-a-half years for Cattle Stealing and Receiving. (2nd charge) Two-and-a-half years for Cattle Stealing and Receiving. Cumulative
Date of Conviction: 17 April 1873, before Beechworth Criminal Sessions, Judge Williams.

Quinns and Kellys when he wanted a meal and a bed. Young Ned Kelly may well have listened to his stories, one Lloyd descendant says that it was Power who first talked of the Republic of Victoria idea, later credited to Ned Kelly. He became Power's 'apprentice bushranger' mate. Power was helped by a young lad on several of his 1870 hold-ups, and on 2 May 1870 fifteen-year-old Ned was arrested at Greta and charged with being involved in robberies and helping Harry Power. The case was dropped after some delays due to a lack of positive identification of Ned.

The Greta arrest was not Ned's first apearance in court. On 26 October 1869, at the age of fourteen, he had appeared before the Benalla justices on a charge of assault and robbery, but this case also was dropped for lack of evidence. The police kept a close eye on him, as they did on all the Kellys and their relations, and on 10 November 1870 they hauled him before the Wangaratta court on two charges of assault and one of using obscene language. He received six months in gaol plus another twelve months 'in default of sureties to keep the peace.' His family promised to pay these sureties, and Ned was released after six months.

His brother Dan was not slow to imitate his elder brother. His first appearance before the courts, for illegally using a horse, was when he was only ten years old, at Wangaratta in 1871.

The judge discharged him, perhaps with a friendly warning because of his youth, but Dan was

■ *Kate Kelly (from* The Sun *1911).*
(Courtesy La Trobe Collection, State Library of Victoria)

no more ready to learn than Ned was. Their brother James appeared on the same charge and was also released.

After that, the three youngsters were fairly regularly in trouble. When James was only thirteen he was sentenced to five years on two charges of cattle stealing. He was released before the conclusion of this term, which was recorded against him at Beechworth on 17 April 1877, and was in trouble again, when at Wagga Wagga, New South Wales, on 27 June 1877, when he

BEECHWORTH COURT HOUSE

received a sentence of three years for horsestealing.

Dan was charged three more times before his death at Glenrowan. On 13 October 1876 he was before the Beechworth court, accused with stealing a saddle, but discharged. There was another charge for the same offence, when he was tried at Beechworth in March 1877. He was again discharged. In October 1877, the Benalla court gave him three months for wilful damage.

Ned Kelly, at sixteen, was sent down from Beechworth on 2 August 1871 to serve three years for horsestealing, but on his release he must either have kept out of trouble or broken the law a lot more skilfully. The police did not have another opportunity to arrest him until September 1877, when he went on a drunken spree in the Benalla pubs and ended in court for being 'Drunk, and assaulting police.' He got away with a fine of £3.1.0d. But the stage was set now, and the actors were ready to play their parts. The poverty stricken little Irish community appears to have been ripe for some kind of explosion, and when it came it would include Ned Kelly's mates Joseph Byrne, Stephen Hart, and Aaron Sherritt. Aaron was then regarded as a suitor of Ned's sister Kate, although she was only about fourteen at the time.

Many different stories have been told about Kate. Constable Alex Fitzpatrick of the Benalla police may have had his eye on Kate also. He

■ *James (Jim) Kelly, as an old man.*
(Courtesy La Trobe Collection, State Library of Victoria)

was an Irishman, and Irish police were hated by their fellow Irish, and looked upon as betraying their own. Fitzpatrick has been accused of raping Kate, and a descendant of the family told the author that some descendants believe that a child was born of this unwilling union, but that the incident was suppressed rather than bring Fitzpatrick to justice and thus expose Kate to the shame of her ordeal. Professor Molony's theory, in his book *I am Ned Kelly* suggests that Constable Flood was the father of Annie Gunn's baby (Annie was Ned's older sister) and this may mean the two stories have become mixed.

Like so much of the Kelly story, the truth of this matter has been obscured by time. However there is no doubt that Kate was regarded very sympathetically in the neighbourhood. Miss Sarah McMonigle, who died in 1964 at the age of ninety-two, wrote in a letter now in the author's collection that Kate was "A sad, moody girl." A Mrs. Henderson, who knew Kate when she worked as a housemaid a few miles west of Greta, wrote of her that 'Kate was a nice girl, all the stories of her drinking, etc. were lies, she was upset by the whole set-up of the gang.'

By an unhappy coincidence, Constable Fitzpatrick was the man sent to arrest Dan Kelly on 15 April 1878, on another charge of horse stealing. He found Dan in the Kelly home, with family. Like other aspects in the Kelly story there is confusion on what exactly happened that night, but in any case Fitzpatrick received a wound to the wrist in a scuffle. Police evidence later would be denied by the Kellys, it seems likely that everyone was lying about what happened and that the truth will never be known. Ned is supposed to have arrived home, with Bill Williamson and Bill Skillion, and threw Fitzpatrick out. Of course the policeman reported it to his superiors, and warrants for the arrest of Dan and Ned Kelly, their mother, their neighbour Bill 'Bricky' Williamson, and Ned's brother-in-law Bill Skillion,

STAND AND DELIVER

■ *(Right) Police Contable Scanlan.*
(Courtesy Victoria Police, PRD)

■ *(Below) Police Sergeant Kennedy.*
(Courtesy Victoria Police, PRD)

Mrs Kelly, Williamson and Skillion were arrested, and held in custody for three months before being tried for the 'attempted murder' of Fitzpatrick. Judge Redmond Barry, who was eventually to sit in judgement on Ned Kelly, sentenced his mother to three years imprisonment and told her that he would have given Ned twenty-one years if he had been in court, according to George Wilson Hall, the Mansfield newspaper editor. Another claim reports that the Judge said he would have given Kelly fifteen years. It was an extraodinary outburst by a judge.

In the meantime, Ned and Dan had taken to the bush with some mates, working on a gold claim, clearing and fencing a big horse paddock, and setting up a whisky still to raise money for Mrs Kelly's appeal. Ned had plenty of time to brood over the Fitzpatrick incident, and, later, over the stories he heard about the way police treated his mother. When the word came through of her imprisonment, Ned's hatred of the police would be confirmed for all time. The police were determined to track down Ned Kelly and his mates. In October 1878, a party of four Irish-born police constables entered the Wombat ranges in search of the Kelly Gang, and came up against the four Australian-Irish youths near Stringybark Creek. The shoot-out did not last long.

The gang surprised Mounted troopers McIntyre and Lonigan while the other two were away from the camp. On being challenged, Lonigan drew his revolver, dived for cover and was getting up to fire when shot by Ned. McIntyre agreed that he would try and persuade Kennedy and Scanlon to surrender, on their return. But Kennedy drew his revolver, a gunfight began, and Scanlon was shot. Kennedy dismounted, his horse broke away, and McIntyre managed to mount it and rode away. Kennedy was mortally wounded in a running gun battle with Ned. Realising that the Sergeant couldn't live, Ned decided, right or wrong, it would be more humane to put him out of his misery. He shot him at point blank range. He covered the body with a cloak, some say a mark of respect which bears out his claim that it was a mercy killing.

It was the murder of the police that meant the gang would be proclaimed outlaws, that any citizen could take up arms against them.

Those on the side of the law urged every possible effort to hunt down the Kellys and kill them like vermin. One only has to look at the vast volume of letters in police headquarters, Melbourne, to see the effect that the murder of the policemen had on their colleagues. Police from all parts of Victoria applied to the Commissioner to join the hunt for the murderers and take revenge for their comrades. The newspapers, and members of respectable society, joined in the outcry for swift justice to be done.

On the other side there were those who saw Ned and his mates as protectors of the free-ranging life of the bush, and of the descendants of poor Irish convicts and emigrants who were harassed by authority. Ned himself took this attitude and threatened to oppose the laws, the banks, and even the railways, which were seen as destroyers of traditional bush life. During the next eighteen months he began to see himself able to defy the great oppressive forces of law and order and even to create a new republic in which men and women could live as they pleased.

The Kelly gang had never numbered more than four men, but Ned's influence was so great that when they invaded Jerilderie he said he had come to capture New South Wales. He often would make broad statements for effect, knew that he could shake people up with a good rant. Given an audience, he invariably performed — often with a very clear purpose in mind. The Jerilderie exploit followed a raid on Euroa, where they had robbed a

NEW SOUTH WALES, } Proclamation by His Excellency Sir
to wit.   HERCULES GEORGE ROBERT ROBINSON,
                     Knight Grand Cross of the Most
                     Distinguished Order of Saint Michael
                     and Saint George, Governor and Com-
                     mander-in-Chief of the Colony of New
                     South Wales and its Dependencies, and
           Governor. Vice-Admiral of the same.

WHEREAS Edward Kelly, Daniel Kelly, Stephen Hart, and Joseph Byrnes, have been proclaimed outlaws in the Colony of Victoria: And whereas warrants have been issued by James Bambrick, Esq., J.P., at Wodonga, Victoria, charging Edward Kelly, Daniel Kelly, and two men whose names were then unknown, with the wilful murder of Michael Scanlon, Police Constable of the Colony of Victoria, and the said warrants have been duly endorsed by Captain Brownrigg, Police Magistrate at Albury, to have force in the Colony of New South Wales: And whereas Victorian warrants duly backed for execution in New South Wales, were subsequently granted for the apprehension of Stephen Hart and Joseph Byrnes, charging them with the murder of the aforesaid Michael Scanlon: And whereas the above-named offenders are still at large, and have recently committed divers felonies in the Colony of New South Wales: Now, therefore I, Sir HERCULES GEORGE ROBERT ROBINSON, the Governor aforesaid, do, by this by my Proclamation, issued with the advice of the Executive Council, hereby notify that a reward of four thousand pounds will be paid—three-fourths by the Government of New South Wales, and one-fourth by certain Banks trading in the Colony—for the apprehension of the abovenamed four offenders, or a reward of one thousand pounds for the apprehension of any one of them; and that in addition to the above reward a similar reward of four thousand pounds has been offered by the Government of Victoria; and I further notify that the said reward will be equitably apportioned between any person giving information which shall lead to the apprehension of the offenders and any members of the police force or other persons who may actually effect such apprehension or assist thereat; and that if, in attempting to effect the capture of the said offenders, any member of the police force should be wounded, thereby incapacitating him from earning a livelihood he will be pensioned; or in the event of any member of the police force losing his life in the execution of such duty, his widow or family depending upon him for support will be provided for by the Government.

Given under my Hand and Seal, at Government House, Sydney, this eighteenth day of February, in the year of our Lord one thousand eight hundred and seventy-nine, and in the forty-second year of Her Majesty's Reign.

By Command,

GOD SAVE THE QUEEN!

■ (Above) On the trail of the Kellys. Police officers and Queensland trackers engaged in hunting the bushrangers.
From left Senior Contable King, Sub-Inspector Stanhope O'Connor, (Queensland), native troopers Hero, Barney, Jacky, Jimmy and Johnny (with arms folded), Superintendant J. Sadlier, Chief Commissioner F.C. Standish (Victoria)
(Courtesy Victoria Police, PRD)

■ (Right) Proclamation signed by Governor Robinson, by command of Henry Parkes dated 18/2/1879 naming the Kelly Gang as Outlaws.
(Courtesy Archives of NSW)

■ *Ned Kelly 8/8/1874*
He won a 20-round boxing match against Isaiah 'Wild' Wright. Ned Kelly once boasted of his boxing ability that 'while I had a pair of arms and bunch of fives at the end of them they never failed to peg out anything they came into contact with . . .'
(Courtesy Victoria Police, PRD)

bank as they did in Jerilderie. In the latter place they tied up the local police and drove the small population into the bar room of the Royal Mail Hotel.

In the hotel, Ned addressed his proclamation to the outside world, in what has become known as the Jerilderie Letter. He claimed that he and everyone associated with him had been cruelly wronged, and the long letter has some colourful material such as blaming everything upon a 'parcel of big ugly fat-necked wombat-headed big-bellied magpie-legged narrow-hipped splay-footed sons of Irish bailiffs of English landlords'. There are however, elements of a manifesto in the letter, a foreshadowing of the rebellion and a clear threat of what lies ahead.

An interesting point is that, although the name of Ned Kelly springs to mind when the subject of bushrangers is mentioned, he and his gang did little or no bushranging in the traditional style practised by Frank Gardiner, Harry Power, Ben Hall, etc. There was no sticking up of mail coaches and robbing of travellers. The Kellys didn't see themselves as bushrangers. Their robbing of just two banks, only two months apart, would serve to remind people that they were against authority. But none the less, the money they stole was used amongst their family and friends.

Even the police came to recognise the Kelly phenomenon as something different and used the significant description 'outbreak' to define it.

The Gang retreated to their bush hideout. Many sympathisers knew where they were, but the police had a long search ahead of them. The gang broke from cover of the bush in order to kill Aaron Sherritt (whose story is told later in this book) on the night of Saturday, 26 June 1880. This would bring major police resources to the area to mount a pursuit.

A special police train was despatched on Sunday, when no other trains ran, with the bulk of

■ *General plan of the battleground at Glenrowan. An illustration of the period.*
(Courtesy La Trobe Collection, State Library of Victoria)

police being picked up in Benalla to travel to Beechworth via Wangaratta. The train had to pass through Glenrowan, and here would be Ned's climactic strike at his enemies — joined by the tiny selector army who would be summoned to Glenrowan by rocket signals when the train was wrecked. This was the strategy, almost a military operation. Ned and Steve Hart started the Glenrowan holdup while Joe Byrne and Dan Kelly were still on their way from Beechworth.

The railway tracks were ripped up to derail the police train, and the people of Glenrowan were herded into the parlour of the hotel owned by Mrs Jones. The night was spent drinking free grog, singing songs, and dancing, in a great party atmosphere, but with some apprehension being experienced.

No doubt numerous people would have looked curiously at the set of armour Ned and his mates had forged out of plough mould-boards — the blunt, curved wedge that turns the sod after the share has sliced through it. The gang believed that the suits of armour would protect them from police bullets.

Ned made the mistake of allowing the local schoolmaster Thomas Curnow to take his wife and child home. Curnow took a candle and a piece of red cloth and ran to the railway and stood waving the improvised lamp at the approaching train, thus saving it from being derailed and saving from almost certain death many of those police on board.

The police quickly detrained and set to lay seige of the Glenrowan Inn. The battle of Glenrowan began with both sides firing defiantly at each other. Joe Byrne was the first of the gang to die (see his story earlier in this book). Dan Kelly and Stephen Hart were almost certainly dead by the time the police set fire to the Inn. This episode is covered in Hart's story in the book.

When the signal rockets were fired, in error, at the start of the battle, Ned Kelly left the hotel to turn the sympathisers back. He was already seriously wounded in the arm and foot. He returned to try and

STAND AND DELIVER

■ *Glenrowan Railway Station and Jones Hotel. The Kelly Gang's last stand at Glenrowan.*
Photographer Wadeley stood on the south side of the line to get this amazing photo of one of the most historic events in Australia — as it was in progress. By this time, a wounded Ned Kelly was being attended to by Dr. Nicholson, in the station master's office. The spectators on the platform represent only a portion of the entire crowd. Note the ladder placed against the verandah, offering the chance to view the events from the roof.
(Courtesy Victoria Police, PRD)

get the others out and was in the Inn, about 5 a.m., when Joe Byrne was killed. Dan and Steve did not follow him when he left, and at dawn, he made his last attempt to save them. After bleeding from severe wounds for more than four hours, wearing ninety-seven pounds of armour, in near-zero temperatures, he limped back to attack thirty-four police besieging the inn.

The police would have been in awe and fear of the armoured figure when it appeared from the misty light of dawn, firing wildly at them. He did not escape their bullets and finally he fell, mangled by twenty-eight shot wounds.

Puzzled by this strange apparition, they pulled off the helmet and found they had captured the dreaded Ned Kelly. With the Glenrowan Inn burnt to the ground, the end of the Kelly Gang was at hand. Ned survived his wounds and on 28 October 1880 he stood trial for killing Mounted Constable Thomas Lonigan almost exactly two years earlier. He retained his sense of grievance, and his conviction that the murder had somehow been justified because he had been wronged, until the end. When Judge Redmond Barry asked Ned whether he had anything to say 'Before sentence of death should be passed upon him,' he replied that he and the judge would soon meet again at a higher court, where they would find out what was right and what was wrong.

The argument about the rights and wrongs of the Kelly affair continue to this day, and one may find plenty of people in the Kelly Country, indeed anywhere in Australia, who believe that all his actions were justified. Murder can never be justified. Some people in the north-east knew the Kelly family well, long after the events of 1880, because Ned's mother lived until 1923 and his brother James lived until he was eighty-seven, when he died in Greta in 1946.

James Kelly was the only one of Ellen Kelly's three sons to learn a lesson from the law. When he appeared before Judge Williams in the Beechworth court, on charges of cattlestealing and receiving, the jury found him guilty but added a recommendation for mercy because he was only thirteen. Williams ignored this and sentenced him to five years imprisonment. In those days, this meant that he was gaoled with men much older than himself, many of them hardened criminals of the worst kind, and he must have had to grow up very fast.

Jim Kelly served part of his time in Beechworth until he was transferred to Pentridge, where his

No. 10926		Name	Kelly, Edward	
Height ... 5ft 10	Sentence.	Three Years H.L.	Death	
Weight ... 11 st 4		Serve		
Complexion ... Sallow		Two & a half years		
Hair ... Dk Brown		4D		
Eyes ... Hazel	Date of Conviction.	2. 8. 71	29 October 1880	
Nose ... Medium				
Mouth ... Medium				
Chin ... Medium				
Eyebrows ... Dk Brown	Offence.	Receiving a Stolen horse.	Murder	
Visage ... Broad				
Forehead ... Low				
Date of Birth ... 1856				
Native place ... Victoria	Where and before whom tried.	Beechworth Ged Sess J. Electe Esks	Melbourne Central Crim! Court. Sir Redmond Barry	
Trade ... Labourer				
Religion ... R Catholic				
Read or Write ... Both.				

Scar top of head, Two scars crown of do; Scar front of head, eyebrows meeting. Two natural marks between shoulder blades, Two freckles lower left arm, Scar ball of left thumb, Scar back of right hand, Three scars left thumb.

Single, Mother Ellen Kelly living at Greta, nr Devil's river, Uncle James Kelly a prisr at Pentridge & another James Quinn now at Beechworth awaiting trial and John Lloyd an uncle a prisr at Pentridge & Contr Same day at Wangaratta pol Ct. Vey 3 Ms 3 Ms & 12 Ms. in default of bail — Bail found

When received.	Offences, Sentences, &c.	Extensions by—
		Visiting Justice / Superintendent
		M. D. M. D.
	Brothers James No 10861 Daniel 10991	
Beechworth Gaol	21.5.73 Handing to fellow prisr two pieces of tobacco Sus. dy 7 days 5	7
Pentridge	19.2.73	
thereabouts Battery	25.6.73 Jan wards Sus 2 pris	
	25.9.73 2.2.74 Freedom by remission Regained 2.11.11	
Melbourne Jail 31.10.80	11 November 1880. Executed at 10 am.	

100 AUSTRALIAN BUSHRANGERS 1789-1901

■ *Ned Kelly — The last two portraits. Both were taken on 10/11/1880. The next day he was hanged.*

Both were taken by photographer Charles Nettleton, who ten years earlier had photographed Ned's bushranging tutor — Harry Power.
(Courtesy Victoria Police, PRD)

■ *(Below Right) Note the prison garb and close cropped hair. This was an early prison photo, long before he grew a lengthy beard.*
(Courtesy Public Record Office, Victoria)

record shows that he behaved himself fairly well except for three offences: having cell blackened with gas (?); disobedience of orders; and having paper with writing. He served a total of four days solitary confinement for these fairly innocuous offences, and was freed on 21 August 1876 after serving three years and three months of his sentence. With £5.2.11d prison pay in his pocket he headed for home territory.

He was briefly in trouble again when he went over the border into New South Wales and served a spell in Wagga Wagga gaol and Darlinghurst Gaol in Sydney. He would later receive a sentence also, his last, of five years sentence for horsestealing, before he finally decided to go straight and settle down. He devoted himself to taking care of his mother and he became a respected citizen of the Greta district. A letter from an old lady living in the Kelly Country described Jim Kelly as '... the most beloved man in our district, always ready to help anyone in trouble. Went across to Parkes in a jinker and brought Kate's three children back to Greta West (as it is today) in the jinker. (The baby so small it had to be tied to a pillow.) A distance of hundreds of miles — and he, Jim, a bachelor, and Mrs. Kelly raised the three children.'

There is no doubt that the Kelly story is far from over. Many people still search for more and more details, even over one hundred years after Ned's death by hanging in Melbourne Gaol on 11 November, 1880. As more and more delving into official documentation continues and new evidence becomes available we shall learn more of the real story. After a ten year search the author is finalising a book on Harry Power, which includes a lot of new evidence, including Ned Kelly's association with the bushranger. The respected Kellyana author-historian, Ian Jones, is presently researching a book on Joe Byrne and Aaron Sherritt, in which much new evidence will be released.

111

STAND AND DELIVER

FRED LOWRY

From Return of Bushrangers Guilty of Offence, known as Acts of Bushranging:

No. 94

Lowry Frederick
Country: New South Wales
Age: 27
Religion: Unknown
Particulars: Engaged in numerous Robbery under Arms

From Return of Bushrangers Killed and Wounded:

No. 4

Date/Place of occurence: August 1863, Laggan
Name: Frederick Lowry
Killed or wounded: Shot dead
Particulars offence: Robbery of Mudgee Mail, Western District.
Particulars known: Notorious offender.

'Tell 'em I died game!'
Fred Lowry's last words have assured him of a place in Australian folklore, although there is not very much more known about a man whom the authorities once described as a 'notorious offender.' Apparently he committed a number of bushranging offences in company with Larry Cummins and Jack Foley, until he was shot dead after their robbery of the Mudgee Mail.

Somehow the three men had learned that the Mudgee mailcoach would be carrying Henry Kater, a Mudgee bank officer, on his way to Sydney with a quantity of old bank notes which had been withdrawn from circulation and were to be destroyed. On Monday 13 July 1863 the coach was moving slowly up Big Hill in the Blue Mountains when the bushrangers trotted their horses out of ambush with the cry of 'Bail up!'

Kater's only companion in the coach was a Mrs Smith, who began to scream loudly until Lowry assured her that he did not rob women. This was lucky for Mrs Smith, who was carrying £200 in her handbag. The bushrangers were interested only in Kater's carpetbag, which contained £5700 in old notes.

Lowry joked that he and his mates could make a bonfire of the notes just as easily as the bank could. He was in jovial mood, and when he relieved Kater of his revolver he commented that it was the eighth he had commandeered in similar circumstances.

The bushrangers unharnessed the coach horses, drove them off into the bush, and disappeared after them. The coach crew and passengers plodded to the nearest town with news of the robbery, and the troopers of the South eastern Police District of New South Wales set out in search of the bushrangers.

They took nearly seven weeks to catch up with them, but ended the affair on 29 August 1863. They caught Foley separately, in the manner described in his biography in this book, and caught up with Cummins and Lowry at the hotel on Cooksvale Creek.

Senior Sergeant Stephenson led the party of troopers which trapped Lowry and Cummins in their hotel room. He called on them to surrender, but Lowry was certainly determined to 'die game' and the hotel resounded to gunshots as he and Stephenson exchanged fire. Lowry's bullets wounded Stephenson in the hand and leg, but one of Stephenson's shots hit him in the throat. Larry Cummins surrendered as his mate fell choking and gasping to the floor.

Next morning, the police brought a dray to carry Lowry to Goulburn, but it was already obvious that the bushranger would not survive the long journey. Later in the day the police pulled up the dray at a station homestead, and sent for a doctor, Dr Waugh, to attend Lowry. Waugh examined him and said that he was dying.

Bushranger Lowry, who had been unconscious for much of the time, survived only three hours longer. Just before he died he opened his eyes and croaked out the words, 'Tell 'em I died Game'.

The police carried his body on to Goulburn, where an inquest on 1 September 1863 decided that his death was the result of 'justifiable homicide'. He had been carrying £164.19.6d in his pockets.

Also see John Foley

112

WILLIAM MACK

Born: 1827
Native Place: Dublin
Trade: Shoemaker
Religion: Roman Catholic
Height: 5ft 7ins
Complexion: Dark
Hair: Brown
Eyes: Hazel
Particular Marks: Nil recorded
Previous History: Arrived per ship 1829. Free. Ascertained to be 'Bond'. States he arrived in Sydney when a child but does not know name of ship, to Port Phillip about 17 years ago. Proper name.
Sentence: (1st charge) Twelve years on the Roads, First two years in Irons — for Robbery in Company. (2nd charge) Eight years on the Roads, first year in Irons, to take effect from expiration of former sentence — for Robbery in Company. Two years remitted (vide/chief Secretary's letter 11 November 1856).
Date of Conviction: (1st charge) 10 February 1853, at Melbourne Supreme Court.

■ *An early engraving of Castlemaine.*
(Courtesy Castlemaine Art Gallery & Historical Museum)

William Mack was the partner in crime of Richard Bryant, whose story is told in this book. The two men robbed Jackson's store at Fryer's Creek, Mount Alexander (Castlemaine) of money and gold. There is some doubt as to whether they were the only two men involved, because they faced two consecutive charges of robbery in company at the same time as George Ellison and Thomas Quin. This may be pure coincidence, because there were plenty of assaults and robberies in those uproarious days.

The Melbourne Supreme Court sentenced Mack and Bryant to twenty years imprisonment, and they may have wondered whether they would ever be free again. Bryant was a rebellious prisoner but Mack seems to have behaved himself fairly well. During his first two years he received minor punishments for one case of insolence and one of disobedience, but the next note on his record is to his credit.

On the date 22 October 1856 there is a note that Mack 'Assisted in rescuing the Shipkeeper (Mr Jackson) after he had been thrown out of the row boat on the occasion of the rush. Remission of sentence as recorded.'

The 'rush' was an attempt by a number of prisoners to seize and escape by a rowing boat. The story is told in the biographies of Frank McCallum (alias Captain Moonlite) and Harry Power in this book.

Mack received a generous remission of two years for his part in this affair, but this did not save him from official admonishment for disobedience, in February 1857.

His record notes that in April 1857 he was a witness in the trial of prisoners concerned in the murder of Inspector-General Price. After that there is a list of minor offences and punishments, which no doubt caused the refusal of his first petition for release in October 1859.

During the next two years there were only three charges on his record. On 19 October 1859 he received ten days solitary confinement for disobedience, with a further ten days on 17 May 1860 for having tobacco in his possession. The punishment on 3 May 1861, for the strange offence of 'Talking in school,' is indecipherable. Probably he was subject to one of the early attempts to reform prisoners by teaching them to read and write.

William Mack was to serve only half his sentence of twenty years. On 19 November 1861 he was released on Ticket of Leave to Melbourne. After that date his name does not appear on criminal records which have come to light so far.

Also see Richard Bryant

STAND AND DELIVER

FRANK McCALLUM

— FRANCIS McNEISH McNEILL McCALLUM —

Alias

CAPTAIN MELVILLE

No.528
Born: 1823
Native Place: At Sea/Inverness
Trade: Labourer
Religion: Presbyterian
Height: 5ft 5¾ins
Complexion: Sallow
Hair: Brown
Eyes: Grey
Particular Marks: Two Scars on left side of head, two small scars on right arm.

From Van Diemen's Land record:
Alias: Edward Melville, Mulvell
Name: Francis McCallum
Trade: not recorded
Age: 15 years
Height: 5ft
Complexion: Pale
Head: Oval
Hair: Reddish brown
Whiskers: -
Visage: Oval
Forehead: High
Eyebrows: Reddish Brown
Eyes: Grey
Nose: Small
Mouth: Medium
Chin: Medium
Particular Marks: Small blue mark inside right arm, three scars back right hand.

Frank McCallum, who is best-known in bushranging history as 'Captain Melville,' seems to have had a talent for confusing the authorities. His record is so long and complicated that it is quite difficult to work out where he was on any specific date. Even his native place, as given in the records, has this touch of confusion. It is stated as 'At Sea/Inverness', which may mean that he was born at sea and first landed at Inverness in Scotland. He was using the alias of 'Edward Melville or Mulvell' when he was only fifteen, and this was only one of the aliases used during his criminal career. When Judge Barry tried him for highway robbery, in the Geelong Circular Court on 3 February 1853, he was described as 'Thomas Smith (3rd) tried as Captain Melville.' There is no explanation of the enigmatic '(3rd)', although it may simply mean that two other criminals were using the name of Thomas Smith at that time.

Frank McCallum began his criminal career at a very early age. He was only thirteen when he was tried at Perth, Scotland, for housebreaking, and the record states that he had earlier convictions for theft. On 3 October 1836 he was sentenced to seven years transportation and sent to Van Diemen's Land.

The usual confusion surrounds his date of arrival. One part of his record remarks 'Stated to have arrived per *Royal Sovereign* about 1837 under sentence of 10 years', while another part states 'Arrived in Van Diemen's Land 29 September 1838. No. 2369. Per *Minerva (2)*, tried at Perth 3 October 1836, 7 years for Housebreaking'.

However there seems to be no doubt that he was sent to Point Puer, the penal settlement for juvenile convicts, where he was quickly in trouble. He received twenty lashes for absence and insolence, a further thirty-six for repeated insolence, and seven days solitary for yet another case of insolence. This last offence was recorded on 22 February 1840, but after this date confusion reigns once more. One part of his record states that, after eighteen months in Point Puer, he was drafted to the timber yard at Hobart Town, where he took to the bush with a boy named Staunton. They were recaptured and sent to Port Arthur, with their sentences extended by five years, and young Frank received thirty-six lashes when a fellow-prisoner reported him for 'making free' with Staunton in the hut where they were confined.

Another part of his record tells a completely different story. On 22 February 1841, he committed a felony and had his sentence extended by two years, and on 6 July 1841 his sentence was changed to transportation for life after he had been charged with burglary.

Obviously he kept the warders and magistrates busy, and if his record is correct then he appeared before the police magistrates twenty-five times between 1839 and 1848. The charges ranged from misconduct and disobedience to neglect of work and absconding, and the sentences ranged from thirty-six lashes to lengthy periods of hard labour and time to be served in chains. He absconded three times: in November 1848, January 1850, and April 1850.

So many stories have been told about Frank McCallum as 'Captain Melville' that it is difficult to separate fact from fiction. One story is that, during a year's probation, he lived with Tasmanian Aborigines and his alleged interest in the Aborigines has given rise to

■ Part of the prison record of Frank McCallum, alias 'Captain Melville'. Copious documentation still exists regarding this complicated man.
(Courtesy Public Record Office, Victoria)

another yarn in which he is said to have translated the Bible into one of the Aboriginal languages.

There is no real evidence for either of these stories but they help to show the atmosphere of confused romanticism which now surrounds the young Scotsman. Part of the problem may be ascribed to the fact that parts of the copious records which still survive are now almost illegible.

Apparently he reached Victoria, the goal of so many escaped convicts from Van Diemen's Land, in late 1851, and began his bushranging career.

Again, it was hard to separate fact from fiction, because other bushrangers may have committed some of the robberies attributed to him. Alfred Joyce of Norwood Station claimed that he was robbed by a man who called himself Captain Melville, but the robbery does not appear to have been very significant. In fact it seems to have been rather a friendly affair. Captain Melville exchanged weapons with Joyce and left him a broken-down horse and dilapidated saddle and bridle, while making off with a good horse and harness, food, clothing, a meerschaum pipe, six sovereigns, tobacco, and a watch. Joyce's horse was later found at Ballan.

Captain Melville's territory was the Mount Macedon area of Victoria, where he is said to have commanded a gang, but if all the stories are true he ranged far and wide. There are two Melville Caves, allegedly named after him: one near Mount Kooyoorah, near Inglewood, and the other in Mount Arapiles near Natimuk, and Melville Forest, in the Western District of Victoria, is supposedly named after the bushranger.

The legends that surround Inglewood claim that the bushranger hid his plunder in the rock formations near the summit of a hill, and that he had a horse trained to come to his whistle. The 'hidden plunder' story is also told of places in the Grampians.

Legends of Captain Melville persist through western Victoria, and many people still living there can pass on stories which they were told by their forebears about the exploits of Captain Melville. One of these was told to the author by Miss E. Biggin of Daisy Hill, who wrote 'Grandfather Donald McDonald was working on a

Melvilles Caves, 1866.
(Private collection)

sheep station, when a horseman came up on a nice fleabitten grey brood mare . He said he was Melville, and no one must leave the premises or it wouldn't be well for them. He locked all the doors and the elderly couple were locked in their room. He slept in grandfather's room with him during the night. [In the morning] he sent [McDonald] for the station horses . . . and asked about a fine black animal. "You can have my horse . . . here is a receipt for her." The horse remained in the district and foaled many times'.

At some time in 1852, Melville joined with William Robert Roberts, whose story is told in this book. They committed various acts of bushranging, culminating with a theft from the two golddiggers Thomas Wearne and William Madden. The two bushrangers stopped them on the Ballarat road on 19 December 1852 and robbed them of £33, but gave £10 back so that they could enjoy their Christmas holiday in Geelong.

Melville and Roberts also made their way towards Geelong, collecting tribute from various travellers on the way. By Christmas Eve they were comfortably ensconced in a Geelong brothel, where Melville boasted drunkenly that he had a price of £100 on his head.

One of the prostitutes slipped out to tell the police, who turned up to arrest the bushrangers. Melville made a desperate attempt to escape by dragging one of the troopers off his horse and attempting to mount, but he was subdued and handcuffed.

The Colonial Secretary had already written out a notice of reward 'for apprehension of two bushrangers, who have been committing depredations in the neighbourhood of the Loddon River, and Jim Crow Creek.' They were described as 'One — rather tall, face long and dark, wore a light waterproof coat (shooting coat underneath) grey crossbarred trousers — He was called by his companion "Doctor" and "Frank." One —short, rather stout, fair complexion, hair brown, had a black waterproof coat on. In his hat, which was a cabbage tree, he had a pair of goggles etc.'

The notice appeared in the *Government Gazette* of 31 December 1852, when the two bushrangers already were in Geelong Gaol. The Visiting Justice wrote to the governor of Victoria that 'The two men . . . now confined in the Geelong Gaol on Remand Warrants for several felonies, answer the above description . . . I am of the opinion they, the two men, are connected with the daring robberies and murder lately committed in the vicinity of the Ovens diggings.'

On 3 February 1853, Judge Redmond Barry sentenced Captain Melville to a total of thirty-two years, on three charges of highway robbery. Frank McCallum, then aged thirty, began his sentence on the hulk *Success*, where he started off on the wrong foot by attacking one of the warders and trying to bite off his nose. He was flogged and put in solitary confinement for twenty days.

The hulks *Success, President, Lysander,* and *Sacramento* lay moored together in the bay, and convicts were taken ashore each day to work on building a stone wharf, magazine, and battery. On one of these dreary boat journeys from hulk to shore the convicts made a sudden attempt to escape by taking over the boat. Maxwell, the Assistant Superintendent of the *Lysander,* was following in another boat, and he witnessed the struggle in which Constable Owen Owens was bashed over the head with 'something short' and thrown overboard. John Turner, an English seaman serving a sentence of four weeks for deserting his ship, also was killed in the struggle.

Maxwell and his men soon caught up with the mutinous convicts, and Captain Melville and two others were tried for murder and sentenced to death. The case was referred to the Full Court and McCallum escaped the gallows on a technicality: that the Crown could not show a warrant for the removal of McCallum from one hulk to another, and thus could not prove that he was trying to escape from custody.

The sentence was changed to life imprisonment but Frank McCallum was far from defeated. He made a violent attack on the governor of Melbourne Gaol and would have killed him if the warders had not dragged him off. The years of rebellion against authority seemed to have turned him into a wild beast, and he became notorious for his savage reactions against restraint.

By that time, Frank McCallum must have felt that the life which began as a petty thief in Scotland, and brought him the brief glamour of a bushranger's career, was hardly worth living. In August 1857 he contrived to strangle himself in his cell. Reports of the incident described his body as 'Lean and slight, but highly muscular, being one of those men whom constant exposure and exercise had rendered "wiry" and tough.'

Also see William Robert Roberts

JAMES McPHERSON

James McPherson, known as 'The Wild Scotsman,' was one of the ten children of John and Elspeth McPherson. Young James was thirteen when his parents emigrated from Scotland to Queensland, in 1854. Some accounts say that James became an apprentice stonemason in Brisbane, and this would seem to be confirmed by the fact that he was a stonecutter in later life. Others say that he worked with his father on a property in the bush, and that he learned to be a skilled horseman and bushman. It is possible that the second occupation succeeded the first, especially since James was a shearer and bush worker when he turned to bushranging. He became known variously as Alpin, Alphin, or Alphen McPherson or Macpherson, Bruce Kerr, McGregor, Scotchie, and John or Jack McPherson, but the official documentation always refers to him as 'James McPherson, otherwise called The Wild Scotsman'.

One report attributes his descent into bushranging to a romantic and impetuous turn of mind. Apparently he liked to read stories about bushrangers and built a picture of them as 'men whose example it would be honourable to follow,' which may be the reason why he claimed — or had claimed for him — that he had been a member of Ben Hall's gang.

Another story is that he became a bushranger after a dispute with the manager of a property on which he was employed, and left without his wages. Perhaps one thing led to another, with the sense of injustice inspired by the quarrel causing him to follow his bushranging heroes into a career of robbery under arms.

Among the first of James McPherson's long series of offences was the holdup of a hotel owned by a publican named Willis. In company with other men he raided the hotel and shot Willis when he resisted. The bullet struck Willis in the mouth and the gang left him bleeding badly as they ransacked the hotel and galloped away.

McPherson was about twenty-one at the time, and despite the reward posted for his capture he evaded the troopers for several years until he was caught and charged with robbery of the mails. It was not the first time that he had held up a mailman and sorted through his bags in search of money.

Sentenced to twenty-five years in the St Helena Island prison settlement in Moreton Bay, for some reason he attracted a lot of sympathy and a many people, including clergymen, politicians, and landowners, signed petitions for his release.

One of these, in the State Archives of Queensland, states that 'The said James McPherson was tried at Maryborough in the colony on the thirteenth day of September [1866] before His Honor Sir James Cockle Knight Chief Justice; for that on the twenty-seventh day of November [1865] on the Gayndah Road near Degilbo in the district of Wide Bay in the colony of Queensland feloniously and under arms did stop a certain mail with intent to rob, and did steal therefrom certain post letterbags the property of the Postmaster General of this colony contrary to the statute in that case made and provided for and was found guilty whereupon the said James McPherson was sentenced to twenty-five years penal servitude.'

Despite this petition and subsequent appeals McPherson had to serve eight years of his sentence. His excellent behaviour, which led to the Sheriff of the gaol describing him as one of the best-conducted prisoners in his charge, must have helped his sympathisers' efforts on his behalf; and he was released on 22 December 1874.

For the rest of his life he was a reformed man. As a stockman on Ruthven Downs Station, at the age of thirty-seven, he married seventeen-year-old Elizabeth Ann Horsfeldt on 21 December 1878, and took her to live at Hughenden. Their first child, Elspeth Ann, was born there on 2 April 1880, and four sons and another daughter were born during the following eleven years.

The family had moved to Burketown, where James worked as a stonecutter and carrier. The Burketown people were well aware of his bushranging past.

His peaceful and hardworking life ended on 23 July 1895. He was riding home from the funeral of a friend, Daniel Sullivan, who had died in a horse and cart accident, when he was badly injured in a horse accident. There are various accounts of the accident, but one of the most consistent is that the horse, a flighty thoroughbred mare, took fright and ran away with him. It ran into a gully and up the bank, fell back, and rolled on McPherson. He sustained a fractured skull and severe internal injuries, and died four days later. He was buried beside his friend Daniel Sullivan in the Burketown cemetery.

STAND AND DELIVER

HARRY MANNS

From Return of Bushrangers

NO.105

Country: New South Wales
Age: 22
Religion: Protestant
Former Calling: Labourer
Particulars: Executed. Bullock Driver and Stockman. Relatives farmers in Lachlan district.

Various books have given different accounts of the background and even of the age of Harry Manns. Frank Clune, for example, says in *Wild Colonial Boys* that he was thirty-one, and in *King of the Road* that he was twenty-four. The official records show that he was twenty-two, the son of a small farmer in the Lachlan District, that he had been a bullock driver and stockman and 'stockman to Mr McCaush,' and that he had been 'brought up to Horse and Cattle stealing.'

That evocative statement may have been written by an exasperated police official who felt that everyone born in central New South Wales had been brought up as a 'cattle duffer' or 'gully raker' as the men who made free with other people's livestock were sometimes known.

Harry Manns was certainly associated with various bushrangers who roamed the area, especially the group which Frank Gardiner organised for the daring robbery of the Gold Escort. Gardiner enlisted Manns for this exploit, and he received his share of the gold and banknotes although various writers disagree upon how much he was carrying when he was caught. Roy Mendham says that he had '100 ounces of gold and £400 in notes,' while Frank Clune states that the amount was '£134 in banknotes in his pockets and 215 ounces of gold in the valise in his saddle.'

Inspector of Police Sir Frederick Pottinger, who was fighting a kind of guerrilla warfare with the bushrangers who infested the western police district, drove his small force to the utmost in an attempt to run down the Gold Escort robbers. On 7 July 1862 Pottinger and two troopers came face-to-face with Harry Manns and John and Charlie Gilbert. After a brief interrogation John Gilbert galloped away, but the police arrested Harry and Charlie and took them to Merool Station. Next morning they escorted them towards Burrangong, but John Gilbert and his mates ambushed the party and freed the two bushrangers.

Harry headed for Gundagai, but the police were determined to 'get their man' and they tracked him to Wombat Diggings. They put him on trial in Sydney, on 3 February 1863, with his mates McGuire, Fordyce, and Bow, but the jury disagreed and could not reach a verdict. A second trial was scheduled for 23 February, at Darlinghurst.

By that time, Harry Manns had been in captivity for months. He had been lodged first in Bathurst Gaol and then brought down to Sydney, and he was fed up with prison life and legal quibbling. During the trial he interrupted the judge, became abusive, said he was tired of the proceedings, and finally condemned himself to death by growling a confession of guilt. The jury returned a verdict of guilty against all the bushrangers, but the administration commuted the death sentences except for that passed against Manns. He had confessed his guilt, and so he must hang.

The people of New South Wales were horrified by this heartless decision of the Executive Council. Six members of parliament and a number of prominent citizens begged for his reprieve, and 15,000 people took only two days to sign a petition for commutation of the sentence. The authorities ignored all these pleas for mercy and the time was set for Harry's execution: nine a.m. on 26 March 1863.

When Harry's last day dawned he was attended by Archdeacon McEnroe, Archpriest Therry, and Father Dwyer. They accompanied him as he walked from his cell to the gallows, carrying a crucifix, and mounted the scaffold to confront the masked hangman. About thirty witnesses heard him say 'I thank all my friends and the good people of Sydney who have tried to save my life. May God bless them all.'

The execution was a horrid shambles. The hangman had not adjusted the noose properly, and when Harry fell through the trap the noose slipped partly up over his face and head. The struggling body swayed and writhed in agony as Harry slowly strangled. The witnesses heard loud gasping and saw blood staining the hood over Harry's face.

The body convulsed for ten minutes, became still, and then recommenced its awful struggling and writhing. The prison surgeon and four warders took hold of the body, adjusted the noose around its neck, and let it fall again. A few minutes later the surgeon pronounced life extinct.

The nightmare scene would never be forgotten by those who witnessed it. Archpriest Therry is said to have prayed 'May God forgive them, may God forgive all who took part in and saw this dreadful happening.' Harry Mann's tortured body was placed in a coffin and taken to Redfern railway station. It was buried in the cemetery at his birthplace, Campbelltown, where a large crowd attended the funeral.

Also see Frank Gardiner, John Gilbert, Ben Hall

EDWARD MELVILLE

Numerous Melvilles were convicted for bushranging and other offences, and this fact has led to some confusion between them and the notorious Captain Melville. He is well known, but not many people have heard of such men as Edward, George, Alfred, and James Melville, who appeared before the Victorian courts at various times, and there were other Melvilles in other parts of the country.

Some bushranging historians believe that Edward Melville was in fact Captain Melville, since the latter used the name of Edward in an early alias. However this seems unlikely, and it is probable that Edward Melville was a comparatively small-time bushranger who committed only one or two offences and was never brought to justice.

The reasons behind the confusion may be found in George Boxall's *Story of Australian Bushranging*, in which Edward Melville appears before Captain Melville. The first incident described was that of 23 February 1852, when the squatter Elliott Aitchison was robbed near Buninyong.

The man who bailed him up robbed him of horses, saddle, bridle, saddle bags, a watch, a bill of exchange for £30, and some money. Aitchison identified the bushranger as 'Edward Melville, who had been working for a neighbouring squatter, Mr Winter, of Winter's Flat, and was well known in the district. A reward of £30 was offered for his apprehension.'

The second incident was that of 18 December 1852. In Boxall's words, Captain Melville 'rode up to a sheep station near Wardy Yallock, and asked Mr Wilson, the overseer, who was the owner. "Mr Aitcheson," was the reply'.

Captain Melville and his mate Roberts then held up Wilson, the station owner David Aitcheson, and sixteen shearers, tied them up, and stole two horses with saddles and bridles.

The confusion undoubtedly has arisen because of similarity between the names Aitchison and Aitcheson and the fact that a Melville was involved in both instances. But Elliott Aitchison was able to identify Edward Melville as a man known as a worker in the district, which would hardly have been the case with Captain Melville. Perhaps Edward actually carried out some of the robberies for which the 'Captain' was blamed.

As for Alfred and James Melville, they cannot be classified as bushrangers. On 16 April 1866, Judge Williams gave Alfred two years on the public works for setting fire to a stack of hay, while James Melville received two years hard labour for unlawfully wounding and was imprisoned in June 1869.

STAND AND DELIVER

GEORGE MELVILLE

On 20 July 1853 the Gold Escort operated by the Melbourne Gold Escort Company left the McIvor diggings (Heathcote) en route to Kyneton, where it would join with the government Gold Escort and drive on to Melbourne. Thomas Flookes drove the team pulling a dray loaded with gold, escorted by a police sergeant and three men led by a Mr Warner.

About thirty-five kilometres from McIvor the dray had to turn a sharp rocky corner in the road, and as Flookes drove up to this rocky point he saw that a shelter similar to that of an Aboriginal mia-mia had been built by the side of the road and a big log thrown across the track. Flookes tried to negotiate his team around this obstacle, but as he did so a hail of fire erupted from the shelter. Flookes received a fatal wound and the men of the escort soon gave up the attempt to fight back and galloped away.

A number of men emerged from behind the shelter and looted the dray of 2223 ounces of gold and about £700 in notes. They included George 'Frenchy' Melville, a thirty-one-year-old ex-convict from Tasmania; William Atkins, twenty-eight, another ex-convict; George Wilson, thirty-two; and John and Joseph Francis who were also known as John and Jeremiah Murphy.

It is possible that several other men were involved. When John Francis, a Ticket of Leave convict, was captured, he is supposed to have told the Commissioner of Police, Captain McMahon, that the gang included 'Joe Grey (alias Nutty, to be found at Tommy Condon's in Little Bourke Street), one named "Billy," boarding with the proprietor of the Bush Inn, Bob Harding (at McEvoy's tent opposite to the Commissioner's at McIvor), Ned McEvoy, George Elson (fighting man who had one tooth out), George Melville, George Wilson, and two others, names unknown...

If the gang was indeed as large as Francis claimed then it is no wonder that the Gold Escort guards turned tail, but the whole story of the McIvor Gold Escort is so confused that it is hard to know the truth. Reports of the capture of Joseph Francis say that he was captured in Queensland, and released after informing on the rest of the gang, and also that he was 'arrested at Jeffries' Station on the Campaspe ... by Cadet William Symons, and, as he was being conveyed to Melbourne, committed suicide.'

Some of this confusion is understandable because most of the official documents concerning the

■ *(Left) Judge Edward Williams who sentenced Melville, Atkins and Wilson to be hanged on 3/10/1853.*
(Courtesy La Trobe Collection, State Library of Victoria)

■ *(Opposite) George Melville. Every bushranging book will show this photo as being 'Captain Melville' (Frank McCallum), who supposedly committed suicide in the Old Melbourne Gaol in August 1857. In actual fact it is the death mask of George ('Frenchy') Melville, leader of the gang who robbed the McIvor Gold Escort on 20 July 1853. George Melville was hanged on 3 October 1853 at Old Melbourne Gaol, where this original death mask can be seen on display.*
(Courtesy La Trobe Collection, State Library of Victoria)

£500 REWARD.—The Melbourne Gold Escort Company will pay the sum of 250*l.* for the apprehension and conviction of the parties who robbed the M'Ivor Branch of the Escort, on Wednesday last; and a further sum of 250*l.* for the recovery of the stolen property, or a proportionate sum, for the recovery of any part thereof. SAML. ARGYLE, W. LE BOUEF, JAMES FINLAY, Directors.
Melbourne, 23nd July, 1853.

8:05

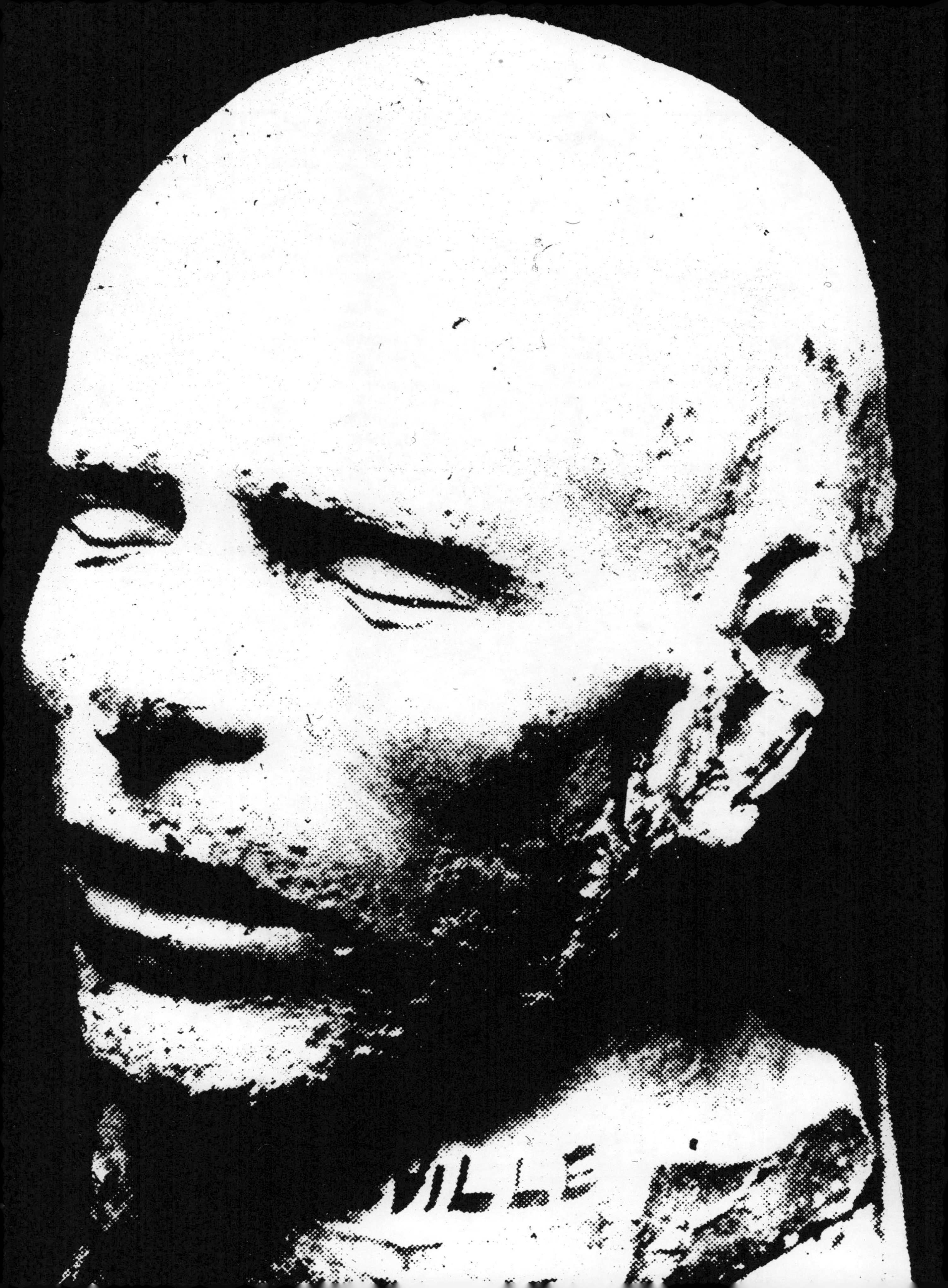
VILLE

STAND AND DELIVER

■ *(Opposite) Attack on the Gold Escort between McIvor and Melbourne on 20 July 1853. The Melbourne Gold Escort Company offered a £500 reward for the capture of the bushrangers. (See page 120.)*
(Courtesy La Trobe Collection, State Library of Victoria)

■ *The McIvor diggings' 26 July 1853. Julius Hamel made this impression of the McIvor (Heathcote) goldfield just a few days after the infamous robbery of the McIvor Gold Escort, which was robbed on 20 July 1853.*
(Courtesy La Trobe Collection, State Library of Victoria)

case are missing. The prison records of the gang have disappeared, and the Trial Briefs covering the trial of the bushrangers cannot be located. It is not altogether uncommon for criminal records and files to be missing, perhaps because some relation influenced their removal from storage.

However it is certain that the Gold Escort robbery sparked off a manhunt which soon resulted in the capture of some of the bushrangers just as they were about to escape from the country. The police arrested John Francis and George Wilson and their wives aboard the *Madagascar* in Hobson's Bay, and George Melville and his wife aboard the barque *Collooney*. They found William Atkins and his wife Agnes at a boarding house in Melbourne, with their passages for England already booked in the *Hellespont*.

The captured men and their wives were carrying a total of £2501.10.0d in gold, banknotes, sovereigns, and bank drafts, plus '7 bags of gold, value not stated.' The Melbourne Gold Escort Company did not recover the bulk of the stolen gold and so it is possible that other members of the gang, as named by John Francis, got clear away with their share of the booty.

Apparently John Francis told Captain McMahon all about the robbery and then committed suicide by cutting his throat, which may be the reason why his brother Joseph also is alleged to have suicided. Only three men, Atkins, Melville, and Wilson, could be brought to trial before Judge Williams, who passed sentence on many bushrangers during his long career on the bench. They were well represented by defence counsel. Thomas Fellowes defended Atkins, Archibald Michie defended Melville, and Richard Ireland defended Wilson.

These three barristers were to have brilliant careers in law and politics, but they could not break down the prosecution case against the three bushrangers. Williams sentenced them all to hang for the murder of Thomas Flookes.

At eight a.m. on Monday 3 October 1853 they were hanged before a large crowd of spectators. An account published many years later said that 'Atkins died as soon as the bolt was drawn, but Wilson and Melville struggled for several minutes. The hangman was compelled to draw the legs of Melville down with considerable force before life was extinct.'

The McIvor Times of 13 June 1862 told the gruesome story of Mrs Melville's treatment of her husband's body. She recovered it from the Sheriff, took it to an oyster shop in Bourke Street where they had been living, decorated it with flowers, and placed it on public view. 'Many hundreds of people indulged in morbid curiosity by visiting the place, and quite a thriving trade was done in oysters while the body was on view. As she served her customers Mrs Melville indulged in a tirade of abuse of the police and their methods to the annoyance of Captain McMahon ...'

After that incident, the bodies of executed felons were buried within the prison walls.

■ *A woodcut of 'Mad Dan' Morgan printed when Morgan was on the loose as a bushranger.*
(Courtesy La Trobe Collection, State Library of Victoria)

DANIEL 'MAD DAN' MORGAN

Australian folklore has given the name of 'Mad' or 'Mad Dan' to Daniel Morgan, but it may be rather an unjust nickname. He was certainly a ruthless bushranger and murderer, but his acts were no worse than Ned Kelly's murder of three policemen and not as bad as those of the cannibals like Pearce and Jeffries and the killers of friends like Dignum and Comerford, who burnt their victim's bodies. He is said to have shot men while they were asleep, and to have committed arson and killed stock, but other bushrangers cold-bloodedly murdered men,- men like James Kelly senior who served fifteen years for arson and Captain Moonlite who shot a horse he could not handle. Morgan's bushranging career lasted from 19 July 1860 until 9 April 1865, but many of the acts which he committed were no worse than those recorded against such men as Ben Hall and Thomas Clark.

For example, the list of his offences between 18 June and 26 August 1863 shows that he 'Robbed two horses from 7 youths near 10 Mile Creek... Robbed three men at Wagga Wagga... Robbed one man of horse and gold watch... Robbed a man of a horse near Piney Range... Robbed Wallandool Station of horses, saddles, etc... Stuck up Magistrate Bayliss near Urana, but took nothing... Gunfight with Bayliss and party, in which the Magistrate received a gunshot wound.' None of these offences, or even the total of them all, would seem to warrant the 'Mad Dan' nickname.

It may have been bestowed because of his hatred of the police, and because of his ominous physical appearance. In Margaret Carnegie's book *Morgan — The Bold Bushranger* she says that 'He was distinguished by his immense black beard flowing to his breast, his hair hung over his shoulders in gipsy ringlets. His height was nearly six feet, the nose a demonstration, massive and straight but terminating in a peculiar hook which curved over the upper lip, this with his small clear blue eyes gave him the appearance of a ferocious bird of prey...'

He was arrested only once, after his robbery of a hawker near the Castlemaine goldfields in 1854. He appeared before Judge Redmond Barry on 10 June 1854 under the name of John Smith, and received the sentence of twelve years hard labour with the first two years in irons.

Apparently this sentence caused Morgan to develop the hatred of police which affected him during the rest of his life. The volume containing his prison record for that sentence is one of those missing from the archives, but Margaret Carnegie says that he became an embittered man and that 'fellow inmates give a picture of an isolated and bitter man, brooding over his wrongs and injustices.'

The absence of official records causes a problem in researching Morgan's background, and much new research is still required. Margaret Carnegie lists a number of aliases and nicknames by which he was identified at various times, including 'John Smith, Sydney Bill, Sydney Native, Dan Owen, Down-the-Hill Jack, Down-the-River Jack, Bill the Native, Bill the Jockey,' and so on. The quantity of these fanciful names, and the number of offences listed against him, make one wonder how much of his story belongs to bushranging legend rather than to reality.

In his book *Morgan the Murderer*, Edgar Penzig states that Margaret Carnegie's work in wrong, and he comes up with the unusual suggestion that Morgan was just an alias — adopting the surname of the seventeenth century pirate, Henry Morgan! Penzig's book sheds some new light on the subject but many gaps remain in this complex bushranger's career. Morgan always protested his innocence of the crime for which he was imprisoned, and when he was released on Ticket of Leave to the Ovens–Yackandandah districts on 23 June 1860 he began his long campaign of revenge against society. On 19 July 1860 he was posted as 'Illegally at Large,' and soon after this the reports began to flow in of bushranging offences committed by the man called 'Mad Dan' Morgan.

■ *John Wendlan with the shotgun he used to shoot Dan Morgan.*
(Courtesy Victoria Police, PRD)

■ *Dan Morgan — the corpse was propped up and a revolver placed in his hand, so a dramatic photograph of the dead bushranger could be taken. Small copies of this photo were sold as souvenirs to an eager public.*
(Courtesy Victoria Police, PRD)

On 26 August 1863, Magistrate Henry Baylis was wounded in a shoot-out with Morgan and a mate, between Urana and Wagga Wagga. Baylis escaped and was to be awarded a gold medal for his courage in the face of danger. Morgan's bushranging escapades continued in earnest.

By 1864 he carried a price of £500 on his head, and this was soon to escalate to £1000. This was because of his murder of John McLean, on Round Hill Station near Albury. He shot and wounded a station worker, Heriot, and then burst into tears and apologised for the 'mistake.'

By way of making amends he told John McLean to go for a doctor, but as McLean turned to obey, Morgan changed his mind and shot him in the back. Morgan's mood changed again and he tried to look after his victim, but McLean died.

These bewildering changes of mood seem to have been typical of 'Mad Dan,' and have caused some bushranging historians to believe he was insane. However there can be no doubt of his hatred of police, and on Friday 24 June 1864 this led him into the coldblooded murder of Police Sergeant David McGinnity, who with Constable Charles Churchley, was riding homewards along the Tumbarumba road when they met Dan Morgan. McGinnity did not recognise the bushranger and greeted him casually.

Morgan's reply was 'You are one of the bloodthirsty wretches looking for bushrangers.' He drew his revolver and shot McGinnity, who fell dead from his horse. Churchley fired twice but missed Morgan, and then turned and galloped away. He was charged with cowardice, but perhaps he can hardly be blamed for making his escape.

Morgan showed his strangely divided character yet again. He placed the sergeant's cap in the middle of the road so that any passerby would look for the body, but stole the policeman's horse, revolver, and rifle.

After the murder of McGinnity he continued his bushranging career, but the list of offences alleged against Morgan is far too long to relate in a brief biography. It is now impossible to say how many offences he actually committed, and how many of those could be attributed to his imitators.

His reputation was enough to send a thrill of horror through the people of the bush, and it may be that they blamed every raid and robbery upon Morgan without knowing whether he had been anywhere near the site.

The police were hot on his trail after his murder of the sergeant.

■ *'Capture and death of Morgan the Bushranger', drawn by N. Chevalier.*

The Victoria Police said they would catch him within a couple of days if he returned to that colony, and he responded by boasting that he would 'take the bloody flashness out of the police.' As though to challenge them, he made his way back to Victoria, to the Ovens district.

The police, backed up by a party of armed settlers, were soon on his trail again. By the time he reached Peechelba Station on the Ovens River, on 8 April 1865, they were only a couple of hours behind him.

Peechelba Station, owned by Ewen MacPherson, was a fine property with a seventeen-mile river frontage, well stocked with sheep and possessed of a fine homestead. The story goes that Morgan arrived late in the day, pulled his revolver on MacPherson's son, and herded the whole family and station personnel into the homestead, where he enjoyed a meal and forced them to entertain him with piano-playing and singing. It is said also that the nursemaid of the MacPherson children asked his permission to put them to bed, and that when he allowed her to do so she ran away to warn the police.

At eight-fifteen on the following morning, Sunday 9 April, he drove the men of the station out of the homestead at pistol-point, and walked with them across the yard to mount his horse and make his getaway. Unknown to Morgan and the station people the police party had arrived during the night, and they were staked out around the homestead in readiness for his appearance.

They included a local settler, John Wendlan, who had armed himself with a single barrel muzzle loading percussion shotgun taken from one of the men's huts.

As Morgan appeared, Quinlan stepped from behind a tree, took careful aim, and pressed the trigger. The shot hit Morgan in the back and came out through his throat.

The police carried Morgan into the woolshed and laid him on a mattress, where he lay throughout the morning with about fifty people crowding around to have a look at 'Mad Dan.'

He died at a quarter to two in the afternoon.

The stories about Morgan had created such a sensation that hundreds of people flocked to see the corpse when it was carried to Wangaratta, and many of them behaved as badly as he was supposed to have done. Souvenir hunters cut off locks of hair, and Police Superintendent Cobham persuaded a doctor to flay off Morgan's face skin and beard so that he could 'peg it out on a sheet of bark like an opossum skin to dry.'

Dr Dobbyn, the coroner, wanted Morgan's head for examination by the professor of anatomy in Melbourne

University, to study the theory that Morgan was a 'humanised gorilla.' Dr. Henry, for Dr Dobbyn, cut the head from the body, had it shaved bald by a barber and a plaster cast made of the shaven head, and then sent the head to Melbourne.

One account says that while the headless corpse lay in the police stables, awaiting burial, some other ghoul cut off the scrotum and made it into a tobacco pouch. Edgar Penzig in his book *Morgan the Murderer* disputes that it ever happened.

Dobbyn and other medical men were suspended from duty because of their interference with the body, but were later reinstated. A Board of Inquiry gave its opinion that the mutilation of the body of Daniel Morgan was 'of a brutal disgusting character and an outrage on public decency.'

JAMES MORGAN

Born: 1829
Native Place: Birmingham
Trade: Labourer
Religion: Roman Catholic
Height: 5ft 4½ins
Complexion: Fair
Hair: Brown
Eyes: Grey
Particular Marks: Wart on back of right hand.
Previous History: Arrived per ship Lady Raffles 1842. Bond on arrival and Conviction. A Returned prisoner from Van Diemen's Land. Proper name James Gavagan recognised by J.G. an absconder from VDL per Asia 4. 1836 — 7 years. Tried in Melbourne about 1845 and sentenced to 15 years per Flying Fish to VDL, From where he absconded.
Sentence: 15 years on the Roads of the Colony, first three years in Irons, for Robbery of the ship Nelson.
Date of Conviction: 28 May 1852.

The criminal record of James Morgan shows that his real name was James Gavagan and that he was a 'returned prisoner,' or absconder, from Van Diemen's Land.

There were plenty of those in Victoria during the goldrush era, but the authorities do not seem to have made any special effort to round them up unless, like Gavagan alias Morgan, they got themselves into trouble on the mainland.

Even in such cases they seem to have been simply given a term of imprisonment and, as often as not, released on a Ticket of Leave which allowed them to remain on the mainland.

Morgan was an accomplice of John James in the *Nelson* robbery, of which the story is told in James' biography in this book. Morgan was captured with the rest of the gang, and sentenced to fifteen years imprisonment with the first three years in irons. He was received on board the hulk *President* on 15 December 1852.

The guards in the *President* and the other hulks, and in the penal establishments ashore, had to supervise a collection of unruly prisoners of whom a good many had long criminal records. Such men did not bow their heads to authority without making some effort to show their contempt for it, and their reactions ranged from 'disorderly behaviour' to mutinies and escape attempts of the type in which the prison guard Owen Owens was killed.

James Morgan was not prepared to submit without a struggle and for the seven years which he served in the hulks or in Melbourne Gaol he was repeatedly hauled up before the Chief Warder the Assistant Superintendent, or the Superintendent for one offence or another.

The long list of offences recorded against him began on 6 March 1853 when he received five days solitary confinement on bread and water for using 'insolent, obscene, and threatening language to the Chief Warder.'

After that date, Morgan's list of numerous offences includes exciting a disturbance, fighting, being disorderly, talking, and over and over again, the use of threatening, abusive, insolent, profane, or improper language. Between August 1856 and July 1860 he was charged sixteen times, and received sentences ranging from three days solitary confinement to six months hard labour in irons.

On 27 November 1860 the Colonial Secretary granted him a Ticket of Leave for the district of Melbourne, and no doubt the prison guards heaved a sigh of relief when they saw him go down the hulk gangway for the last time.

Also see John James

MUSQUITO

George Boxall says that Musquito, the black bushranger, was 'transported to Van Diemen's Land for the murder of a black gin (possibly his wife, which is no crime according to native law) in 1823, and having been employed on a cattle station in New South Wales, was appointed stock keeper. Later he was employed as a tracker, and aided the soldiers in capturing some of the bushrangers. For this he was so persecuted by his fellow-convicts that life became a burden to him. He appealed to the authorities for protection; but as this was not accorded to him, he became a bushranger himself ... After about two years of bushranging, Musquito and Black Jack, the two leaders, were captured!'

The *Hobart Town Gazette* of 13 August 1824 wrote 'We are exceedingly happy to state that Musquito, the Sydney black, who had speared and killed so many unfortunate storekeepers, has at last been taken and lodged in gaol ... He was brought into town yesterday severely wounded.'

On 3 September 1824, the newspaper reported 'Musquito, who was lately taken and wounded by a black boy named Tegg, was this day removed from the Colonial Hospital to the Country Gaol. It is supposed he will recover.'

Boxall states that Musquito was defended by Gilbert Robertson, who claimed that the murders he committed were in self-defence. But the jury found him guilty of 'Aiding and abetting in the wilful murder of William Holyoak at Grindstone Bay on 15th November 1823.'

According to Boxall, Musquito replied to the sentence of death with the oft-quoted comment 'Hanging no bloody good for blackfellow.' When he was asked why it was not as good for blackfellows as whitefellows, he replied 'Oh, very good for whitefellow — he used to it. Unfortunately for Musquito he also had to become 'used to it' when he was hanged in Hobart in 1825.

■ *This notice-board, c. 1828, promises equal justice to black and white alike. Colonel George Arthur addressed this message to the natives of Van Diemen's Land; who within Arthur's lifetime had been reduced to a population of merely fifty.*
(Collection: Queen Victoria Museum and Art Gallery, Launceston)

STAND AND DELIVER

JAMES NESBITT

■ *(Opposite) James Nesbitt. One of the young men who was influenced by 'Captain Moonlite'. His prison record ends with the note 'shot dead by the Police', like numerous other young wild colonials.*
(Courtesy Public Record Office, Victoria)

No.11234
Born: 1857
Native Place: Victoria
Trade: Labourer/Tobacco manufacturer
Religion: Roman Catholic
Education: Read and write
Height: 5ft 9½ins
Weight: 10st 10lbs
Complexion: Fresh
Hair: Brown
Eyes: Hazel
Nose: Thick
Mouth: Medium
Chin: Medium
Eyebrows: Dark brown
Visage: Long
Forehead: Medium
Particular Marks: Build medium, scar top of head, two scars side of head, 2 inches long. Two moles back of neck, two brown spots right cheek bone; scar upper right lip, scar left jaw, freckle top of shoulder and left side neck.
Previous History: Native. Single, parents and three sisters in Carlton, James Nesbit proper name. 28/07/73, one month 12/06/75, 14 days impt.
Sentence: (1st charge) Three months Hard Labour, for Larceny. (2nd charge) Four years Hard Labour, for Robbery in Company. (Sentenced as James Lyons.)
Date of Conviction: (1st charge) 8 September 1873, Prahran Police Court.
(2nd charge) 15 July 1875, Melbourne Criminal Sessions, before Mr Justice Stephens.

James Nesbitt began his criminal career early in life, with a sentence of a month's hard labour for larceny when he was sixteen. He was barely out of prison for that sentence, handed down on 28 July 1873, before he was back again for another three months hard labour for larceny, to which he was sentenced on 8 September 1873. After that he stayed out of trouble until June 1875, when he received fourteen days for being drunk and disorderly.

The young labourer and 'tobacco manufacturer,' which probably means that he worked in a tobacco processing plant, was born in Buninyong, Victoria, in 1857. He must have had a discouraging family background. During the trial of Captain Moonlite's gang, of which James Nesbitt was a member, the *Melbourne Argus* reported that his father James Nesbitt senior had been charged at the Melbourne City Police Court with having thrashed and abused his wife and sent to gaol for six months.

On 15 July 1875, James Nesbitt appeared before Mr Justice Stephens at the Melbourne Criminal Sessions, under the alias of James Lyons. He was on the serious charge of robbery in company, and Stephens gave him four years at hard labour.

He served his time in Melbourne Gaol, Pentridge, Williamstown, and Pentridge again, and his record shows that he was a fairly troublesome prisoner after his first sixteen months confinement. On 11 December 1876 he received forty-eight hours solitary confinement for disobedience, and after that he received a series of punishments for relatively minor offences such as idleness, talking, improper language, quarelling, leaving his seat at divine service, and the peculiar charges of 'Claiming paper improperly' and 'Having trousers improperly.'

He was released on 17 September 1878 and set free with prison pay of £3.13.9d. Nobody knows how he occupied the next few months, but he was waiting for the release of a man whom he had met in Pentridge. His Pentridge record shows that on 13 August 1878 he had his 'Indulgences deferred one day' for giving tea to a prisoner named Scott, and this was Andrew Scott who called himself Captain Moonlite and enlisted young James Nesbitt into his bushranging gang.

No doubt the two men discussed a bushranging venture while they were in Pentridge, and Captain Moonlite lost no time in forming his gang after his release from Pentridge in March 1879.

The story of Captain Moonlite's gang is told in Andrew Scott's biography in this book. For young James Nesbitt, membership of the gang led to his death at the age of twenty-two.

James Nesbitt, like the rest of Moonlite's young accomplices, was devoted to his leader. He always showed himself ready to obey his leader's slightest wish. When the police surrounded the gang at Wantabadgery homestead, Nesbitt made a desperate attempt to cover Moonlite's escape by rushing out of the homestead with his rifle blazing to divert the police. Constable Bowen shot him dead, and Moonlite avenged him by shooting the policeman.

When the battle was over, Moonlite asked to see Nesbitt's body. The police led him to a shed behind the homestead, where Moonlite looked at the corpse and muttered 'He died trying to save me, he had a heart of gold.'

James Nesbitt's criminal record ends with the note 'Engaged in bushranging with Andrew G. Scott at Wantabadgery, New South Wales, and shot dead by the Police.'

Also see Andrew G. Scott, Thomas Rogan, Graham Bennett Thomas Williams (2nd),

JOHN NEWTON

> Born: 1820
> Native Place: Northumberland
> Trade: Carpenter
> Religion: Not recorded
> Height: 5ft 6ins
> Complexion: Dark
> Hair: Dark brown
> Eyes: Dark brown
> Particular Marks: Scar on upper left arm.
> Previous History: Arrived at Port Phillip per ship *Sir George Seymour* in 1844. An exile from Pentonville Prison.
> Sentence: Five years on the Roads of the Colony, for Horsestealing.
> Date of Conviction: Convicted at Melbourne, 22 October, 1850. (Actually he was convicted at Geelong, before Judge William a'Beckett. Refer Frank Gardiner's conviction, as Francis Clarke, same charge, same date.)

*I*n Frank Clune's book *King of the Road* that writer described John Newton as 'about eighteen, a freckle-faced youth with flaming red hair ... worn long in the fashion of that first generation of Australian-born sons of pioneer colonists.' However the prison record has a very different story to tell. Newton was thirty when he was convicted, an 'exile' from Pentonville prison in London, with physical characteristics quite unlike Frank Clune's description.

John or Jack Newton was one of the earliest associates of Frank Gardiner when the latter began his long career of bushranging. He took part in the theft of a mob of horses from Lockhart Morton's station which is described in Gardiner's biography in this book, and if Jack and Frank and their mate Bill Troy had got away with this robbery then Jack Newton might have joined Frank Gardiner in later escapades.

But the police tracked them down and Jack stood trial with Frank before Judge William a'Beckett at Geelong. On 22 October 1850 the judge sentenced both men to five years on the roads of the colony, and when they were returned to the Geelong lock-up they must have thought wistfully of how lucky Bill Troy had been in escaping from custody before he could be tried.

Newton and Gardiner were transferred to Pentridge on 4 February 1851, and Newton appears to have been a model prisoner. There is only one charge on his record, that of 29 June 1852. The warders had found a quantity of tobacco in his possession, but he received nothing worse than a reprimand.

His good behaviour earned him a Ticket of Leave after serving less than two years of his sentence, and he walked out of Pentridge on 14 October 1852. Unlike many bushrangers he seems to have learned a lesson from his spell behind bars, because his name does not appear again on the criminal records of the period.

Also see Frank Gardiner

100 AUSTRALIAN BUSHRANGERS 1789-1901

PATRICK O'CONNOR

> Colonial Secretary's Office,
> Melbourne, 24th September, 1853.
>
> **TWO HUNDRED POUNDS REWARD.**
>
> WHEREAS two Prisoners of the Crown did, on the 15th instant, seize the schooner *Sophia*, then lying in the river English, in Van Diemen's Land, and in her make their escape to this Colony, in which they landed on the 20th instant, near Western Port, and during the afternoon of the 23rd instant, did attack and rob the station of Mr. King, situated a few miles beyond Brighton, and shoot one of his servants, a Reward of £100 is hereby offered for the apprehension of each of the above offenders.
>
> DESCRIPTION OF THE FIRST MAN.
>
> Name, supposed to be PATRICK O'CONNOR; age, thirty years; height, five feet seven inches; fair complexion; red hair, whiskers and moustachios; full face; has one of front teeth gone; wore a dark pea coat over a blue shirt, and a wide-awake hat; has a scar down the nose; had a blanket rolled up before his saddle, and was armed with a double-barrelled gun and revolver.
>
> DESCRIPTION OF THE SECOND MAN.
>
> Name, HARRY; age, twenty-three years; height, five feet five inches; fair complexion; brown hair, long and curly; no whiskers; thin face, with peculiarly large nostrils; wore a light Petersham coat, and was armed with a rifle and three pocket pistols.
>
> They took away with them two bay horses, one particularly large, and the other of a moderate size.
>
> By His Excellency's Command,
> JOHN FOSTER.

After Patrick O'Connor and his murderous mate Henry Bradley killed the ploughman at Brighton (see Bradley's story earlier in this book for further details) the news of the murder soon reached police headquarters in Melbourne. The *Melbourne Argus* reported:

'... the whole police force of the city, the detectives as well as the mounted troopers, have been indefatigable in their endeavours to bring to justice these daring and hardened Vandemonians. 'A party of five troopers on Saturday received information that two men, answering the description of the bushrangers, had travelled in the direction of Deep Creek. They were traced by the courageous band as far as Wright's public house, but had turned on their steps and retraced the road, proceeding the same night as far as Jackson's Creek. On the Sunday morning they reached Gisborne, where those in pursuit met Mr Nicholson and Cadet Thompson, who joined the party and went to the Black Forest Inn, having received information that the men had gone in that direction. The landlord, Mr Hunter, had observed them to pass about two hours before those in pursuit arrived, and they scoured the forest for some five or six miles around, but without success.'

The pursuers did not know that Bradley and O'Connor had already been to Mr Clarke's station, posing as two shepherds looking for work. When he refused their services they shot at him, the bullet passing through his hat. A gardener, who had been working nearby, ran to help Clarke and was shot through the chest. The bushrangers fired six more times at Clarke but missed every time, and then went to one of the huts, bailed up seven men, and stole lead from which they cast some more bullets.

They then galloped on to Kane's station, where they held up eleven men and tied them up while they ransacked the station premises. But the police were hot on the trail, and they arrived to find the station people still trussed up. O'Connor and Bradley had run into hiding.

Howitt, in his *Two Years in Victoria*, wrote

'... as they were being unbound one of the inmates cried out "There are the bushrangers!" and immediately shots were fired by the two men who were some thirty yards from the door. Other shots followed, and Cadet Thompson was shot in the left breast; the ball, passing through his body, lodged in the wall behind him. The fusillade made the police horses bolt and the two bushrangers got clean away. The police reported the happenings to Kilmore Station and tramped on to Mr Cairns' station, where they found out that the bushrangers had robbed a nearby tent of all its provisions. Cairns lent horses to Sergeant Nolan and the rest of the police party, and Howitt continues 'In a short time the party came upon four men, two on horseback, the others being on foot. Two of these turned out to be the bushrangers, one of the men being mounted on Ostler's horse. The party then rode on as fast as they could, and succeeded in overtaking the two villains about three miles up the road. They instantly turned, and fired.'

The police charged full tilt at the bushrangers, with Sergeant Nolan wielding his sword. He struck at O'Connor with it but the bushranger parried with his pistol. In a brief but violent affray the police overcame the two men. '... four pistols were found upon Bradley, who resisted with much determination, till Ostler threatened to blow his brains out if he did not surrender.'

It was the end of the road for Bradley and O'Connor, who were hanged in Melbourne on 24 October 1853. The place where they are supposed to have landed in Victoria is now known as Bushrangers Bay.

Also see Henry Bradley

■ *Implements of containment and correction.*
(Collection: Queen Victoria Museum and Art Gallery, Launceston).

ALEXANDER PEARCE

The Convict Conduct Register of Van Diemen's Land shows that Alexander Pearce was regarded as an unregenerate delinquent. A transcription of the various entries would show that he was a 'pockpitted' man, of a height given variously as five feet three and three-quarter inches and five feet four inches.

He arrived in the *Castle Forbes* in 1819 on a sentence of seven years transportation. Between 18 May and 29 November 1821 he suffered a total of 150 lashes for various offences.

He had received a number of less memorable punishments apart from the 150 lashes, and the authorities must have thought that it was time to send him as far away as possible. They despatched him to Macquarie Harbour, but he was there for only a matter of months before escaping in company with Bob Greenhill, Mathew Travers, Thomas Bodenham, Bill Cornelius or Kennelly, James Brown, John Mathers, and Alexander Dalton.

The escapees fought their way through dense bush for eight days and nights, with nothing to eat until one of the escapees said he was so hungry he could 'eat a piece of man.'

Bob Greenhill, who was carrying the party's only weapon, an axe, soon put this notion into practice. He killed Dalton while he slept, and then he and the others managed to make a fire to cook their horrid feast.

When the two bush-rangers had consumed the choicest portions of Alexander Dalton they began to look around for another victim, and Greenhill killed Tom Bodenham. They must have begun to look at each other very queerly by that time, and wondering who would be next to end in the bellies of his companions. Greenhill, the self-appointed butcher, chose John Mathers as his next victim, but his first blow did not kill Mathers and with a horrible irony the remnants of the gang gave him half-an-hour to say his prayers before Greenhill finished him off.

Matt Travers was the next to die. He was suffering from a swollen leg, the result of an insect bite, and he was unwary enough to lie down to rest the painful limb. Greenhill quickly followed what was by then a familiar routine: a blow on the head to kill him, a slash across the throat to bleed him, and dismemberment of the corpse so that they might eat him.

After they had eaten Travers, Pearce decided that it was time to take over the role of butcher before he became the victim. Greenhill slept on the axe, but one night Pearce grabbed it from beneath his body and brained him with one blow. A few days after this he was filled with such self-disgust that he decided to hang himself with his belt, but changed his mind.

The surviving convicts reached the settled areas, where Pearce left them and teamed up with two other escapees: Davis and Cheetham. They lived by raiding farms until the soldiers caught them. Nobody knew anything about the acts of cannibalism and so Pearce was charged only with being in possession of stolen sheep, and returned to Macquarie Harbour.

During this third spell of captivity he found that he had an unconquerable craving for human flesh, and he persuaded a convict named Thomas Cox to escape with him. They had not gone very far before Pearce killed Cox and settled down to eat the body, and the soldiers caught up with him before he had consumed the whole of the mutilated corpse.

The prison authorities sent Pearce back to Hobart to stand trial, and when he stood before judge and jury he made little attempt to defend himself: He even told his horrified listeners that man's flesh was delicious and that it tasted far better than fish or pork.

Pearce's confessions created a sensation, and attracted a huge crowd to watch him hang in Hobart early in 1824.

■ *Alexander 'Cannibal' Pearce. The charge letter against him stated in conclusion that, 'Sentence of Death pronounced upon the prisoner, and that his body when dead be dissected.' The order was carried out on the gallows in 1824.*

STAND AND DELIVER

JOHN PEISLEY

George Boxall recorded that John Peisley was 'described as a fine-looking man at a distance, but when examined closely there was a shifty, disagreeable look about his eyes.' The frequent misspellings of his name, which was rendered as Paisley, Peasley, and Piesley, led to a good deal of confusion and have even caused some bushranging historians to allege that two separate bushrangers, named Paisley and Piesley, were hanged in 1862.

He was first in trouble when he was twenty, when he was sentenced to five years for horse stealing. This sentence was passed on him at Bathurst Quarter Sessions on 13 September 1854, and it appears that he escaped from custody and was recaptured before he was sent down to Darlinghurst.

The sequence of his criminal record is confusing because a note on 20 March 1857 states 'Discharged to Parramatta Gaol,' but on 8 December 1857 he was before the Supreme Court, Sydney, on a further charge of horse stealing, and received another sentence of five years 'to commence at expiration of present sentence.'

It would seem that he was released for long enough to steal another mob of horses, caught again, and returned to prison to serve out the remainder of his first sentence plus another five years.

He spent a part of this second period on Cockatoo Island, where it is likely that he met Frank Gardiner. An unsuccessful escape attempt, by 'taking to the water,' added nine months in irons to his sentence, but he was released on Ticket of Leave to the district of Scone on 23 November 1860.

The authorities made a bad bargain by granting him a Ticket of Leave. Johnny Peisley teamed up with Frank Gardiner and the two of them, with other bushrangers, became notorious in the Abercrombie district and other parts of New South Wales. The *Return of Bushrangers*, in the section 'Offences by Gardiner,' mentions Peisley four times in 1860-61:

1

Where Tried: Quarter Sessions Bathurst, 13 September 1854
Sentenced: Five Years on the Roads
Offence: Horsestealing
Trade: Labourer
Religion: Protestant
Native Place: O'Connell Plains
Complexion: Ruddy fair
Hair: Light sandy
Eyes: Grey
Height: 5ft 9½ins
Remarks: Several small scars back of right wrist, scars on middle finger same hand, several scars on finger of left hand, nail of middle finger and end of same crushed.

2

Where Tried: Quarter Sessions Bathurst, 18 February 1855
Sentenced: One month Parramatta Gaol to commence on expiration of former sentence.
Offence: Escaping from Custody while under sentence. Age 20.
16/02/1855 Received from Darlinghurst Gaol.
13/11/1856 Probation to commence 1 February 1855. 20/03/1857 Discharged to Parramatta Gaol.

3

Where Born: Native of Colony
Year Born: 1834
Native Place: O'Connell's Plains, N.S.W.
Religion: Protestant
Trade: Labourer
Admitted When/Where: 13 February Carcoar
Trial: County Court, Murder. Death. 13/03/62
Disposed of How/When: Executed 25/04/62

In an early record is the following Police Description:
'Native of Bathurst, 26 years of age, 5 feet 8½ inches high, pale complexion, flaxen hair, bluish-grey eyes, long featured, nose a little pock-marked, with a scar on the bridge, scars on right hand and arm, middle finger on left hand disfigured, arms and legs hairy.'

'On the 16th of July, Sergeant Middleton and Trooper Hosie of the Western patrol were attacked and severely wounded at the Fish River by the offenders Gardiner and Peisley — Peisley escaped but Gardiner was captured and afterwards released by two armed men one of whom was Peisley . . . On the 14th of September, Mr O'Sullivan of the Lachlan was taken into the bush between Marrugo and Cowra and robbed by this offender [Peisley].

The hut of William Dawkins, situated at the gap near Marrugo was forcibly entered and one of the inmates named John Dawkins robbed . . . On the 30th October James Eldridge, J. Laverty, and Catherine Vardy were robbed near Binda by the offender Peisley and another . . . December 28, 1861.

This offender had a quarrel with two brothers named Stephen and William Benyon at their farm near Bigga (Abercrombie) he fired upon them with a double-barrelled gun severely wounding Stephen Benyon and mortally wounding his brother William Benyon.'

Peisley's reaction to all these accusations may be seen in a letter he wrote (or had written for him) on 4 September 1861 to the editor of the *Bathurst Free Press & Mining Journal*. He said:

'Through your valuable paper I must make it known that, if it be my lot to be taken, whether dead or alive, I will never be tried for the rescue of Gardiner, in the light in which it is represented; nor did I fire at Trooper Hosie . . . I am no doubt a desperado in the eyes of the law, but never, in no instance, did I ever use violence, nor did I ever use rudeness to one of the fair sex, and I must certainly be the Invincible Prince to commit one-tenth of what is laid to my charge . . . I love my native hills, I love freedom and detest cruelty to man or beast.'

This letter did not convince the police, who offered £50 reward for the capture of Peisley and printed his description in the Police Gazette of January 1862:

■ *'Attacking the Mail'. Artist S.T. Gill captured the feeling of the robbery, one of his many goldfields era watercolours.*
(Courtesy La Trobe Collection, State Library of Victoria)

'. . . about 28 years of age, about 5 ft. 10 ins. high, stout and well made, fresh complexion, very small light whiskers, quite bald on top of head and forehead, several recent marks on face, and a mark from a blow of a spade on top of head; puffed and dissipated-looking from hard drinking; invariably wears fashionable Napoleon boots, dark cloth breeches, dark vest buttoned up the front, large Albert gold guard, cabbage-tree hat and duck coat. Sometimes wears a dark wig and always carries a brace of revolvers.'

Whether Peisley actually committed all the crimes attributed to him or not, his reputation became so bad that everyone was on guard against him. On 29 January 1862, at Tarcutta in the Wagga Wagga district, he stopped at the premises of a Mr McKenzie and asked for a meal. McKenzie recognised him from his description, but said nothing and had him served with a meal.

While Peisley was eating, McKenzie slipped away for help and returned with some other men. They grabbed Peisley as he was lifting a cup of tea to his mouth. He was tried in Bathurst Circuit Court on 13 March 1862, and the story goes that when he was sentenced to death he said defiantly, 'I'll die game.'

On the scaffold, he began to make a speech in self-defence, repeating his claims that he had never taken a shilling from or done violence to a woman and never used violence until he killed Benyon, until the clergyman attending him advised him accept what must happen.

His last words on the gallows in Bathurst Gaol, on the 25 March 1862 were 'Goodbye gentlemen God bless you'.

Also see Frank Gardiner, John Gilbert, Ben Hall

GEORGE PENNY

*T*he prison records of two men named George Penny are still available, but it cannot be said with certainty whether either of these men was the accomplice of William Armstrong and George Chamberlain in their murder of the goldbuyer Cornelius Green. The story of that event is told in the biography of Armstrong in this book.

A minor reference to George Penny, as 'Sydney Penny,' was made in a letter written by Chamberlain to a man named Paynter, before the police had caught up with the murderers of Green. He wrote that he felt sure the 'snaffle men' (police) would not catch up with him 'this time,' and that he would return 'some fine moonlight night, in about six months, and also that the articles which Paynter had planted for them, among the rocks, they would not find.'

The garbled letter referred to Sydney Penny being chained in a room in the new police quarters, and Chamberlain seemed to have some notion that he would either escape or that the police would not have enough evidence against him. But the fate of George or 'Sydney' Penny still remains a mystery.

Also see William Armstrong

STAND AND DELIVER

HARRY POWER

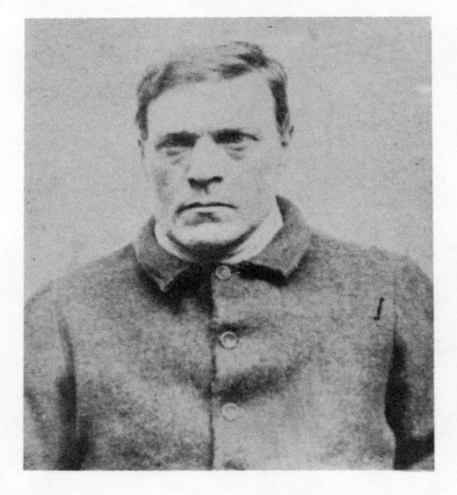

Henry Johnson (alias Harry Power). An early prison record photo.
(Courtesy Public Record Office, Victoria)

Henry Johnstone (or Johnson, or Johnston), alias Harry Power, also known as 'Old Harry' and Power the Bushranger, was unusally old for a bushranger. Many concluded their careers when they were about thirty, most even younger, but Harry Power was still going strong when he was almost fifty. He was twenty-one when he arrived in Van Diemen's land in 1842, transported for stealing one pair of shoes.

Like many other convicts he gave false information, one record states he was convicted for robbing a bank in company, and that he later absconded in Van Diemen's Land and lived in the bush for two years. His convict record in Tasmania tells a different story. He served at various properties as an assigned convict and also at a convict outstation.

Finally, in 1848, he received a Ticket of Leave and eventually found his way to the mainland. If he broke the law during the next thirteen years or so he must have done so skilfully, because there is no charge recorded against him. Apparently he was a horse dealer at Geelong for a number of years, and it may be that this occupation led him into handling horses of somewhat shady origin.

There has been conflicting and confusing recording of his first major confrontation with the law. Many years of delving into the official documentation regarding his career has yet to confirm what exactly happened in March 1855 when he is supposed to have shot a police trooper. Almost every avenue has been followed in an attempt to find details. Many of the official records have 'disappeared' from the Public Record Office.

Writers for many years have recorded that Harry Power was stopped on the road near Daisy Hill, in the Maryborough district of Victoria, when the police noticed that the horse he was riding matched the description of a valuable mount which had been reported stolen. When asked to show a bill of sale for the horse, Power responded by challenging their right to stop him on the public road. After a few more words he drew a revolver. They tried to arrest him, several shots were fired, one of the troopers fell wounded, and Power escaped.

As the volume of Prisoners Records which contains the first Victorian prison record of Power is 'missing' from the Public Record Office, it is not possible to gain further information. Details on subsequent prison records only contain some of the required information. Various official records perused give some conflicting details. One says he was convicted at Maryborough Court, another says Melbourne. No police or court records have shown any reference to the Daisy Hill incident.

The police did eventually catch up with him again and he was finally charged with 'Wounding with intent to do grievous bodily harm.' This brought 'Henry Johnstone' a sentence of fourteen years penal servitude and he was sent to the hulks.

On 22 October 1856 he was in a launch with many other convicts being taken ashore, from the convicts hulks, to work. Mr Jackson, in charge of this working party, was in a row boat towing the launch, and he noticed that the convicts were all crowding into the bow. He shouted to them to get back and trim the launch properly, but they ignored him and seized the towrope.

They pulled the towboat back to the launch and began jumping into it, throwing Jackson into the water and killing a guard, Owen Owens, and John Turner, one of the convicts at the oars.

Henry was one of those accused of killing him, the official records still using the name of Henry Johnstone. He would become notorious as Harry Power at a later date. In the trial that occured later he managed to talk his way out of the accusation and there was apparently no firm evidence that he was guilty.

He received a Ticket of Leave on 25 March 1862, and disappeared from official records until he appeared in Beechworth Court in February 1864, charged with horsestealing.

He had sold a horse to a miner at Harrietville, and gave a bill of sale signed Henry Johnson. He had stolen it from Henry Huon, a squatter at Wodonga. It was at this stage when he was known and charged as Harry Power. Constable Bell, stationed at Belvoir, stating that he knew the prisoner, and said that he lived on part of Mr Huon's run and went by the name of Power. He received a sentence of seven years.

He was transferred to Pentridge and may have been released before his time, but for some reason he decided that he had enough and decided to escape.

On 16 February 1869 he made good his bid for freedom. Almost every author since then has said he

100 AUSTRALIAN BUSHRANGERS 1789-1901

■ *Capture of Power the Bushranger, an illustration as it appeared in the* Illustrated Australian News *in June 1870.*
(Courtesy La Trobe Collection, State Library of Victoria)

■ *(Opposite) Harry Power in leg-irons. Photo taken on 5 August 1870 by the official police photographer, Charles Nettleton, who held the contract for over 25 years. He later photographed Ned Kelly. Nettleton had a cell at Pentridge Gaol fixed up as a permanent dark-room, outside which his subjects were stood in the sun against a granite wall, such as this photo of Harry Power.*
(Courtesy Victoria Police, PRD)

■ *Powers Lookout — a prominent landscape feature overlooking the King River valley.*
(Courtesy La Trobe Collection, State Library of Victoria)

POWER'S LOOKOUT.

The volume of the Prisoner Register (Males) recording early convictions of Power, is missing. Following details are taken from the 1870 conviction.

<u>Born</u>: 1819
<u>Native Place</u>: Waterford
<u>Trade</u>: Nil recorded
<u>Religion</u>: Roman Catholic
<u>Education</u>: Read and write with difficulty
<u>Height</u>: 5ft 6¼ins
<u>Weight</u>: 10st 10¾lbs
<u>Complexion</u>: Sallow
<u>Hair</u>: Brown to grey
<u>Eyes</u>: Blue
<u>Nose</u>: medium
<u>Mouth</u>: Medium
<u>Chin</u>: Large
<u>Eyebrows</u>: Light and scanty
<u>Visage</u>: Long
<u>Forehead</u>: High
<u>Particular Marks</u>: Small scar over right eyebrow, two small scars left side of forehead, one scar on left eyebrow, scar right side of head, flesh mole between eyebrows, small scar left cheek bone, scar right cheek, lost two upper front teeth, several moles on breast and back. Large burn mark, upper right arm, large scar on left elbow from gunshot wound, top of third finger left hand mutilated, large bunion on each foot (very conspicuous).

◆

<u>Previous History</u>: *Per* Isabella *from London to Van Diemen's Land 1840 — Seven years for Robbing a Bank in Company, as Henry Power, Admits having absconded in Van Diemen's Land and been two years in the bush, came over to Twofold Bay, thence to Sydney, overland to Port Albert in 1848. Previously convicted as Henry Johnstone/Henry Power.*
<u>Sentence</u>: *(1st charge) Five years Roads for Robbery under Arms. (2nd charge) Five years Roads for Robbery under Arms (cumulative) (3rd charge) Five years Roads for Robbery under Arms (cumulative).*

◆

<u>Date of Conviction</u>: *2 August 1870, before Beechworth General Sessions; Mr Hackett.*

141

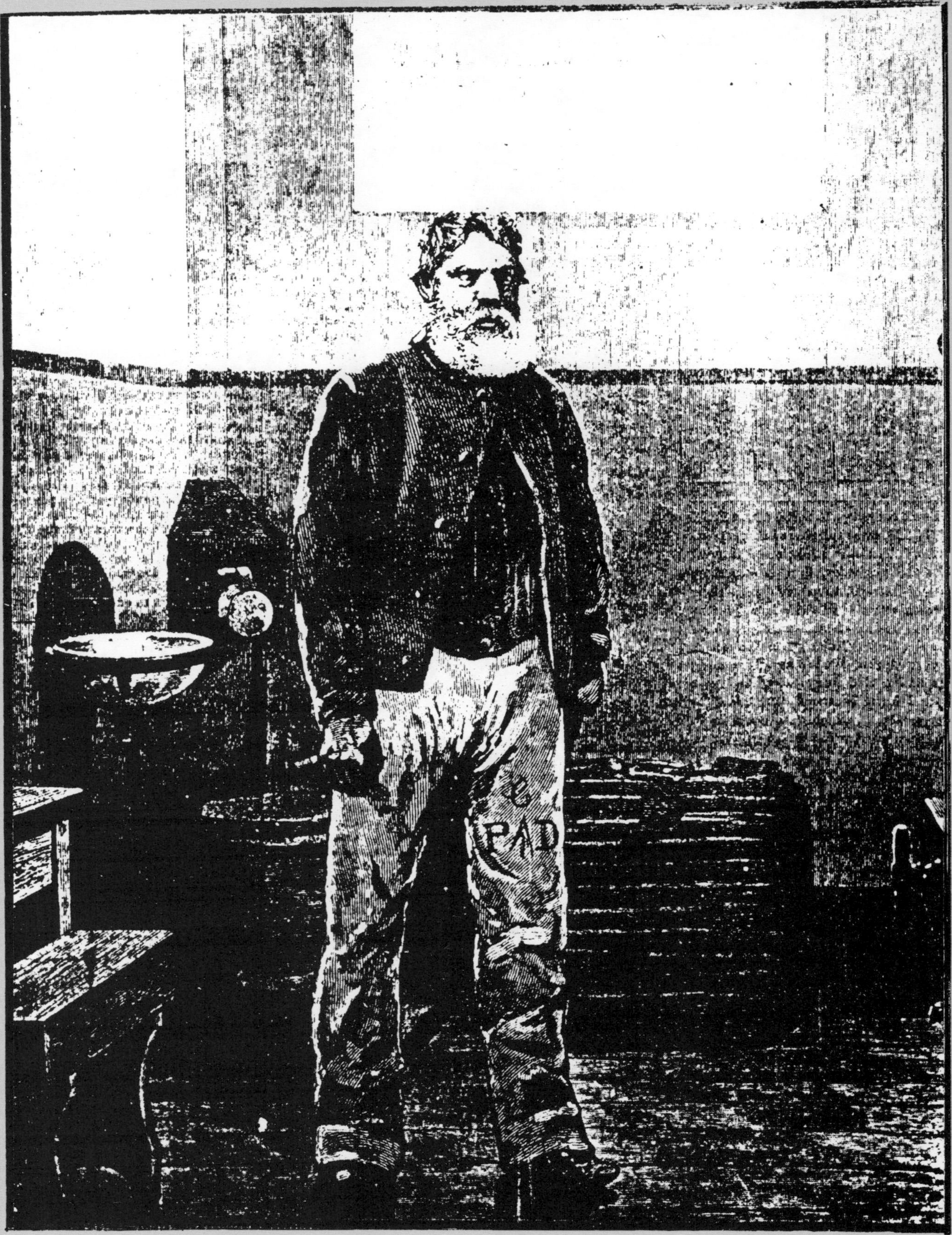
PAD

(Opposite) A Bushranger in Old Age. An illustration of Harry Power in Pentridge Gaol not long before his release in 1885.

Another prison record photo of Harry Power, dressed in prison garb. His strong facial features include a still defiant look in the eye.
(Courtesy Public Record Office, Victoria)

escaped by hiding underneath rubbish in a cart being used to carry garbage out of the prison to the dump. However, the truth is now available, and official documents show a different story. In an interview many years later Harry himself stated that 'they were building a wall ... I had hidden in a hole by the wall, and the minute they passed me coming in, I stepped out, and was over the Merri Creek in a minute ...'

Official documents written at the time by Gaol officers and Government officials state in part ... 'he evidently sneaked down under the wall and got away through the gap near the bridge after the Bridge Gang had passed in.' Another report stated that 'his braces were found under the wall near the bridge ...' Other reports confirm in detail his escape.

Much other information about the career of Harry Power is now coming to light and the author has has been delving into Power's career for the past ten years. A seperate detailed biography of the bushranger is now near completion. Only some of the details will be dealt with here.

Harry Power then commenced his career of bushranging in earnest and would become in time, one of the most notorious and active bushrangers in Victoria. He has often been written of as a bit a larrikin, bluffing his way around the countryside. When a close study is made of all the robberies he committed and the hundreds and hundreds of miles he covered over some of the most rugged terrain, it is soon evident that there was much more to the man. There is also ample evidence to show just what an influence he actually did have on a young Ned Kelly.

One newspaper in the north-east of Victoria reported in June 1869 that 'a wager of £2 to £1 is freely offered in Wangaratta, that Power, the bushranger, will be captured within a week.' The bet would not be a winner for some. Harry Power would go on a wide-ranging robbing spree for many months until June 1870.

On 7 May 1869 the Bright-Beechworth coach was stopped near Beechworth by a man who presented a double barrelled gun at the driver and ordered him to bail up. It was one of many such robberies that Harry Power would commit.

At Bowman's Forest Gap, near Beechworth, on the morning of Saturday, 28 August, 1869, Harry robbed the Beechworth-Buckland coach and four passengers, and any person who happened to ride along the road was also waylaid.

His reputation had spread far and wide and the size of the territory over which he travelled, even by todays standards, was immense. He carried out robberies as far south as Blackwood and Kyneton, to Bairnsdale in Gippsland, throughout the mountain settlements of the north-east, and as far north into New South Wales as Adelong. He had a good knowledge of the territory of the north-east and spent a lot of his time around the Mansfield, Bright, Beechworth, Seymour areas and all districts in-between.

By September, Frederick Standish, the Chief Commissioner of Police, wrote to the Government requesting that they post of £200 reward for the bushranger's capture, noting that several recent outrages had also been attributed to Power the Bushranger.

In November 1869 he robbed the mail coach near Jamieson, and committed numerous other robberies, and on 22 November the Chief Commissioner of Police asked that the reward be increased again to £500. Harry Power took little notice as he continued his depredations. He robbed four men on the road between Tallarook and Broadford. In December he was reported to be near Castlemaine. The police were frustrated and becoming more and more embarassed by their lack of ability to capture Power the Bushranger. One police letter refers to the dispatch of guns being sent to various police stations, and requests that the staff be trained to use them.

The Parliamentary Debates show that there was much argument regarding the inability of police to capture Power, who had now become their main target. Police blamed the sympathisers and abettors in the district in which he roamed. Power had friends who were willing to help. He had been in prison with Tom (senior) and Jack (senior) Lloyd and knew the Quinn, Lloyd, and Kelly families. He was given assistance by many families, as far distant as Omeo, in East Gippsland.

In March 1870 he was still roaming and committing robberies. He stole horses frequently, and many travellers on the Sydney road were robbed. He even robbed a mounted police constable, near Yea and stole his revolver. He repeated it with another policeman at a

Harry Power. The last of his prison record photos, this one shows him shortly before his final release in 1885. This one shows an old man with grey hair and beard. He still retained that defiant look in his eye.
(Courtesy Public Record Office, Victoria)

different location. He was snubbing authority. Authority did not like it, and the police force was faced with mounting pressure to capture him.

One newspaper commented that Power was 'almost ubiquitous. One day he is heard of at Mansfield, the next at Seymour, and then near Albury.' The list of robberies was immense.

He robbed the same coach twice within a few weeks.

In March 1870 he robbed Robert McBean, the owner of Kilfera station, and took his horse, bridle, saddle and gold watch. It was that watch, which meant so much to McBean, that would lead to the downfall and capture of Harry Power. He sent word through Jack Lloyd that McBean could have his watch back for £15. McBean was influential, he met with the Chief Commissioner of Police, and added more pressure for the villain to be captured. For quite some time, victims had commented on Power having a 'young mate' with him, to hold his horse, whilst Power robbed them. It was a young teenage Ned Kelly that was finally arrested on 2 May 1870 and charged with assisting Power. Due to a number of problems, including two witnesses not wanting to appear in court, the charge was not proved and dropped for lack of evidence.

It is interesting to note that most writers have stated that Ned did not give police information on where they could find Power, yet from police documents recently found there is reason to now believe that they did get information, as various letters from police confirm, including one from the Chief Commissioner . . . 'From what Kelly stated since his apprehension . . .' it went on to describe where Harry was likely to be found. Harry Power always believed it was 'young Kelly' who gave police information.

Jack Lloyd (senior) has been regarded by most historians as being the man who finally gave information which led to Harry's arrest, and documents give an indication to other relatives being involved — the Quinns. It is possible from the material available that the information received by police may have come from a combination of sources — Ned Kelly, Jack Lloyd and James Quinn (senior).

Power's hideout was a bush shelter near the Quinns, where he thought he was safe because the Quinns owned a peacock which they claimed to be 'as good as a watchdog.' However the peacock did not screech a warning of approaching troopers, and Power was rudely awakened to see police revolvers levelled at him. He accepted his fate, and offered his captors breakfast.

A telegram was sent to Melbourne which would have pleased the authorities, which stated in part that...'Power, alias Johnston, arrested on Sun. the 5th inst at seven thirty (7.30) a.m. In the King River Ranges Glenmore Run by Superintendants Nicholson and Hare and Sergeant Montfort and is now in the Wangaratta watchouse.'

He was later taken to Beechworth where a large crowd gathered in the street to see him, he was in strong spirits, calling to the crowd that the only way the police could have captured him was when he was asleep. He was charged with robbery under arms and he stood trial at the Beechworth General Sessions on 2 August 1870.

Two days later he entered Pentridge under sentences totalling fifteen years imprisonment, and the police magistrates added another six months hard labour for his escape from Pentridge in 1869.

He was to serve almost the whole of the fifteen years and six months and was not released until 9 February 1885. His prison records lists ten offences between 1872 and 1879: six having tobacco or smoking in unauthorised places, three of quarrelling or fighting, and one of 'Giving rations out of cookhouse.'

He was released at the age of sixty-six, with £7.14.5d in his pocket, having spent almost half of his life in one prison or another.

He attracted attention from the public as a 'guide' on board the prison hulk *Success*, on which he had once been a convict. He later went to Swan Hill. The end came for the old man who had once been one of the most active bushrangers, when in October 1891 a body dragged from the Murray River was believed to be that of 'Henry Power'. The Coroner stated he had died from drowning, and that 'there is nothing to show how he came into the river.' There was a question mark beside the name, and the records do not give all the answers. There is no record available to show his final burial place.

He had outlived his 'apprentice' Ned Kelly, who was hanged in 1880, by eleven years.

JAMES REGAN

Born: not known (Age on record as 26 years)
Native Place: (Not recorded, but possibly Leeds)
Trade: Hairdresser
Height: 5ft 4ins
Complexion: Brown
Hair: Dark brown *Head:* Oval
Whiskers: Dark brown
Forehead: High
Eyebrows: Black
Eyes: Hazel
Nose: Medium large, broad

Mouth: Wide
Chin: Medium large
Particular Marks: (tattoos). JR MR heart, BR half-moon, three stars, fish inside right arm; crucifixion, star on breast. Man, cask rum, above elbow and man, woman, fish, Mermaid, anchor, Mermaid, two fish, anchor below left arm.
Previous History: Per Elphinstone 24 May 1836. Lancaster Quarter Sessions — 6 July 1835, 14 years.

Transported for stealing Purse and Money. Gaol report: convicted before, Hulk report: Orderly. Married. Stated this offence, stealing purse and two pounds, prosecuted by a woman, once before for a gold watch etc., 12 months, once 3 months for Bastardy, I am not married, I lived with a woman who came to me in Gaol, Single. Surgeon's report: Conduct far from being satisfactory, character apparently little improved.

James Regan was one of a gang led by James Atterall, whose story is told earlier in this book. His prison record covers the period from March to June 1838, but for some unexplained reason it does not mention his involvement in the bushranging activities on Brown Mountain.

He was charged with the wilful murder of one Richard Morley, but the condition of his prison record makes it hard to read the details.

One entry, for 6 June 1838, reads: 'Charged by Robert Thornhill and others with stealing one sovereign of the value of twenty shillings and other monies of the goods and chattels of the said Wm. Thornhill being at the time of the committing of the said felony in the said dwelling house and therein being put in fear by the said James Regan.'

Another entry on the damaged prison record which could be read with difficulty may have some relevance to the 'said felony.' In part it states:

'Having on the 12th April last maliciously and wilfully murdered one Richard Morley.'

Whatever the relevant facts may have been, there is certainly no doubt that James Regan hanged with his bushranging associates on 21 June 1838.

Also see James Atterall

CODRINGTON REVINGSTONE

A man with such a grandiose name as Codrington Revingstone sounds as though he must have belonged to one of the notable English families. If so, then he was obviously a black sheep. An intriguing mystery surrounds him because nothing is known of his background and there are no surviving criminal records under his name.

He may have been an escaped convict, or he may have been a free settler who took to the bush. One part of the mystery is that his name obviously was well-known to the people of Victoria in 1850, because a newspaper report called him 'the now formidable Codrington Revingstone,' and yet the name does not appear in any official records.

Perhaps it was simply an assumed name, by which he announced himself when he bailed up his victims.

The newspaper report, in the *Melbourne Morning Herald* of Friday 22 November 1850, is headed THE PORTLAND MAIL ROBBED AGAIN!

The story runs 'Intelligence was received in Melbourne last evening that the mail from Portland to Melbourne has again been plundered by the now formidable Codrington Revingstone, the same worthy who on two former occasions despoiled it. It appears that about half-past five o'clock on Monday evening, as the Mailman was proceeding about three miles at the other side of Mt Sturgeon, he was suddenly rushed upon by an armed man, whom he at once recognised as his former friend.

'Presenting a pistol the robber demanded him to stand and deliver. The Mailman had no other alternative than to comply, when the other very deliberately cut open the bags, helped himself to what he thought to be of any value, and handing back the rifled mail, ordered the Mailman to lose no time and drive on about his business... It is high time that the Executive adopted some means for effectually protecting Her Majesty's mails, as the public interests cannot be permitted to be at the mercy of every marauding ruffian who thinks proper to adopt the highway for a profession, and laugh at the authorities...'

Apparently the 'formidable' bushranger Codrington Revingstone continued to 'laugh at the authorities' until he disappeared into the unknown recesses of colonial history.

Travellers along the Princes Highway between Port Fairy and Portland today, pass by a major sign of 'CODRINGTON'. Few, however, would realise its connection with the past.

STAND AND DELIVER

JOHN ROBERTS

An almost unbelievable coincidence resulted in twenty-five-year-old John Roberts serving time for a robbery which he perhaps did not commit. He was arrested for participation in the *Nelson* robbery, of which the story is told in John James' biography in this book, and he stood trial with John James, James Morgan, and James Duncan. If he was indeed innocent of the crime then he must have despaired when he heard the judge sentence him to 'Fifteen years on the roads of the colony, the first three years to be served in irons.'

He was convicted on 28 May 1852, but it appears that his defenders had strongly believed his plea of innocence and that they continued to press his case to the administration. A writer who called himself 'Old Chum,' who described the *Nelson* robbery in the *Melbourne Truth* in 1910, wrote that 'The person wrongfully convicted very much resembled the guilty party for whom he had been mistaken; and we believe, if the two were together, it would be next to impossible to distinguish them. This we mention upon the authority of the gentleman who defended the prisoners, and who had no object in stating what was untrue.'

The 'gentleman who defended the prisoners' believed so strongly in the coincidence of John Roberts having an 'identical twin' somewhere in the colony that he made the administration think twice about the conviction of John Roberts. 'Old Chum' wrote 'After a few weeks this man — John Roberts— was pardoned, the authorities either having been satisfied that it was a case of mistaken identity or else they gave him the benefit of the doubt.'

John Roberts' prison record states '3rd August 1852. Sentence remitted by His Excellency the Lieutenant Governor, vide the Colonial Secretary's letters of that date.'

John Roberts returned to freedom after little more than two months imprisonment, but at this distance of time the researcher may well wonder about the truth of the coincidence which secured his release. Some questions still remain unanswered. If Roberts was indeed innocent, how was it that the three other men in the dock with him did not say so? It seems hardly likely that his likeness to his 'twin' was so complete, in appearance and voice and mannerisms, that fellow-thieves would not have noticed the difference. And, if the people concerned knew that Roberts had a 'twin' somewhere among the population of the colony, how is it that they did not track him down? There is no doubt that 'truth is stranger than fiction,' but the Roberts case does seem to stretch the long arm of coincidence a little too far.

Born: 1827
Native Place: Manchester
Trade: Carpenter
Religion: Protestant
Height: 5ft 5ins
Complexion: Fair
Hair: Light brown
Eyes: Grey
Particular Marks: A scar on left forehead, a scar on left arm, a cut on left thumb.
Previous History: Arrived per ship Maitland *in 1847. An exile from Pentonville Prison.*
Sentence: 15 years on the Roads of the Colony, first three years in Irons. for Robbery from the Ship Nelson.
Date of Conviction: 28 May 1852.

The presumed innocence of John Roberts is further overshadowed by the fact that, thirteen months after his release, he had to stand trial once more. 'Old Chum' tells the story as follows:

'Some time after his release from the hulks he was convicted of complicity in highway robbery at Buninyong. He was sentenced to 10 years, and he, with 10 other prisoners, was being conveyed to Geelong, and were halted at Ray's Hotel, on the road, for refreshments. Roberts begged to be allowed to write a letter to a magistrate who resided in the vicinity. His request was granted, and his right hand freed from the wrist-cuffs.

The prisoner to whom Roberts was chained managed to slip his hand out of the cuff, and Roberts, thus freed, jumped through the window and bolted for the bush. Only one constable had been left in the room in charge of the prisoners, and he could only shout out an alarm. Roberts' luck, however, was not in, as he ran into the arms of the foot constable who had been recently stationed at this point, and he held Mr Roberts until the pursuing constables came up.'

It may perhaps be thought that John Roberts, with his request to write a letter to a magistrate, was simply a plausible rogue, and that he had somehow hoped to evade the second sentence as he had done the first.

He was lodged in Geelong Gaol and then transferred to the hulk *Sacramento,* on 5 November 1853. On 31 December he received a taste of solitary confinement, for assaulting the sergeant.

He served the next four years in the *Sacramento,* in Geelong Gaol, in Pentridge, and in Collingwood Stockade. He was a comparatively well-behaved prisoner, with only four minor charges against him, but his prison record ends with the comments '25th March, 1858. Died 2 p.m. 27th March 1858. Inquest held on the body of the prisoner, verdict returned that the deceased died from Chronic dysentery at the Collingwood Stockade . . . being at the time a prisoner of the Crown in legal custody.'

Also see John James

William Robt Roberts

Born: 1816
Native Place: Manchester
Trade: Shoemaker
Religion: Roman Catholic
Height: 5ft 8¼ins
Complexion: Fresh
Hair: Light brown
Eyes: Blue
Particular Marks: Scar on temple. Skull and crossbones, two flags, sword and pistols, cross. E.B.B.D., spade and pick, cross on right arm. Crown and two flags, wreath and anchor, heart, soldier and woman on R.D.E.B. on left arm.
Previous History: Arrived per ship Tenesserim 1844. Bond. By name of alias Robert Duneau, seven years to Van Diemen's Land. To Victoria August 1852 per Gazelle.
Sentence: (1st charge) Highway Robbery - Twelve years on the Roads first three years in Irons. (2nd charge) Highway Robbery - Ten years on the Roads to take effect from former sentence. (He later received a remission of this sentence) (3rd charge) Highway Robbery - Ten years on the Roads; first two in Irons, to date from expiration of previous sentence.
Date of Conviction: 3 February 1853, at Geelong Circular Court, before Mr Justice Barry.

The main claim to fame of William Robert Roberts was that he was a bushranging partner of Frank McCallum, who assumed the name of Captain Melville. How and when they met, and what offences they committed early in their partnership, can now only be guessed at.

The partners rode into bushranging history when they raided the station owned by David Aitcheson, near Wardy Yallock, in December 1852. They rounded up Aitcheson, his overseer Wilson, and sixteen shearers, and Roberts held them under the gun while Captain Melville systematically cut up a coil of rope into lengths. They tied up the menfolk with these, and compelled Mrs Aitcheson and other women to prepare a meal while they searched the house and took whatever they wanted. After eating the meal they helped themselves to Aitcheson's horses and saddles and rode away.

Christmas was coming, and the two bushrangers were cocky enough to ride into Geelong to enjoy the festive season after robbing travellers on the Ballarat road. They were captured in a brothel and lodged in the old gaol until the court opened in February.

George Boxall, then a boy in Geelong, witnessed their progress to the court. He wrote 'I remember going to see "the bushrangers" conveyed across the flat and up the hill to the court-house to stand their trial. The were seated in a dray, heavily ironed — there was no "Black Maria" in Geelong in those days — and drawn by two horses. There were several armed policemen on the dray, and others marched before and behind. The court-house, of course, was crowded, and, as boys were not admitted, I was not present . . .'

The two bushrangers faced one of the most severe judges of the day: Mr Justice Barry, who was to become Sir Redmond Barry and pass sentence on Ned Kelly. He sentenced Roberts to a total of thirty-two years imprisonment on three charges of highway robbery.

On 12 February 1853 Roberts stepped aboard the hulk *President* to start his sentence. He seems to have been a well-behaved prisoner, because his record shows that during the first seven years of his sentence he was charged only five times. Four of the offences were minor ones: Having a piece of tin in his cell, using profane language, having bread concealed, and quarrelling. The only major charge was the enigmatic one of 'On board the *President* at time of general issue,' for which he received a sentence of '30 days solitary rations by order of Chief Secretary.'

Roberts had at least one friend out in the free world: a Reverend R. Russell of Evandale, Tasmania. His record showed that he maintained a steady correspondence with Russell throughout 1856 and 1857, and it may be that Russell exerted some influence on his behalf. If so, then it bore fruit on 7 May 1858, when Roberts' record states 'Letter authorising a remission of ten years.'

Roberts would still have had a long time to serve, but either his good behaviour or outside influences persuaded the authorities that he was a fit subject for a Ticket of Leave. A man whose name appears to have been A. S. Turnham, although it is hard to distinguish on the records, found a job for him and he was released on Ticket of Leave on 19 January 1864.

Further research might discover the identity of Turnham, the reason why he was interested in Roberts, and the nature of the job which he obtained for the bushranger. Apparently his charitable gesture did not help Roberts to reform, because the *Police Gazette* dated 7 June 1870 states that Robert Roberts, alias Melville was arrested in Deniliquin, New South Wales.

But that is another story.

Also see Frank McCallum

THOMAS ROGAN

Thomas Rogan was one of the unfortunate youngsters who fell under the spell of 'Captain Moonlite', as Andrew Scott called himself. The modern criminologist would recognise Rogan as a classic 'juvenile delinquent:' a youngster with an unhappy family background and with little self-confidence, ripe to be influenced by some older person and persuaded that his criminal activities were a way of striking back at society.

Boxall believes that Rogan was born in Hay, New South Wales, and that he met Scott in Melbourne. George Calderwood, in his comprehensive book *Captain Moonlite*, gives a different account. He states that Scott and his gang were heading up through north-eastern Victoria towards New South Wales when they became involved in a fight outside a grog shanty near Albury. '... the fight brought a newcomer to their side, twenty-one-year-old Thomas Rogan, who became known as Number Five ... Rogan was a nervous character who had been bullied by his father, a small tradesman in Errol Street, Hotham. His real name was Baker, but when he left home and ran foul of the police at Beechworth he had changed it to Rogan.' His prison records confirms his native place as Victoria.

Like some other young members of Moonlite's gang, Rogan had been in trouble before he joined up with the bushrangers and this no doubt exacerbated his sense of grievance against the world. The companionship of youngsters much like himself, under the leadership of a 'father figure' in the shape of Andrew Scott, may have given him a feeling of security such as he had never known before.

If so, then it was not to last for long. It concluded with the 'Battle of Wantabadgery,' of which the story is told in Andrew Scott's biography in this book. After Moonlite surrendered, nervous young Tom Rogan was found hidden under a bed, armed with a loaded rifle and revolver which he had not tried to use.

Two of the bushrangers, and a policeman, had died during the shoot-out. The police took Rogan, Scott, Graham Bennett, and Thomas Williams down to Sydney for their trial, which opened on 8 December 1879 before Mr Justice Windeyer.

The trial proceeded in an atmosphere of such hostility that Rogan, Williams, and Bennett sat with bowed heads, unable to withstand the angry stares of people in the public gallery. The long trial ended when Windeyer asked each of the accused whether he had anything to say before sentence of death was passed on him. Rogan replied 'He [Scott] was my friend, the only one I ever had.'

Windeyer sentenced all four men to die, but the sentences on Bennett and Williams were commuted to life imprisonment. Inexplicably, the Executive Council did not see fit to save young Tom Rogan, who had not killed anyone, from the gallows. Perhaps his record weighed the scales against him.

A petition of mercy had no effect, and it is said that when Rogan heard of its failure he collapsed into the arms of his confessor, Father Ryan.

George Calderwood wrote '... for several days after, Rogan was morose and violent in turn. His mother and sister travelled from Melbourne to visit him, and when he saw them he told then forcibly that he resented their belated interest in his welfare. His lurid language shocked even the hardbitten prison guards. Both women left the prison in tears and begged the Sisters of Mercy to comfort them.

'Rogan's mother had brought a petition for the reprieve of her son containing over ninety signatures. When an investigation of the petition was made by the police it was revealed that many of the names had been signed by the same person.'

The end came for Thomas Rogan and his hero, Andrew George Scott, on 20 January 1880, when the hangman pulled the lever which launched them both into eternity.

Also see Andrew George Scott, James Nesbitt, Thomas Williams (2nd).

No. 2171

Born: 1857
Native Place: Victoria
Trade: Bootmaker
Religion: Roman Catholic
Education: Read and write
Height: 5ft 11¼ins
Weight: 156lbs
Hair: Black
Eyes: Brown
Alias: Brown, Baker
Where and When Tried: Supreme Court, 11 December 1879
Offence: Murder
Sentence: Death.
Previous Convictions: Beechworth General Sessions, April 7, 1875 for Larceny — Three months Hard Labour. Beechworth General Sessions, 28 February, 1877 for Horsestealing and Larceny — two years labour and six months Hard Labour accumulative.
Remarks: Executed 20 January 1880.

No. 2171 Name Thomas Rogan als Brown als Baker

Date when Portrait was taken, 26th Novr 1879

8270/79

Native place: Victoria
Year of birth: 1857
Arrived in Colony { Ship: / Year:
Trade or occupation previous to conviction: Bootmaker
Religion: R. Cath.
Education, degree of: R & W
Height: 5 feet 11¼ inches
Weight in lbs. { On committal: 156 / On discharge:
Colour of hair: Black
Colour of eyes: Brown
Marks or special features: —

Where and when tried: Supreme Ct. 11 Dec. 79
Offence: Murder
Sentence: Death
Remarks: —

Executed 20 Jany 80.

(No. of previous Portrait   )

PREVIOUS CONVICTIONS.

Where and When.	Offence.	Sentence.
Beechworth Gen Ses. Apl. 7 1875	Larceny	3 months H.L.
Feb. 28 1877	Horse Stealing and Larceny	2 years L and 6 months H.L. acumulative.

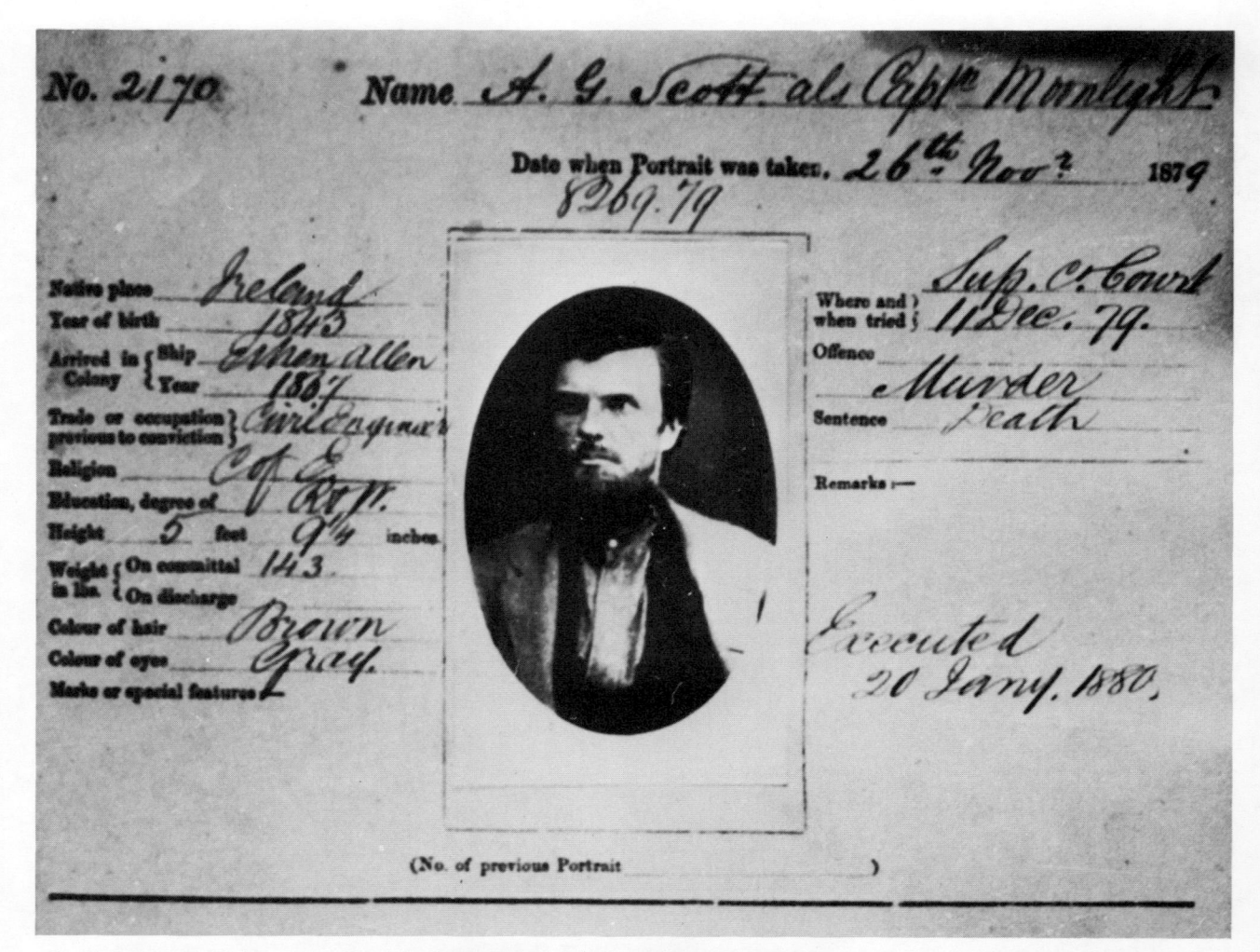

ANDREW SCOTT (CAPTAIN MOONLITE)

No.462

Born: 1845
Native Place: Down, Ireland
Education: Read and write
Religion: Church of England
Trade: Civil Engineer
Height: 5ft 8¾ins
Weight: 10st 8lbs
Complexion: Fresh
Hair: Brown
Eyes: Blue
Nose: Medium/pointed
Mouth: Medium
Chin: Medium
Eyebrows: Light brown
Visage: Long
Forehead: Medium
Particular Marks: Scar right elbow, scar near outside corner of right eyebrow, fleshy excrescence top of left shoulder, three moles back of neck, scar back of left armpit, mole left shoulder blade, scar centre of back, several small moles left side of back, mole right side of back, mole left side of cheek, mole right side of abdomen, two moles left side of abdomen, moles outside lower left arm, scar back of right hand, gunshot wound left breast, gunshot wounds on both shins, right ankle has been broken, same of right foot which turns in when walking.
Previous History: Per Black Eagle from London to Auckland, New Zealand in 1861, served in N.Z. Volunteers from 1861 to 1867. From South Sea Islands to Sydney 1868. To Melbourne in 1868 in Ethan Allen Barque. Single, no relatives in the Colony. Admits a sentence of 18 months in N.S.W. in 1870 for Uttering a Valueless Cheque. Not a militate (not to have force as evidence) offence having been committed after that for which Scott is now convicted — by order of Inspector General.
Alias: Captain Moonlite
Sentence: Stealing Gold and Monies value One Thousand Pounds from the London Chartered Bank. (This charge is crossed out on his record and changed to Robbery being armed with an offensive weapon). Ten years Roads, cumulative on previous sentence.
Date of Conviction: 23 July 1872, before Sir R. Barry, Ballarat Circular Court.

The man who called himself 'Captain Moonlite' was perhaps the strangest character among the Australian bushrangers.

An excuse can be found for most bushrangers in that they came from deprived backgrounds, or were in rebellion against the convict or social system, but there seems to be no excuse for Andrew Scott. He was a well-educated man of good family, widely travelled, trained in a good profession, at ease in the best of society, courageous and charming. It is believed he had a split personality, but also possible that he was what is now known as a sociopath: a person totally incapable of telling the difference between right and wrong.

A good deal of fiction and guesswork is blended with the facts that are known about Scott, beginning with his birthdate. Most writers give it as 1842, but on his prison record it is stated as 1845. This means that he was thirty-five when he was hanged in 1880.

He was born in County Down, Ireland, the son of a clergy-man who expected Andrew to follow him into the church. However he followed his father's other ruling passion, that of the study of hydraulics, and was trained as a civil engineer. One of his dubious claims is that as a young man he went to Italy and joined Garibaldi's freedom fighters, and with this early taste of warfare behind him he sailed to New Zealand to fight as a volunteer in the Maori Wars.

The 'Previous History' given in his prison record states that he served in New Zealand from 1861 to 1867, but if this is the case then he could not have fought also in the American Civil War (1861-1865), as stated in various biographies.

It seems certain however, that he was in America, whether as a soldier or otherwise, and it is said that he copied the name of Captain Moonlite from a crook whom he met in California. This man, Archie Telford, is supposed to have left notes signed 'Moonlite' at the scenes of his escapades, with the idea of confusing the police.

Scott arrived in Sydney in 1868 and went on to Melbourne and then to Bacchus Marsh, where he arrived on 17 July. His familiarity with religion secured him an appointment as a lay preacher on a salary of £130 a year, and he also opened an office as a civil engineer. Local society welcomed him and he soon made himself popular with his tales of adventure, his persuasive preaching, his lectures on irrigation schemes and letters to the local papers. Whatever Andrew Scott may have done with himself before he arrived in Australia there is no doubt that he was always a fluent speaker.

The church moved him to Egerton, to preach to the miners, but he found them an unresponsive audience. As usual he imposed himself on local society, which including Ludwig W. Julius Bruun, the eighteen-year-old agent of the London Chartered Bank.

Scott always got on well with men younger than himself and Ludwig Bruun may have felt himself honoured by the acquaintance. He could not have expected the incident which occurred at eight o'clock on the stormy evening of 8 May 1869, when he went to the bank premises and was about to open the door when he felt the muzzle of a pistol digging into his back. A voice said 'Don't make a sound or you're a dead man.'

Bruun immediately recognised the voice of Scott, and laughed with relief. But Scott growled 'Don't laugh, you bloody fool. Open the door and get inside quickly.'

The light inside the bank showed that the robber's face was covered with a mask of black crepe, but Bruun still recognised Scott. The latter forced him to hand over £697 in notes and sovereigns and gold worth £518, and then took him to the schoolhouse and made him write 'I hereby certify that L. W. Bruun has done everything in his favour to withstand our intrusion and the taking away of the money which was done with firearms.'

Scott signed this note 'Captain Moonlite,' tied Bruun to a chair, and made his getaway, The incident shows Scott's divided personality in that he was willing to hold up his friend Bruun but did not want him to suffer for it.

His scheme did more harm than good. The police refused to believe Bruun's story and even accused the schoolmaster, James Simpson, also a friend of Scott, of having written the note. They arrested and charged both men, who steadily protested their innocence and blamed Scott. The lay preacher was called as a witness at their trial, where he told the court that Bruun's story was nonsense. Scott's reputation was good, the court believed him, although the judge discharged Bruun and Simpson for lack of evidence. They still had to suffer from the incident because they remained under a cloud of suspicion and lost their jobs.

Scott abandoned his Egerton pulpit and went to Sydney, where the spoils of the bank robbery enabled him to cut a dash in local society. He pretended he was a wealthy squatter, gained membership of the exclusive Union Club, and entertained actresses at after-theatre parties.

In tune with his identity he bought an ocean-going yacht, renamed her *Why Not,* and set off on a cruise to Fiji with a charming companion. But he had paid for the yacht with a dud cheque and his cruise stopped short at Sydney Heads, where police boarded the *Why Not* and took her back to port.

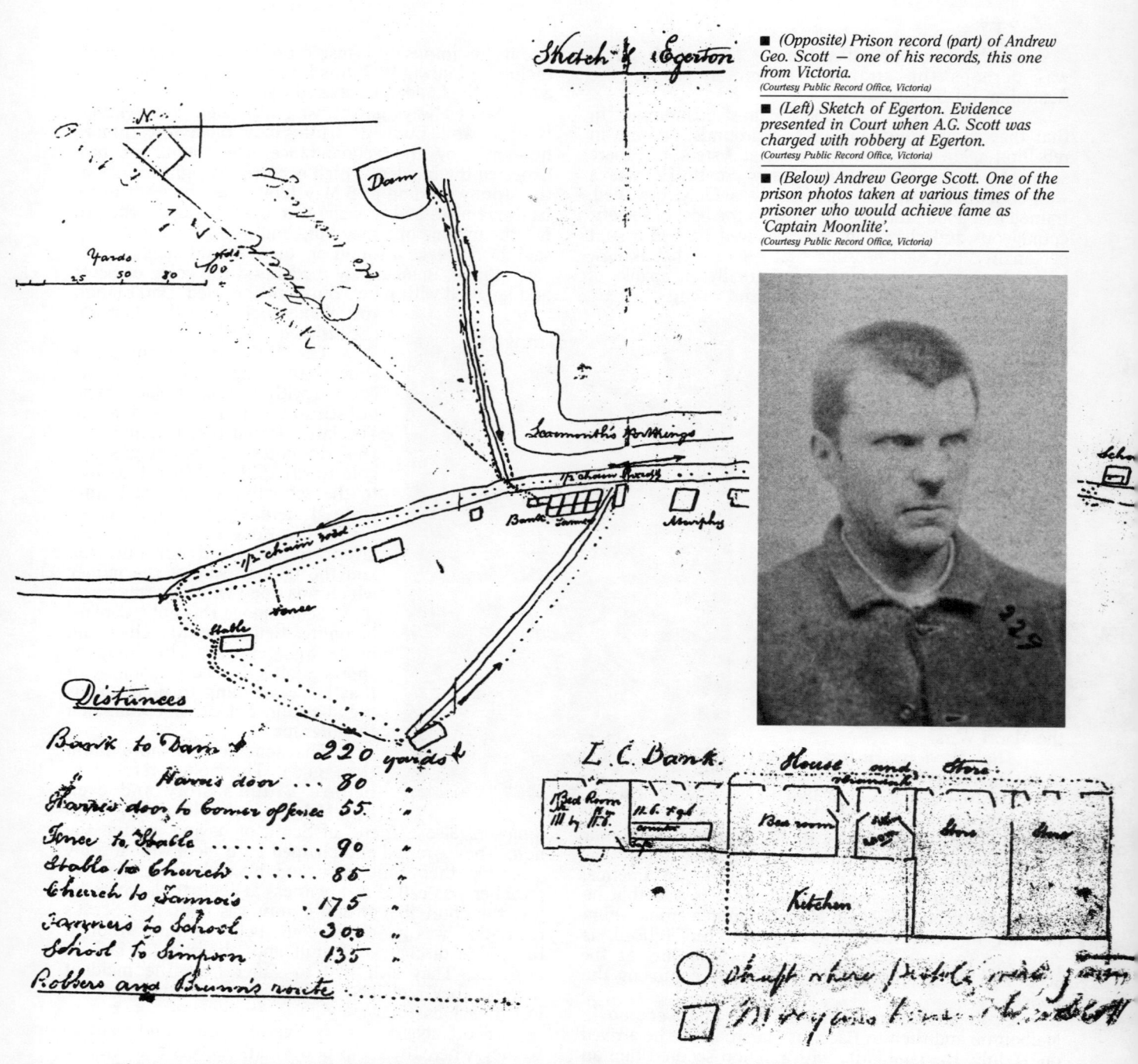

■ *(Opposite) Prison record (part) of Andrew Geo. Scott — one of his records, this one from Victoria.*
(Courtesy Public Record Office, Victoria)

■ *(Left) Sketch of Egerton. Evidence presented in Court when A.G. Scott was charged with robbery at Egerton.*
(Courtesy Public Record Office, Victoria)

■ *(Below) Andrew George Scott. One of the prison photos taken at various times of the prisoner who would achieve fame as 'Captain Moonlite'.*
(Courtesy Public Record Office, Victoria)

The court sent Scott to Maitland Gaol for eighteen months, but he found a temporary way out of prison by feigning insanity. The doctors sent him to Parramatta Lunatic Asylum, but he could not keep up the pretence for longer than four months and was returned to Maitland.

He was released in March 1872, and immediately re-arrested by Detective Patrick Lyons of the Victoria Police. Lyons had a warrant for Scott's arrest over the Egerton robbery, and he took him to Ballarat for trial.

His arrival in Ballarat created a sensation, and there was another sensation when he escaped from the new Ballarat gaol, with a prisoner named Dermoodie, before he could be brought to trial. On his own he made his way towards Bendigo, stealing a revolver and a double-barrelled gun en route. They were near his bed when the police found him asleep in a hut, and a trooper told the newspapers 'When we caught Captain Moonlite he was a sorry sight and looked like a Nunawading wood carter.' The description would hardly have pleased the fastidious Scott.

He appeared before Judge Redmond Barry, who determined to make an example of this man who had committed armed robbery of a bank and betrayed his friends. Barry sentenced Scott to ten years imprisonment, and he entered Pentridge on 8 August 1872. On top of the ten years for 'Robbery being armed with an offensive weapon' he faced an extra twelve months for escaping from Ballarat Gaol.

Scott served less than seven years of these sentences, despite repetitive bad behaviour in Pentridge and Melbourne Gaol. His record lists twenty-one offences, ranging from insolence, idleness, misconduct, disobedience of orders, talking, and assault, to the more specialised ones of 'Having coffee,' 'Having tea improperly,' 'Having trousers, socks, etc.,' 'Making ironwork without authority,' 'Letting water out of bath.'

A more favourable comment shows that he was given three months remission of sentence 'for assistance to an officer assaulted by a prisoner,' but there is no clue as to why he was discharged early, on 18 March 1879.

He had nothing but his prison pay of £2.10.10d, but he quickly found a way to profit from his experiences. With the help of a well-known theatrical agent, Richmond Thatcher, he gave a series of public lectures on the appalling conditions in Pentridge and the brutal treatment of prisoners by warders. Apparently the public lapped them up.

The police arrested Scott, when an actor named Bates was found with a broken neck, and again when the Lancefield Bank was robbed. But they had no evidence against him and had to set him free.

Scott had linked up with young James Nesbitt, whom he met in prison, and he also began to attract other restless youths. These were Thomas Williams, aged nineteen, Graham Bennett aged twenty, and the youngest of them all: Gus Wernicke, fifteen. Later they were joined by Thomas Rogan, twenty-one.

There is no adequate explanation of Scott's attraction for these youngsters, or why he chose such juvenile company. It is easy to think that there might have been homosexual undercurrents, and voluminous official documentation on his history, has a tendency to confirm it. It is likely. He may have also chosen them because he could impress them easily with his romantic stories and boasting, and they looked upon him as a daring and gallant man, an admirable father-figure. They were inexperienced youngsters with no knowledge of life outside petty crime, the raw colonial townships, and restrictive family backgrounds.

Many different stories have been told about Andrew

■ *A rare document — A.G. Scott, alias 'Captain Moonlite' tried to use this forged Bank of Australia note, which was altered from ONE POUND to TEN POUNDS.*
One of two documents (see over page) from a private collection.

Scott's decision to form a bushranging gang, and of its exploits as it moved through Victoria in the second half of 1879. Whether true or false, such stories are of little significance except in the way that they lead up to the final act in the strange tragi-comedy of Captain Moonlite, in what has become known as the Battle of Wantabadgery.

It has been said that Andrew Scott suffered throughout his life from painful headaches whenever he became worried or frustrated, and when he felt that he was being denied his rightful place in the centre of the stage. If this is true, then such symptoms would indeed show that he was suffering from some deep psychological trauma. The events of the few days following the gang's arrival in the Wagga Wagga district may show that he was close to a final breakdown.

By Thursday 13 November 1879, Scott and his gang were well into New South Wales. They rode past Wagga Wagga, stuck up the store at Claredon, and headed towards the little township of Wantabadgery halfway between Wagga Wagga and Junee. On the Saturday morning they rode through the out-paddocks of the property belonging to C.F. MacDonald, who was away from home, and took over the station. They planned to stay there long enough to eat and sleep, but first rounded up as many people as they could find, so that nobody could escape to warn the police. They herded MacDonald's brother Alexander, Samuel Miles the station storekeeper, Percy Baynes the station manager, and seventeen station workers and their womenfolk into the home. C.F. MacDonald returned home while this was going on and the gang pushed him in with the rest, and followed him with David Weir, the Claredon storekeeper, who rode up to the property and was horrified to find it occupied by the men who had robbed his store.

Scott and Rogan then rode into Wantabadgery in the station buggy, and held up the Australian Arms Hotel. They forced James Patterson, the owner, to open the bar, and then took him and his wife and children back to MacDonald's station in the buggy. On the way back they detoured to pick up John Reid, the station overseer, who was apparently unaware of what had been going on at the homestead.

By that time, Scott was obviously in a condition of extreme nervous tension. As the occupation of the station continued, the captives naturally found it hard to obey the bushrangers' orders to keep silent and Percy Baynes talked softly to one of the others. Scott flew into a rage and put Baynes on 'trial,' threatening to shoot or hang him for the offence. He slashed at Baynes with a

■ *The captors of the 'Moonlite' gang, 1879. NSW Police — (left to right standing) Wills, Williamson, Barry. (left to right seated) Rowe, Headly, Gorman, John. (seated centre) Sergeant Cassin.*
(Courtesy NSW Police, PRD)

knife, drawing blood, but the arrival of two more horsemen saved Baynes from whatever might have been his fate.

These horsemen were Andrew Beveridge, a neighbouring landowner, and a companion. They were taken captive and Scott took a fancy to Beveridge's fine horse. He decided to take it over, but when he tried to mount the horse it was so scared and skittish that he could not control it. He drew his revolver and killed it with a shot through the head.

The bushrangers had now crowded so many people into the homestead that they could not control them properly, and Alexander MacDonald managed to escape. He headed for a nearby station to spread the news, and one of the men there, Ruskin, made a foolhardy attempt to rescue the prisoners. Scott captured him and made him face a farcical trial, with the other captives as jury, on a charge of unlawfully carrying firearms. Of course the 'jury' found him not guilty, and Scott told him that he was lucky not to face a firing squad.

The bushrangers knew that MacDonald would have told the police about them, and their strange weekend at MacDonald's station concluded with the arrival of a party of troopers. The police, conscious of the number of innocent people within the house, had to move warily, but there was an exchange of shots before the bushrangers burst out of the homestead with their booty, including any extra firearms they could lay hands on, and galloped away with the troopers in hot pursuit.

The bushrangers evaded them for a while and caught up with a station owner named Edmund McGlede, who was riding along apparently unaware of the events on his neighbour's station. They compelled McGlede to take them to his homestead, and made his wife serve them with a meal before the police arrived and the battle resumed. The people from MacDonald's station, and others who had heard what was going on, had a grandstand view of events from a nearby hillside.

Besieged in the McGlede homestead, the bushrangers returned a hail of fire to the police bullets which slammed into the house. The group of youngsters showed that they were prepared to fight to the end for their hero Captain Moonlite. Gus Wreneckie ran from the shelter of the house to find a better position from which to shoot at the police, and shot Constable Barry's horse from under him. Barry fired back and the bullet hit young Gus, who is supposed to have cried out 'Oh God, I am shot and I am only fifteen!' He was critically wounded and he died a few days later.

Graham Bennett, watching Wreneckie from a window, received a bullet which shattered his arm. He fell back and his companions carried him into the bedroom of Mr and Mrs McGlede. James Nesbitt ran out of the house in an attempt to divert the police, but Constable Bowen shot him dead and a moment later fell from a bullet in the neck, fired by Captain Moonlite.

The savage little affray ended when Moonlite and Thomas Williams surrendered. The police stormed into the house, and found Tom Rogan under a bed, with weapons that he had apparently not used, and Bennett groaning from the pain of his shattered arm.

Sergeant Carroll, in command of the police, organised transport of the captured bushrangers and wounded men to Gundagai, where Wreneckie and Bowen died. Carroll then took the remaining four on to Sydney, where such an enormous crowd awaited their arrival that Carroll had to brandish a pistol to keep them away from the bushrangers.

The bushrangers appeared before Mr Justice William Windeyer on 8 December 1879. Windeyer listened patiently to Andrew Scott's long and flamboyant speeches in his own defence, but these did not impress the jury who found all four men guilty of murder. Scott made a passionate plea for mercy for his young comrades, but Windeyer had no option but to sentence them all to death.

Williams and Bennett escaped the final penalty when their sentences were commuted to life imprisonment, but Scott and his young friend Thomas Rogan died together on the Darlinghurst gallows on Tuesday 20 January 1880. The reputed site of Scott's grave is in Rookwood cemetery, near Lidcombe, New South Wales. Thomas Williams was to meet the fate described later in this book.

Also see James Nesbitt, Thomas Rogan, Thomas Williams (2nd)

■ *Prison photo of Andrew Scott, the only photo known of him with just a moustache.*
(Courtesy Public Record Office, Victoria)

■ *One of two rare documents (see previous page) This cheque is signed by A.G. Scott, alias 'Captain Moonlite'. A check of documents signed by Scott confirmed this is typical of his signature.*

The cheque is from a private collection.

WILLIAM SCOTT

The Archives of New South Wales contain a small reference to William Scott in the *List of Offences of Bushrangers* which is preserved there. It describes him as thirty years old, a native of New South Wales, a sawyer by trade, and a Roman Catholic. The brief particulars state: 'One of Clarke's Gang — supposed to have been murdered by them — a prizefighter and drunkard — sister married a publican at Berrima.'

According to George Boxall, Bill Scott's first recorded offence was committed on the Bendigo diggings. Two diggers, James Mason and John Brown, were sitting outside their tent one evening enjoying their supper, when Bill Scott came plodding along the track towards the township. He looked tired and hungry and so the two diggers invited him to 'Sit down and have a feed.' He accepted, and repaid their generosity by slipping his hand under the edge of the tent while he was eating and finding a bag containing 110 ounces of gold. This was a fairly hefty cache, equivalent to about three kilograms, but he managed somehow to secrete it in his clothes or swag before he continued his journey. Mason and Brown noticed their loss before Scott was out of sight, and they soon caught him and took him into Bendigo.

This story, like so many about bushrangers, may or may not be true. It states that Scott was gaoled for five years, but an exhaustive search of the criminal and prison records of that era has failed to discover any prisoner named William Scott undergoing a five-year sentence for gold stealing. The relevant records, of course, may have been 'Lost, stolen, or destroyed.'

It is equally impossible to find any recorded trace of William Scott's dubious career until he became involved with the most ruthless and daring bushrangers of them all: the Clarke brothers. How and when he became one of their gang is also unknown, but there is no doubt that he participated in some of the numerous robberies and murders committed by the Clarkes. John O'Sullivan, in his fine book about the Clarkes entitled *The Bloodiest Bushrangers*, believes that Scott killed Patrick Kennagh, one of four policemen who met their deaths while in pursuit of the Clarkes. He wrote 'Kennagh had been killed by a large rifle ball that passed through the thyroid cartilage in the neck. The ball had passed downwards through the trachea and upper part of the left lung.'

The life of a bushranger was one of constant tension and suspicion. As Matthew Brady said 'There is constant fear of capture and the least noise in the bush is startling.' Even the men who scoffed at the police for cowardice and incompetence knew that the troopers were bound to win in the end. Every bushranger feared betrayal, by a mate or even a relation who could not resist the temptation of the huge rewards offered for their capture (it must be remembered that £500, in purchasing power, was equal to at least $25,000 in modern currency) and it may be that the Clarke brothers believed that their mate Bill Scott was going to betray them, either for reward or in order to turn Queen's Evidence and escape the consequences of his own crimes.

We can only guess at the truth of the matter, but it is certain that a bushman searching for cattle found the skeleton of William Scott on 9 April 1867 in the territory dominated by the Clarkes. Scott had been a big man, and his remains were clad in a 'black cloth sac coat with brass buttons, a drab black crossbar tweed vest with horn buttons, corduroy trousers strapped with the same material and lined at the bottoms with iron-grey tweed, a Crimean shirt, a drab mauve and black plaid scarf, and strong Wellington boots with brass sprigs and a German silver spur on the right heel.' Medical examination found a fracture of the skull, and one report said there was a bullet in the skull. Many people, including the police, believed that the Clarkes killed Scott because they suspected him of turning informer.

John O'Sullivan adds an amusing footnote to the discovery of Scott's remains. He says that a coffin was taken to the site where they were found, and Detective Lyons was posted there until they could be taken away. When rain set in, Lyons climbed into the coffin for shelter, and was lying within it when two horsemen rode up. He challenged them from inside the coffin and they turned and rode for their lives.

Also see Clarke brothers

■ *'Bushrangers Waiting for the Mails in New South Wales'. An original S.T. Gill watercolour.*
(Courtesy La Trobe Collection, State Library of Victoria)

STAND AND DELIVER

AARON SHERRITT

> **No.13891**
> *Born:* 1856
> *Native Place:* Victoria
> *Trade:* Labourer
> *Religion:* Church of England
> *Education:* Read and write
> *Height:* 5ft 10ins
> *Complexion:* Fresh
> *Hair:* Brown
> *Eyes:* Hazel
> *Particular Marks:* Nil recorded
> *Previous History:* Nil recorded
> *Sentence:* Six months Hard Labour — Unlawfully possession of the Carcase of a cow.
> *Date of Conviction:* 30 May 1876, Beechworth Petty Sessions.

■ *A studio portrait of Aaron Sherritt taken by James Bray at his studio in Camp Street, Beechworth.*
(Courtesy Burke Museum, Beechworth)

*T*he man who the Kelly Gang believed betrayed them, arrived in Beechworth with his parents, when he was still a baby. His father was an ex-policeman. The family took up a small selection at Sheepstation Creek, in the ranges above Woolshed Creek, a few miles from Beechworth. As he grew to manhood Aaron would become one of the wayward colonial youths. He was physically impressive, a likeable person, but he showed some contradictions; one moment he could show his total loyalty, the next utter lack of principle. He exploited police, on whose payroll he was, whilst still friend and assistant of the Kelly Gang. He would go on to play a dangerous game of double-agent.

He became involved in horse and stock theft, and worked with the Kellys, Quinns, Lloyds and Harts, which made him a marked man as far the police were concerned. Aaron took up his own selection when only eighteen years old. Ned Kelly and Joe Byrne helped him fence the selection.

He was only twenty when he was arrested for 'Unlawful possession of the carcase of a cow', and sentenced in May 1876 to six months hard labour by the Beechworth Petty Sessions.

No doubt settlers along the Sheepstation Creek, as elsewhere, were obliged to steal a few of their neighbours' cattle and horses from time to time, simply to keep alive. Their little properties in those rugged bushclad hills were hardly large enough to support them.

Aaron became a firm friend of all the group. He flirted with Ned Kelly's sister, Kate, and later became engaged to the sister of Joe Byrne. Joe was his best friend among the whole community of settlers who scratched out a living along the Woolshed, and defied the law in their forays among livestock of more prosperous citizens.

The continuous skirmishing between settlers and police finally erupted into open warfare when Ned Kelly wounded Constable Fitzpatrick, in the manner described in the Kelly Family biography in this book. The police obtained warrants for the arrest of Ned and Dan Kelly, who took to the bush in company with Steve Hart and Joe Byrne, and established a hideout at Bullock Creek (later called Kellys Creek). Six months later, Ned Kelly killed three of the four policeman sent to arrest him, and he and his gang became outlaws.

In this period Aaron Sherritt was a great help to the Kelly Gang. He was no doubt welcomed at their camps and they would have discussed plans with him. It is pretty clear from evidence that the gang knew that Aaron was stringing the police along and used his contact with them as a useful source of information — for example — in decoying the police away from their crossing place on the Murray River, so they could carry out the Jerilderie raid.

Just what information Aaron had given the police

100 AUSTRALIAN BUSHRANGERS 1789-1901

Murder of Aaron Sherritt. An incorrect illustration as both bushrangers did not have beards, and the door on Sherritt's hut was hinged on the left, not the right.
(Below) An illustration of Sherritt's hut. Both illustrations from the period.

regarding the Kellys is now questionable, however he did become a betrayer as far as the gang, and particularly Joe Byrne, were concerned. One tends to think of a man who could betray his friends as a miserable specimen of humanity, but Aaron was far from that. Police Superintendant Hare told the Royal Commission in 1881 that Aaron 'was a remarkable looking man. If he walked down Collins Street everybody would have stared at him. His walk, his appearance, and everything else were remarkable. He was a man of the most wonderful endurance... I saw the man one night when the water was frozen on the creeks, and I was frozen to death nearly. There was Aaron lying uncovered. I said "Are you mad, Aaron, lying there"?, and he said, "I do not care about coats." ' The 'remarkable looking man' was treading a dangerous path. Apparently he remained in touch with Ned Kelly until the gang returned after their bank robberies at Euroa and Jerilderie. Suspicions of Aaron and his role came to light, and when Mrs Byrne saw him with police in wait for members of the gang, the die was cast. Detective Ward had been using Aaron as the bait to bring the Kellys out of hiding. Kelly sympathisers warned them of Aaron's association with police. They told Aaron of their planned hold-up of a bank in Goulbourn. He told this false story to the police and was rewarded with the sum of £2 for the information.

Ned Kelly reluctantly accepted that Aaron had betrayed the gang. His plan to kill Aaron became the bait that would bring the police to Wangaratta to change trains for Beechworth.

Aaron had married the fifteen-year-old daughter of Ellen Barry and set up home with his new bride. The people openly referred to him as a police spy, and Aaron himself had little doubt now that Ned Kelly would put an end to him. He told Superintendant Hare 'I am a dead man.'

The police posted four armed constables to guard his hut, and sypathisers would have told the Kellys of them, but Dan Kelly and Joe Byrne rode up to Aaron's hut on the evening of 26 June 1880, preceded by a man named Anton Weekes, a settler who lived a mile from Aaron. He was used to lure Aaron into opening the door. The occupants of the hut, fearful of Ned Kelly and his mates, would see only a neighbour, who when he called out, thought he was drunk and had lost his way.

As Aaron opened the door Joe Byrne fired past Weeke's shoulder and killed Aaron before he could say a word. Pandemonium broke loose, the police in fear of their lives, Aaron's wife in a state of shock at seeing her husband gunned down. Joe Byrne and Dan Kelly remained at the hut for almost an hour calling on the police to show themselves and fight. Two of the troopers hid under a bed and forced Aaron's wife and her mother to also. During the Royal Commission in 1881 it was said that 'never was there a more conspicious instance of arrant cowardice than was exhibited by these men on that night...'

Witnesses stressed that had the police made a rush for the doors they would have almost certainly been gunned down and killed. They remained under the bed until the next morning. The fate of the traitor is to earn contempt from both sides. Superintendant Hare summed it up when he said 'The Government of the colony would not have assisted him in any way, and he would have gone back to his old course of life, and probably become a bushranger himself.'

The remains of Aaron Sherritt lie in an unmarked grave next to his father. The Beechworth Progress Association had considered a proposal to erect a headstone over the grave, but the feeling about Aaron in the Kelly Country is still so strong that the idea was abandoned.

Also see Joseph Byrne, Stephen Hart, the Kelly Family.

ALFRED STALLARD

1
Born: 1815
Native Place: Bristol
Trade: Labourer
Height: 5ft
Complexion: Florid
Hair: Sandy
Eyes: Grey
Particular Marks: Scar on left side of chin, and A.S. on left arm.
Previous History: Arrived in Van Diemen's Land in 1836 under sentence of Transportation.
Sentence: Five years on the Roads of the Colony, for Horsestealing, commuted to three years.
Date of Conviction: 16 July 1849 at Melbourne.

2
Born: 1815
Native Place: Bristol
Trade: Labourer
Religion: Protestant
Height: 5ft 1¼ins
Complexion: Fresh
Hair: Brown *Eyes:* Grey
Particular Marks: 'E' on left arm. Wanting middle finger of left hand. A scar under right one on right side of upper lip.
Previous History: Arrived at Van Diemen's Land in 1836. Bond. Per ship Bardostan (?) Convicted at Supreme Court Melbourne 16 August 1849 of Horsestealing and sentenced to three years on the Roads of the Colony. Free on conviction of present crime.

The story of Alfred Stallard has been told by other bushranging historians in connection with that of Christopher Goodison, who appears earlier in this book. However it appears that other writers were not aware that Stallard already possessed a criminal record, as shown in the extract with this article. Entries on his prison record show that he was received at Cockatoo Island on 8 September 1849, on a sentence of three years commuted from five years, but he was actually released less than two years later, on 16 July 1851. He did not take long to team up with Christopher Goodison and rob Mrs Roberts of her gold at Bendigo Creek.

Alfred Stallard appears to have been a plausible rogue and the authorities dealt with him very kindly. He served less than two-thirds of his first sentence of imprisonment, and less than two years of the second sentence before he was released on Ticket of Leave. He regained his freedom on 29 August 1853 and apparently kept out of trouble after this second lesson that 'Crime does not pay.'

The unfortunate Mrs Roberts was not the only woman on the goldfields to suffer at the hands of bushrangers. On 8 October 1852, the *Melbourne Argus* wrote 'Outrages and robberies are still of frequent occurrence, and every day they become more and more daring. A few days ago, a gang of bushrangers walked into one of the three public houses at Sawpit Gully, and commenced ransacking the place all over, and I am told paid themselves well for their trouble. About the same time, three of the same fraternity went into a tent belonging to a man and wife at Fryers Creek, and while the husband was straining his eyes to get an honest nugget, these vagabonds, after a vain resistance from the woman, tied her hands and feet to the bed, and in turn gratified their brutal desires! Where will they stop? I believe the husband had give a description of these three men to the police, offering a reward of £100 for their apprehension, dead or alive.'

Also see Christopher Goodison

STAND AND DELIVER

OWEN SUFFOLK

1

Born: 1829
Native Place: London
Trade: Clerk
Height: 5ft 10½ins
Complexion: Fair
Hair: Sandy
Eyes: Blue
Particular Marks: Anchor on lower left arm.
Previous History: Arrived at Port Phillip per Joseph Somes in 1847, an exile from Milbank.
Sentence: Five years on the Roads of the Colony, for Horsestealing.
Date of Conviction: 19 December 1848.

2

CHARLES VERNON alias OWEN SUFFOLK
Born: 1829
Native Place: London
Trade: Clerk
Religion: Protestant
Education: Read and write
Height: 5ft 11½ins
Complexion: Fair
Hair Light Brown
Eyes: Blue
Nose: Large
Mouth: Medium
Chin: Medium
Eyebrows: Light
Visage: Long
Forehead: Medium
Particulars Marks: Natural brown mark from left breast inclining to back. Anchor lower left arm. Mole on index finger left hand.
Previous History: Per Joseph Soames 1847 an exile from Milbank. Twice previously convicted in Victoria as Owen Suffolk.
Sentence: (1st charge) Five years on Roads — for Horsestealing. (2nd charge) Seven years on the Roads, accumulative on former sentence — for Horsestealing. To serve two years and six months beyond minimum.
Dates of Convictions: (1st charge) 12 February 1858, Portland General Sessions before A.G. Wrixon, Esq. Chairman.
(2nd charge) 21 June 1858, Ballarat Circular Court, before His Honor, Mr Justice Barry.

■ *Copy of the official letter stating that the sentence imposed on Owen Suffolk would not receive a remission of sentence.*
(Courtesy Public Record Office, Victoria)

On a fine day in May 1851 the Portland-Geelong coach was grinding along the rough highway at Bruce's Creek when two men stepped out of the trees lining the road, aimed their pistols at coachman William Freer, and called on him to halt. One of them was nattily dressed 'in a black suit of fashionable cut, and black kid gloves.'

Freer ignored them and whipped up his team, but one of the bushrangers grabbed the lead horse by its bridle while the other yelled at him to stop 'or I'll blow your brains out!'

Freer obeyed this convincing command and followed the bushrangers' instructions to drive the coach off the road into the trees. They forced the passengers to get out, tied them together, ransacked the mailbags and took anything of value, and stole a saddle and bridle belonging to one of the passengers, Thomas Gibson. They used this to saddle up one of the coach horses, and rode another one bareback.

The two bushrangers were Owen Suffolk and his mate Christopher Farrell, whose story is told earlier in this book. The story of Owen Suffolk is that of a complex type of character.

His neat clothing, most unusual for a bushranger, would have been better suited to his original occupation as a clerk. He arrived in Australia when he was only eighteen years old. In 1848, he found himself in gaol for horsestealing.

He was convicted in what is now Victoria but was then part of New South Wales and sent to Cockatoo Island to serve his five-year sentence. Christopher Farrell was there at the same time, and so it is likely that the two young men used the opportunity to plan a career in bushranging. Why Owen Suffolk should have been determined on a life of crime, instead of finding himself one of the clerical jobs available with the merchants and storekeepers of the colony, is one of the mysteries of the criminal personality.

Owen behaved himself reasonably well on Cockatoo Island and his record notes only three offences, all during 1850, of neglect of work, trying to send a letter from the island, and fighting on the square. These charges earned him a total of forty-nine days in the cells before he was transferred to the new stockade at Pentridge. He arrived there on Christmas Eve 1850.

The majority of prisoners in that era, even including some of the most brutal and ruthless, served much less than their full sentences before being released on Ticket of Leave. The thousands of prison records scanned by the author show that this method of releasing prisoners on probation was used with remarkable regularity, and Owen Suffolk would almost certainly have received this kind of second chance if he had been willing to wait for it. In fact he was due to make his application for a Ticket of Leave when he forged a pass out of prison, and walked out to temporary freedom on 2 March 1851.

He contacted his prison mate Christopher Farrell and they held up the mail coach a few weeks later. They enjoyed the fruits of this robbery for no longer than it took the police to find them in Geelong, present them before the court on 20 June 1851, and return them to prison.

Christopher Farrell served his second sentence the hard way and became a violent prisoner. Owen Suffolk quickly showed a willingness to reform, after a refusal to work added two months to his sentence and a transfer to Melbourne Gaol.

The authorities found him very useful in the prison office where he worked as a clerk, and his record remained so clean that they had no hesitation in releasing him on Ticket of Leave on 10 September 1853. They may have congratulated themselves on the success of the system which could set a man free, after serving little more than two years of a ten-year sentence.

Miners at Black Hill, 1854. An original watercolour depicting miners costumes, by Eugene Von Guerard, painted on the Ballarat Goldfields. A fine example of how men and women dressed during the goldrush period.
(Courtesy La Trobe Collection, State Library of Victoria)

But then they began to look at some of the documents on which Owen Suffolk had worked while he was clerking in the prison office, and found some puzzling discrepancies. Owen had been making himself popular among the other prisoners, and perhaps earning a little income on the side, by 'altering prisoners' warrants while employed as Clerk at the Gaol.'

On 30 January 1854 they cancelled his Ticket of Leave. Owen must have thought that nobody would notice his forgeries because he had not even taken the opportunity to slip away from the Melbourne area, and on 28 February 1854 he found himself aboard the hulk *President*, among the hardest of the hardcase criminals who infested the colony at that time.

His good behaviour during his second prison sentence had not only earned him a Ticket of Leave, but commutation of his ten years sentence to one of five years. Under normal circumstances, this would have meant that the cancellation of his ticket would require him to serve out only the balance of a ten-year sentence. But the authorities were so upset by Owen Suffolk's forgeries that the Colonial Secretary rescinded the commutation and restored the full sentence.

Owen had to look forward to years of existence on the coarse meagre convict rations, toiling six days a week on whatever 'government works' the convicts might be employed upon, every minute of his life subject to strict discipline. But he had one weapon with which to fight back: his pen.

Once more he became a model prisoner, apart from one slip on 8 January 1856 when he misbehaved himself in some way, and received four days solitary confinement on bread and water. He spent the greater part of his scanty free time in composing and writing applications for 'indulgence', or remission of sentence, which were quite unsuccessful during the first couple of years of his third stretch of imprisonment. The authorities did not forget the way in which he had made a fool of them. A note on his records dated 5 July 1855 reads 'Application for Indulgence refused, Prisoner not being worthy, having held a Ticket of Leave.'

But Owen was not discouraged and he continued to argue his own case in one appeal after another. He argued that the restoration of the full sentence was illegal because the authorities had officially cut it in half, and the Colonial Secretary referred the matter to the Attorney General. On 24 July 1855 the latter declared 'the rescinding of the commutation to be legal and refuses any recommendation to the Governor.'

Owen continued his paper war, to such effect that the Chief Secretary relented a little and on 30 August 1856 decided to give him one year's remission of sentence. Cheered by this news, Owen kept himself out of trouble with the prison guards, pursued his campaign for release, and was at last rewarded on 18 February 1857. On that date, the prison clerk wrote on Owen's record 'In reply to a petition to His Excellency the Governor, prisoner should receive his Ticket of Leave on 20th December, 1857.'

The young Cockney clerk, still only twenty-eight, tasted the sweets of freedom on 21 December 1857, and it might be imagined that after such a long struggle for release he would have decided that it was time to go straight. But Owen Suffolk, like many criminals, had plenty of intelligence but no common sense. Instead of looking for paid work in the prosperous colony, which was then booming at the height of the gold rush and crowded with so many people that it was easy for a man to rise above his past record, he went wrong again.

His Ticket of Leave had even released him to the district of Ballarat, where there was ample work for anyone with willing hands, but Owen stole another horse and on 21 June 1858 he stood in the Ballarat Circular Court before Mr Justice Barry. He was charged under the alias of Charles Vernon but the police had no difficulty in recognising him.

When he escaped from Pentridge in 1851 he had forged a pass under the name of George Mason, but a careful search of the prison records shows that he did not use this alias again.

Barry sent Owen Suffolk back to imprisonment and it was during his fifth spell of confinement that he earned the name of 'the convict poet.' Probably he realised that there was not much point in writing the usual flow of letters to the Colonial Secretary and other authorities and so he turned to writing verse. He wrote in the flowery style which was greatly admired in that period, and the extent of his vocabulary shows a surprising degree of education or self-education.

Also he occupied some of his free time by writing his memoirs. His fluent pen made the most of his own story and when the book was published in Victoria in 1866 it became a best-seller.

Once more he behaved as a model prisoner. His record shows only a couple of minor charges, 'Having tobacco' and 'Having bread,' for which he was punished by deferment of indulgences for fourteen days, but he still had to serve the whole of his sentence and he was not released again until 4 July 1866. He was under the restrictions of a Ticket of Leave, but the *Police Gazette* 27 September 1866 recorded 'Owen Suffolk . . . has been granted a free pardon by his Excellency the Governor and has left the colony for England.' Perhaps His Excellency was glad to get rid of him.

According to 'Old Chum,' writing in *Melbourne Truth* in 1910. Owen had earned the money to go back to England by the sale of his book. 'Old Chum' remarked that many of the 'exiles' transported from England to Australia in the 1840s became 'highly respectable colonists and wealthy men,' but 'A few, such as Owen Suffolk "the prison poet," were not weaned from their evil courses, and became a burden upon the colony, and a source of trouble to the police. The most specious scoundrel of the lot . . . Owen Suffolk lapsed again in England and one report says to escape punishment for a confidence trick, he faked his own drowning, and with a wealthy widow's money made good his escape to America.

According to the *Melbourne Herald* in 1868, he was still alive, 'enjoying himself in New York'.

Also see Christopher Farrell

VERSES COMPOSED ON BOARD THE HULK *PRESIDENT* ON HEARING A CHILD PLAYING ON THE DECK.

Thou sinless and sweet one—thy voice is a strain
Which yields solace to sadness, and balm to my pain,
From thy unsullied spirit it comes to me here,
Like the music of Eden—soft, holy, and clear.
The storm-stirring thoughts o'er my heart holding sway,
At the charm of its gentleness vanish away!
For its melody, teeming with gladness and love,
Seems the song of the seraph to lure me above.
Beautiful prattler!—that music of mirth,
Yet unchecked by the cares and the sorrows of earth,
Mingles strangely where anguish and wretchedness reign,
With the sigh of the captive, and clank of his chain.
Yet I love to hear it, though captive I be,
Gushing pure from thy young heart all joyous and free.
There's a siren-like sweetness pervading its song,
Which can woo me to virtue, and win me from wrong.
Play on, then—play on, then—for thou dost not know
What it is to be wretched and burdened with woe:
There's the fair world around thee, and blue sky above,
Ever seeming to breathe on thee beauty and love;
And the waters that flash in the sun's golden beams,
Dance beneath thee as bright as thine own fairy dreams;
Yet here there are hearts sank in ruin and crime,
Which once was as gleesome and guiltless as thine.
Beware! then—beware!—when seducingly gay
Vice, with counterfeit smiles, would beguile thee away
From the good and the lovely, from virtue and joy,
To the pleasures of sin, which debase and destroy.
Those holy emotions and pure thoughts which dwell
In the bosom of childhood—oh, cherish them well!
For if there's a true joy this world can impart,
It surely exists in the innocent heart.
Though remorse wring my soul, and though care clothe my brow,

I once was as sinless and joyous as thou;
And knelt, too, like thee, by a fond mother's chair
With tiny hands folded in faith-hallowed pray'r.
Play on, my sweet child! there's a penitent tear
Stealing down my wan cheek as I list to thee here:
There's a prayer in my heart to the Wise One above
To be made like a child in belief and in love.
O ever when gladly this gay world would win
With its tinselled allurements thy young heart to sin,
Turn away from the light of its illusive glare,
And seek in temptation the refuge of pray'r.
Uncorrupted in heart and a stranger to woe,
With the garland of love green and bright on thy brow,
May'nt thou journey through life and thy voice still retain
Its heav'n-given sweetness to soothe grief and pain.

O.H. Suffolk

John Stone

taken July 11th 1886

JOHN VANE

> **Born:** 1843
> **Native Place:** James Plains (N.S.W.)
> **Trade:** Blacksmith
> **Height:** 6ft ½ins
> **Hair:** Brown
> **Eyes:** Hazel
> **Marks or Special Features:** Nil recorded.
> **Previous Convictions:** Bathurst County Court, 12 October 1864, for Robbery under Arms. Sentenced to fifteen years Roads. Remitted Carcoar Bench, 19 May 1875, for Stealing. Sentenced to three months Hard Labour. Bathurst Quarter Sessions, 6 July 1880, for Sheepstealing. Sentenced to five years Roads.

John Vane had every reason to go straight. His parents were 'respectable English Wesleyans,' he was apprenticed to the trade of blacksmith at fourteen and could have earned a substantial living, and he was a personable character described as 'Tall and active, a splendid horseman ... of ruddy complexion with dark hair and an engaging manner ... very different from the popular idea of a bushranger.'

But, as John O'Brien recorded in his book *Men of '38,* young Johnny preferred the tearaway life of the bush lads to a respectable life as a blacksmith. 'Mixing with the rough life of the diggings at the Turon and Tambaroona when a mere boy, bullock driving to Orange and Lambing Flat at 18, he fell easy prey to the blandishments of O'Meally, with whom he had grown up, and Gilbert, whom he was anxious to meet because of his notoriety.'

The youngster later known as 'The Number One,' apparently because his parents lived on a property called The Number One or Number One Swamp, near Carcoar, began his bushranging career with a cattle stealing exploit in company with Mickey Burke and then he robbed a Chinaman. He was by now a confirmed robber. By the time he was twenty his police record was growing steadily. During 1863 he was bushranging in company with Gilbert, O'Meally, Ben Hall, and Burke and they were recognised over and over again. On 24 August they bailed up four storekeepers on the road near Young, on 29 August they broke into J. W. Edmond's house at Demondrille and looted it, on 19 September they bailed up the Cowra-Bathurst mail coach, on 24 September they robbed a store at Calula near Long Swamp, and so the list goes on.

As usual when bushrangers were on the rampage, there was considerable confusion as to which of them committed any particular crime. John Vane was blamed for at least one exploit in which he was not concerned, when a report said 'Vane fired with intent to kill Constable Sutton at Five Mile Water Holes near Carcoar, 6th August 1863. Vane denied taking part in this, and the constable himself was unable to identify him, confusing him with O'Meally.'

However young Johnny took part in plenty of bushranging exploits, with one or another of the Ben Hall-John Gilbert contingent, for which he must certainly bear the blame. They included the raid on Louden's homestead at Grubbenong in September 1863, when they threatened to burn down the house and Johnny 'strummed a farewell tune on the piano' before departing.

Perhaps he thought that a bushranger's life was a gallant existence, but he received a rude shock when the gang raided Commissioner Henry Keightley's house at Dunn's Plains on the evening of 24 October. Keightley fought back with a double-barrelled shotgun and killed Johnny Vane's mate Mickey Burke with a blast in the belly.

For young Johnny this was the turning point, and it is said also that his mind was made up when he had a fight with John Gilbert after the attack on Keightley's house and received a black eye and sixpence as his share of the loot. Apparently he fought with Gilbert because the latter would not let him kill Keightley to revenge Burke's death.

Father Tim McCarthy played a part in persuading the young bushranger to give himself up, although it seems that he did not need much pushing to make him face the music. The fact that he rode into Bathurst and surrendered himself to the police probably is unique in bushranging annals.

He surrendered on 18 November 1863 but he was not tried until April 1864, when he was sentenced to fifteen years on the roads. Chief Justice Sir Alfred Stephens ignored pleas of leniency from Father McCarthy and other community leaders, on the plea that Vane had surrendered himself, and handed down the maximum sentence for robbery under arms.

Apparently he behaved himself in prison and he served only about half of the sentence. A note on his record states 'Remitted 23 February, 1870.'

Despite his early training as a blacksmith he worked as a stonemason after his release from gaol, probably using skills learnt as a prisoner. He worked on St Mary's Cathedral, but it seems that the wild free life of the bush was still calling to him. John O'Brien believes that he had become a reformed character, but in fact he returned to the Bathurst region and was soon in trouble again. His prison record and the Photograph Description Book shows that on 19 March 1875 he received three months hard labour at Carcoar for stealing, and on 6 July 1880 he appeared before the Bathurst Quarter Sessions on a charge of sheepstealing, and received a sentence of five years.

The last report on his prison file shows that he was transferred to Berrima Gaol on 29 July 1880, and after that the records are silent. By the 1890s John Vane was working on a property, and writing details of his bushranging life. In his later life he writes of his regrets at being a bushranger all those years before. Finally, on 30 January, 1906 John Vane died in Cowra Hospital. He was buried in the Cemetery at Woodstock. The exact location is now unknown.

Also see Frank Gardiner, John Gilbert, Ben Hall

STAND AND DELIVER

FREDERICK WORDSWORTH WARD

There has been a vast amount of folklore attached to the life of the man who adopted the *nom de plume* of 'Thunderbolt', — also referred to as 'Captain Thunderbolt'. It is difficult to sort fact from fiction when looking at his career.

He was born Frederick Wordsworth Ward, in 1836 at Wilberforce near Windsor, New South Wales. He began his working life as a groom, horsebreaker and stockman. In 1856 he received a sentence of ten years on Cockatoo Island for horsestealing. He received a Ticket of Leave for the Mudgee district, however he broke his parole and stole two horses. A reward of £25 was posted for his capture. In October 1861, he was back at Cockatoo Island, with a charge of horsestealing adding another three years to his original sentence. On the night of 11 September 1863 he made good his escape, with assistance, accompanied by Fred Britton, who had been serving sixteen years for robbing a mail coach of £500. To add to the conflicting reports surrounding 'Thunderbolt', he apparently had another 'mate' with him, a half-caste woman, who has been written of as Mary Anne, but was also called Mary Ann Bugg, Louisa Mason, 'Black Mary', 'Yellow Long', 'Yelliong', 'Queen Yellow Long', and 'Yellow Louisa'.

The *Armidale Express* referred to her as 'Mrs Thunderbolt', but she apparently took pride in calling herself 'Captain Ward's lady'. Another report states that in fact there were two women in his life — Mary Anne was the part-Aboriginal wife of an ex-Constable, and that 'Yellow Louisa' was also a part-Aboriginal — and the wife of a settler named Robert Mason, who lived near Aberdeen. Like much of Ward's story, the truth is still clouded in mystery. The list of robberies he committed as a bushranger shows he was a busy man. Not all of them can be studied here.

Fred Ward, alias Thunderbolt, went on a wide-ranging career as a bushranger, robbing mail coaches, and sticking up innocent travellers.

In January 1864 he was accompanied by three men, McIntosh, McKay and Long. Robberies were committed in the Bourke district, but later Ward moved back to the New England area. He robbed the mail near Tamworth. On 3 May 1864, with companions Thompson, Hogan and McIntosh he robbed a hotel north of

100 AUSTRALIAN BUSHRANGERS 1789-1901

■ *Fred Ward alias 'Captain Thunderbolt' — a photo taken after his death and autopsy. Note the autopsy incision in the centre of the chest, and the bullet hole in the top left breast.*
(Courtesy NSW Police, PRD)

Narrabri. Other hotel robberies would occur also. Thompson was wounded and caught. He was only seventeen years of age, when he appeared before the Tamworth Court in June 1865.

On one of his finest horses, the stolen racehorse Eucalyptus, Ward robbed Cook's Inn at Quirindi on 18 December 1865, then Davis' Inn at Currabubula on 20 December 1865, and Griffith's Inn at Carroll on 23 December 1865. He seemed to move at astonishing speed.

In August 1866 the Tamworth mail was robbed. A reward of £100 was offered for his capture and £50 for any of his companions.

In March 1866, his 'mate' Mary Anne was brought before the Stroud bench, charged with vagrancy, and sentenced to six months gaol. She was released shortly after her conviction was proved defective. In June, Ward robbed the Tenterfield mail.

In December 1866 robberies continued at Breeza Plain, then Carroll, near Gunnedah. Ward robbed the Tamworth mail on 22 January 1867 and got away with a good haul, including a parcel of gold. Again he robbed the mail three miles from Manilla. Robberies continued at an alarming rate. It should be remembered that some of the robberies attributed to him may have, in fact, been committed by other bushrangers.

By mid-1867 the reward had been raised to £200 for his capture. Another boy bushranger was credited as joining Ward — this time sixteen-year-old Thomas Mason. Later a youth called Kelly joined Ward, yet again, a sixteen-year-old and they robbed more mail coaches, stores inns and station properties.

In December 1869 the reward was increased yet again, this time to £400, and £100 for the capture of any of his associates.

In May 1870, Mounted Constables Mulhall and Walker heard that 'Captain Thunderbolt' was enjoying himself at Blanche's Inn, near Uralla, and rode there to capture him. Ward managed to evade their first attempt and they galloped after him through the bush. Finally Constable Walker ran Ward down in the waters of Kentucky Creek. The constable had cornered his man. They exchanged a few words and when Ward asked if Walker was married, Walker snapped 'Yes!' and Ward said 'Well, remember your family.'

UNDERBOLT

STAND AND DELIVER

■ *A studio portrait of NSW Police Constable Alexander Walker — the man who shot 'Captain Thunderbolt'. He retired from the NSW Police force in 1912, after serving nearly 45 years. At the age of 81 years, he died in Sydney in 1929.*
(Courtesy NSW Police, PRD)

■ *The Sons of Temperance awarded this testimonial to Constable Walker for his bravery against the bushranger Fred Ward. He also received a silver medal from a grateful Government, and New England citizens presented him with a gold watch and chain, and other tokens of esteem.*
(Courtesy NSW Police, PRD)

In the fight that ensued between the two, Walker fired off his last shot. Ward fell and went under the water. When he arose and attempted to grasp the Constable, he was hit on the head by the policeman's empty revolver. He dragged the bushranger out of the water. The bushranger appeared to be dead, and was left on the bank, Walker returned to Blanche's Inn for help in bringing the body in. They returned the next day. Ward had not died immediatley as he had crawled a short distance into the bush He did not survive the trip back to Uralla on 25 May 1870.

Then, as now 'Thunderbolt' had a place in history, and many regard him as a hero. Those that had been robbed by him would have thought otherwise. During Australia's Bicentenary in 1988, in the main street of Uralla, New South Wales, a bronze statue of Fred Ward alias 'Thunderbolt' on horseback was unveiled. This, as well as a granite outcrop called 'Thunderbolt Rock' on a busy highway add to the tourist appeal of the notorious bushranger. Another tourist location is his grave in the Uralla Cemetery.

The Policeman who captured him, Constable Alexander Walker, was rewarded for his courage. He went on to become a Superintendent of Police, and retired in 1912, after nearly forty-five years of police service. He died in Sydney in 1929, when 81 years old.

170

JOHN WHELAN

'He had finally become so callous and hardened that he seemed to regard the lash, the dark cell, and the rest of Price's contrivances with the most perfect indifference.'

That was the comment written by the bushranger Martin Cash, himself one of the hardest of hard men, upon the man who became appropriately known as 'Rocky' Whelan, and recorded in Bill Wannan's *Tell 'Em I Died Game*. Cash knew Whelan on Norfolk Island, where Whelan arrived in March 1834 under sentence of life imprisonment for a string of offences committed as a convict in Sydney. They included 'Being under arms in the bush.'

He was about twenty-six at that time, an Irishman from Wexford transported for a petty crime when he was about seventeen. He showed very quickly that he was 'Rocky' by name and 'rocky' by nature, persistent in a defiance of authority and able to make light of all the punishments heaped on him.

He was on Norfolk Island from 1834 to 1852, when the authorities began to transfer the island prisoners to Tasmania. During those eighteen years he committed at least forty offences and received a total of at least 700 lashes without submitting to authority. He must have lost count of the times that he was sentenced to 'Hard labour in chains,' and periods of extra imprisonment which must have seemed meaningless to a man under a life sentence.

His offences included all the usual prison crimes of fighting, using offensive and abusive language to an overseer, assaulting a fellow prisoner, encouraging men to fight, leaving his work without permission, and so on. But 'Rocky' Whelan added some variations to these by deliberately scalding himself, on several occasions, in order to avoid work. He was also repetitively accused of 'Going to hospital on false pretences' even

---

Born: 1816 (?) (Description taken in May 1855)
Native Place: Wexford, Ireland
Trade: Labourer
Religion: Not recorded
Education: Not recorded
Complexion: Ruddy
Head: Round
Age: 39
Hair: Brown
Whiskers: Brown
Visage: Round
Forehead: Broad and low
Eyebrows: Brown
Eyes: Blue
Nose: Rather long
Mouth: Medium
Chin: Medium
Particular Marks: Crucifixion, MW, MW, MW, head with dart, BW, JW on left arm. Man in whale boat throwing harpoon right arm.
Previous History: Was tried at Wexford Quarter Sessions in January 1829, and sentenced to seven years transportation. He arrived in Sydney on 22 December, 1829 per Larkins 2. (Note: A list of Convicts on Norfolk Island as at the time of the transfer of the Island to Tasmanian jurisdiction, dated 12 August 1844, shows that John Whelan was tried at Wexford Quarter Sessions in January 1829, for stealing worsted, and sent to N.S.W. He was then a Mason's apprentice. He arrived in 1829)

---

though each of these hospital visits earned him a savage flogging.

When he was transferred from Norfolk Island to Port Arthur he seized his first opportunity to escape. On 28 January 1854 he evaded the network of soldiers and watchdogs posted to prevent absconders from crossing Eaglehawk Neck.

Once he was free, he had no way to support himself except by bushranging. He was at large for more than twelve months until he was caught and charged with the robberies of William Kearney and Richard Carpenter.

He was sentenced to death, and the date of execution set as 26 June 1855. Some sympathetic prison visitor conversed with him while he was in the condemned cell, and Whelan persuaded this visitor to write out a petition to the Governor and Executive Council in which he claimed 'That in a long and dreary career (deprived of hope, and urged to desperation by severities) your Petitioner has never been tempted in any instance under any circumstances to injure the person of anyone ... nor has violence at any time been committed by him ...

The governor rejected this petition, and on the evening before Whelan was to hang he decided to tell the truth. He made a horrifying confession to the Vicar General, W. Hall, and the Reverend W. P. Bond. One of these reverend gentlemen wrote it down and signed it with his mark, witnessed by W. T. N. Champ who wrote 'Taken before me in the Gaol at Hobarton this 25 June, 1855 at five minutes past seven o'clock in the evening having been first read out to Whelan who declares that the same is true.'

The confession stated that Whelan '... did, and being then alone, commit the following murders ... An elderly man, between Brown's River, and North West Bay, about two months ago. I shot him in the head, and robbed him ... A young man (I learned afterwards his name was Dunn) on the Huon Track, about six or seven weeks after Carpenter's robbery. I shot him in the head and struck him on the head with the butt of the pistol, then robbed him ... An elderly man at Bagdad six or seven weeks ago. I shot him in the head, and took away a few shillings ... A Hawker near Cleveland, about three days before I was taken. I shot him in the head, and took away several things, most of which are now at the Police Office ... I most humbly and sincerely beg forgiveness of the friends of these victims of my cruelty, and hope that the Almighty will have mercy on my poor soul.'

John 'Rocky' Whelan paid for his crimes on the following morning.

STAND AND DELIVER

JOHN WHITEHEAD

■ *The skull of a convict preserved in Tasmania.*
(Courtesy Archives of Tasmania)

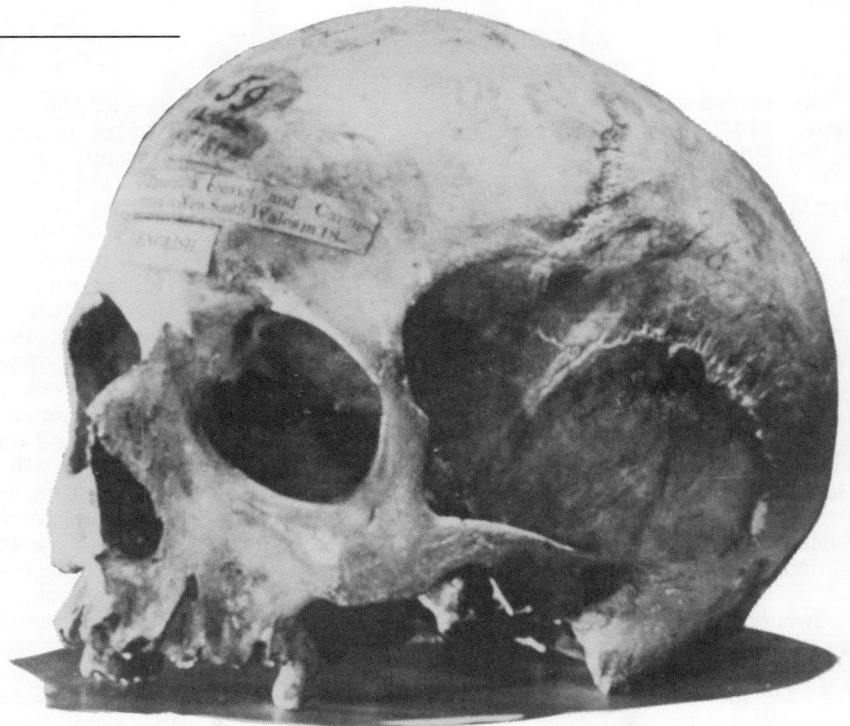

Only brief documentary evidence is available about the man alleged to have led the largest of all bushranging gangs, in Tasmania in 1814. There is even some doubt about his Christian name. Mary Nicholls, who edited the *Knopwood Diary,* believes that it was James, although the prison record shows it as John. The Hobart Town Muster of 1811 also used that name. James Whitehead probably was a man sentenced to transportation for life at the York Assizes in March 1811.

Some of Whitehead's story is told in the biography of Michael Howe in this book, which notes that Howe and Whitehead were given a second chance by the administration but took to the bush again after giving themselves up. Their gang attracted large numbers of escaped convicts, or 'bolters,' and some reports say that it eventually numbered between eighty and a hundred bushrangers.

The early Tasmanian bushrangers, with a few notable exceptions, earned a reputation for utter ruthlessness and Whitehead

> When Convicted: 9 February 1801
> Name: John Whitehead
> Age: 34
> Height: 5ft 6ins
> Complexion: Dark
> Hair: Brown
> Eyes: Hazel
> Native Place: Beverley, Yorkshire
> Trade: Gardener
> To what place committed:
> New Prison
> By Whom: Robinson
> The Crime: Stealing two pair of breeches in the shop of Rowland Allen
> When and Where Tried:
> 18 February 1801
> Before Whom: Hotham
> Sentence: Transportation for seven years.
> How disposed of: Delivered on board the Minerva, 16 May 1801
> Previous History/Remarks: Convicted in October last (1800) and subsequently publicly whipped and discharged. Was transported before by the name of Country Jack, and served his time out.

and his gang were no exception to the rule. The case of John Hopkins, a half-crazy man who was accused of betraying the gang, is only one example of their cruelty. They made a rough pair of moccasins out of bullock hide, filled them with the big ants commonly known as 'bulldog' or 'soldier' ants *(Myrmecia gulosa)* and fastened the moccasins onto Hopkins' feet. He is said to have died in agony.

As related in Michael Howe's biography, the soldiers shot Whitehead in October 1814 and he begged Howe to cut off his head before he could be identified. This gruesome tale is confirmed by a report in the *Hobart Town Gazette* of 13 December 1817, more than three years after the event. The reporter wrote 'A Human head has lately been found near New Norfolk, tied up in a handerchief. The state in which it was found corresponds exactly with the account we are in possession of, respecting what became of the head of "Whitehead," when killed at Mr D. Carthy's at New Norfolk, prior to the proclamation of martial law. We may therefore presume it is the remains of the misled culprit.'

Also see Michael Howe

JACK WILLIAMS

Bushrangers were on the loose in Victoria from as early as 1837, when Dignum and Comerford (who are described in this book) began their bloody career. They were probably the first bushrangers in the Melbourne area, but they were soon followed by others including the gang led by John (or Jack) Williams, a bounty immigrant. Others in the gang included Charles Ellis, an expiree convict, employed as a bullock driver for a wood splitter named Handcock; Daniel Jepps, a 27 year old American sailor, who had also worked at Handcocks, but only for a few days. Both he and Ellis joined up as bushrangers when out looking for a missing mare. The other was Martin Fogarty a young Irish bounty immigrant, who with Williams had been living on a station.

A man named William Camm was associated with the gang, perhaps as a receiver of stolen goods.

The gang perpetrated an act of highway robbery upon the master of the Brig *Scout*, Captain Christopher Gwatkin, and a man named Fred Pittman. Williams and his men stole the gig in which they were riding and robbed them of £63, mostly from the shipmaster. For some inscrutable reason they gave five shillings of the seafarer's money to Pittman, and told Captain Gwatkin to 'Shut up or they'd blow his brains out' when he complained.

The gang also committed a robbery at Dandenong, where they stopped a Mr Darling, a druggist from Melbourne, and a friend Thomas Napier, who were out riding to look at cattle. Darling was astride a fine horse which caught Williams' eye, and he told Darling to show off its paces. The man was cute enough to pretend that he could hardly control the horse and Williams soon lost interest. The bushrangers relieved the pair of £3.6.0d and a silver watch, took a companionable swig of rum with their victims, and handed five shillings back so that they might refresh themselves.

Williams and company later cantered along the main road to the Plenty River, stopping to loot anyone met along the way and diverting to raid properties along the road. They are credited with robbing nine homes and twelve people on this foray, and they camped for the night with a rich booty of watches and chains and some money.

On the following morning they arrived at the homestead of Mr Campbell Hunter, just as he and his guests were about to commence breakfast.

On Saturday, April 30; five men who would later be called the "Fighting Five" had set out in pursuit of the bushrangers. The men who had been sworn in as special constables were Henry Fowler, Peter Snodgrass, Robert Chamberlain, Oliver Gourlay and James Thompson.

By stopping at Hunter's station for breakfast the bushrangers had given the men time to catch up with them. A gun-battle of great ferocity took place, and one of the bullets killed Jack Williams. The bushrangers were now outnumbered, as a dozen more men had arrived to join the seige, led by Constable George Vinge.

Jack Williams' mates lost some of their confidence and agreed to a parley with the beseigers. A man named John 'Hoppy Jack' Ewart volunteered to go into the hut and talk with them.

Realising they had little hope of escape, they agreed to surrender. Their captors, on searching the bushrangers, found four watches, five gold sovereigns, twenty-three shillings, three pairs of spurs, two compasses, and sundry other items.

John Ellis asked to see his dead mate Jack Williams. When he saw the dead body in the store, he knelt and kissed it.

An Inquest into the death of Williams was commenced on 2 May, 'in view of the body of John Williams, a bushranger', before Coroner N.B. Wilmot. The verdict of the Coroner's jury was that 'the said John Williams being armed and having committed sundry depredations as a Bushranger was shot through the body by one Mr. Robert Chamberlain, settler, whilst in the pursuit of justice, who of inevitable necessity and justifiably did kill and slay the said John Williams, a Bushranger.'

On 13 May, after their trial, Ellis, Jepps and Fogarty were sentenced to death by Judge Walpole Willis. William Camm was also caught and for his unexplained possession of a considerable amount of booty, was sentenced on 17 May to transportation to Van Dieman's Land for fourteen years.

After some delays and appeals the three bushrangers were hanged on 28 June. Martin Fogarty had burst out crying saying he 'did not cry through fear of death, but after his friends at home'.

In Daniel Jepps' final speech to the gathered crowd he said: 'you see before you three young men in the prime of life and strength about to suffer on the scaffold for the crime of bushranging. I trust you will take warning by our ultimate fate, and avoid those crimes which have brought us to this end.'

STAND AND DELIVER

THOMAS WILLIAMS 1ST

> Born: 1825
> Native Place: Manchester
> Trade: Carpenter
> Religion: Roman Catholic
> Height: 5ft 8ins
> Complexion: Fresh
> Hair: Light
> Eyes Blue
> Particular Marks: Back freckled
> Previous History: Arrived per ship Constant, 1845. Bond.
> Sentence: (1st charge) Twelve years on the Roads, first two years in Irons, for Highway Robbery.
> (2nd charge) Six years on the Roads to date from expiration of first sentence, for Highway Robbery.
> Date of Conviction: 18 November 1852

The story of the first bushranger named Thomas Williams has been told in this book in the biography of his mate John Flanigan, in which it runs up until the time when Williams began a thirty-year sentence for highway robbery.

He was to serve time aboard the hulks *President, Success,* and *Sacramento* and in the Melbourne Gaol. During his time in those penal establishments, a little more than four years, he committed twelve fairly minor offences against the regulations including the usual examples of 'Insolence' and 'Disobedience and highly insubordinate conduct,' and received a total of sixty-nine days solitary confinement. For some other offences, such as 'Having bread and meat' and 'Disobedience and disrespect,' he was only admonished.

Perhaps the differences between the punishments depended very much upon the men in charge of him at any given time. From his later behaviour it would seem that he was at last driven to desperation, although he took no part in the attempted escape in which Owen Owens was killed (see Frank McCallum) and was in fact noted as having been of 'Good conduct' on that occasion.

In January 1854, the notorious John Price became head of the penal department in Melbourne. Chaplains and other prison officials had already denounced him for his horrifying treatment of convicts on Norfolk Island, but the authorities had turned a deaf ear.

■ *Inspector-General John Price, murdered by convicts in March 1854.*
(Courtesy La Trobe Collection, State Library of Victoria)

In March 1854, a number of convicts from the hulks in Hobson's Bay were taken ashore for their usual labour on the 'government works,' but they downed tools in protest at their prison conditions. Price went amongst them to 'reason' with them and they battered him to death with their tools.

Thomas Williams was one of these convicts. At his trial for the murder, he attempted to make the authorities see that the event had been almost inevitable. He had spent much of his sentence confined in his cell aboard one or another of the hulks, including a full three years in the *President*. It is understandable that men felt themselves forced to rebel against such conditions.

According to J. V. Barry, in *The Life and Death of John Price,* Williams spoke with 'desperate eloquence.' He said 'The blood that has been shed on those hulks is now crying for vengeance. The officers and warders are all picked men by the late Inspector-General [Price]; picked by him because they would suit his purposes, and as long as Mr Blachford, Holles and Hyland are on board so long will prisoners be sent to this court to be tried . . .'

But his eloquence did not save him from the gallows and he died, with Henry Smith and Thomas Maloney, at eight a.m. on 28 April 1857. He was thirty-two years of age.

Also see John Flanigan

No. 2173

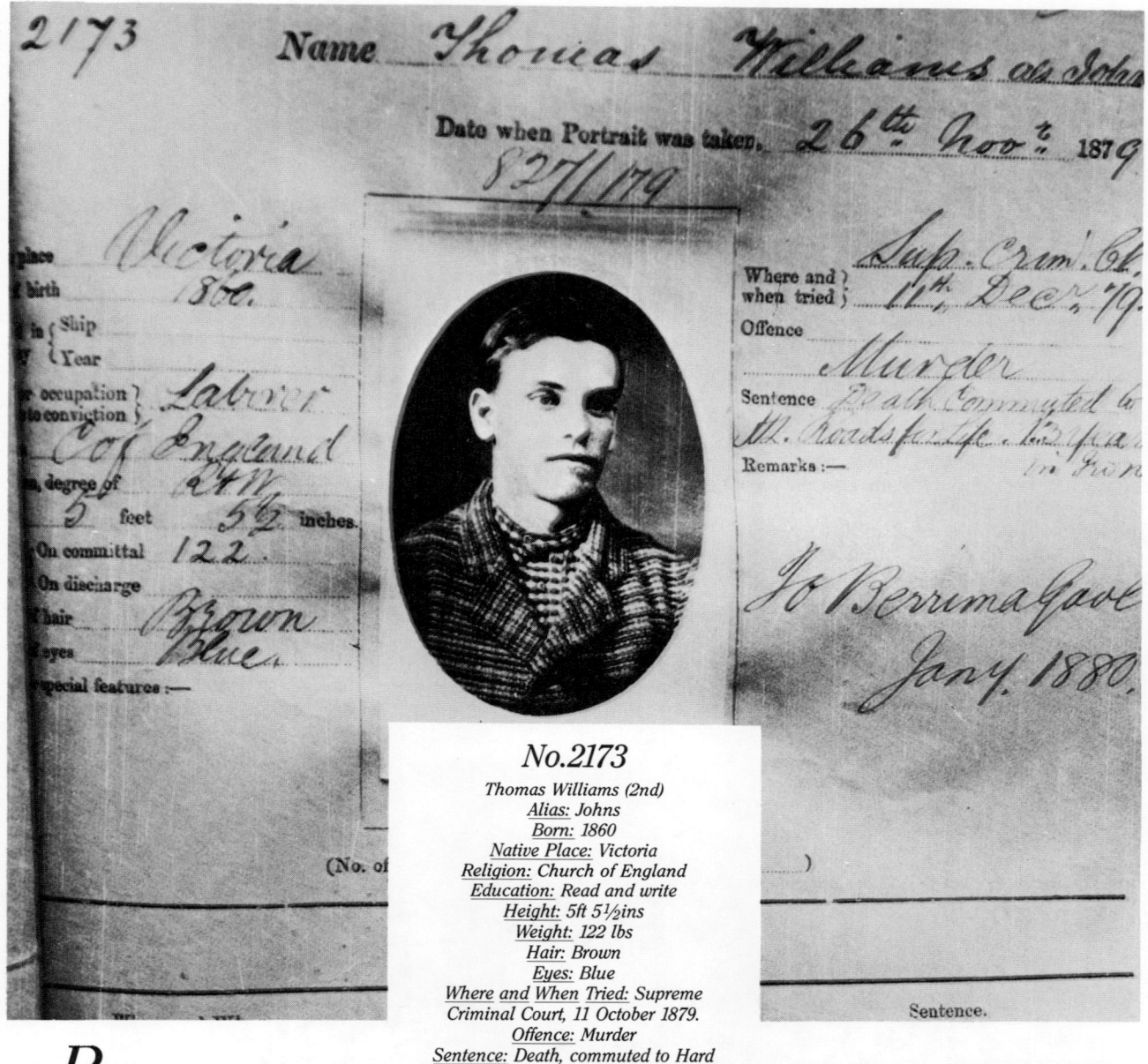

Thomas Williams (2nd)
Alias: Johns
Born: 1860
Native Place: Victoria
Religion: Church of England
Education: Read and write
Height: 5ft 5½ins
Weight: 122 lbs
Hair: Brown
Eyes: Blue
Where and When Tried: Supreme Criminal Court, 11 October 1879.
Offence: Murder
Sentence: Death, commuted to Hard Labour on Roads for Life, first three years in Irons.

Research for this book frequently unearthed details about the lives of the bushrangers which were overlooked by other writers on the subject. One of these facts concerned the eventual fate of young Tom Williams, who joined Andrew Scott and followed him as one of 'Captain Moonlite's' misguided young men.

Apparently Williams met Scott when the latter was lecturing on his experiences as a Pentridge prisoner. Scott advertised for a 'Lecturer's assistant usher' and it was young Thomas Williams' fate to succeed in his application for the job.

The subsequent events are outlined in Scott's biography in this book. Scott and Rogan went to the gallows: Williams and Bennett to 'Hard Labour on Roads for Life, first three years in Irons.'

Williams entered Berrima Gaol in January 1880, and in every other account of his life the story has ended there.

But new evidence shows that the story was far from over. Twenty-year-old Thomas Williams had a violent streak which had not been eliminated by his experiences with Captain Moonlite and his narrow escape from the hangman. Early in 1885 he made a savage attack on another prisoner, and a note on his record states that he appeared in court for 'Wounding a fellow prisoner with intent to Murder.'

This unhappy footnote to the story of Captain Moonlite ends on 14 July 1885, when Thomas Williams was hanged for attempted murder.

Also see James Nesbitt, Thomas Rogan, Andrew Scott

STAND AND DELIVER

EDWARD WILSON

*T*he interwoven mysteries and confusing statements surrounding the *Nelson* robbery, outlined in the biography of John James in this book, still remain to be untangled. There was the peculiar case of John Roberts, also described in this book, who was accused of complicity and then released because of a supposed 'identical twin' who might have been involved, and the peculiar circumstances concerning Edward Wilson and William Barnes (see Barnes' biography earlier in the book). The people of Melbourne could not make up their minds as to how many men had taken part in the robbery, and it would seem that they were prepared to accuse almost anyone of participation.

As the story of William Barnes relates, he and Edward Wilson were arrested for having stolen some money and papers from James Britton, and committed for trial on that charge. The *Melbourne Argus* accused them of being 'two of the *Nelson* robbers.'

The mystery deepens when one notices that Edward Wilson's record does not mention either of the robberies. He was convicted for forgery, and it appears that 'Edward Wilson' was an alias.

He was received on board the hulk *President* in December 1852, with ten long years of imprisonment stretching ahead, but his record between then and 17 October 1857 is almost unblemished. He received only two admonishments for misconduct.

He stepped out into freedom, with a Ticket of Leave in his pocket, in October 1857, and vanishes from history. Perhaps he was as confused as everyone else by the events which had caught him up in their train.
Also see William Barnes, John James

Born: 1817
Native Place: London
Trade: Cook
Religion: Nil recorded
Height: 5ft 5½ins
Complexion: Fresh
Hair: Brown
Eyes: Grey
Particular Marks: Mermaid, sailor, anchor, heart, AB right arm. ABWB left arm.
Previous History: Arrived per ship Duke of Kent 1839. Bond. Proper name Alfred Bowers. Per *Isabella* to Van Diemen's Land 1833. Seven years. Again Hobart 3 May 1844 — Seven years. Free by servitude 30 May 1851, vide Compt. Generals letter 08/01/56.
Sentence: Ten years on the Roads of the Colony, for Forgery.

JOHN WILSON

(Details combined from two records, 1830 and 1833)
Born: 1813 (?)
Native Place: Layland/Lincoln
Trade: Labourer
Religion: Not recorded
Age: 17/20
Height: 5ft 3½ins/5ft 6ins
Complexion: Dark/Swarthy
Hair: Dark Brown
Whiskers: None
Visage: Round/Long
Forehead: High
Eyebrows: Brown
Eyes: Grey/Light hazel
Nose: Long
Mouth: Large, underlip thick
Chin: Medium size
Particular Marks/Remarks: TW, sun, moon, seven stars and mermaid right arm, half moon, cross, anchor, left arm (tattoos). Ring, finger left hand
Previous History: Transported for stealing a pair of Quarter boots - Tried at Lancaster on 21 April 1830 — Sentence: 14 years. Arrived Australia per *Persian* 7 November 1830.

■ *(Opposite) The Old Gaol, Kingston, Norfolk Island. A Charles Kerry photograph.*
(Courtesy La Trobe Collection, State Library of Victoria)

The judge at Lancaster Assizes sentenced John Wilson to fourteen years transportation for the paltry offence of 'Stealing a pair of quarter boots,' and he found himself in Australia only seven months later at the age of seventeen. The young Lincolnshire labourer was small but full of fight, and he was either an unregenerate villain or determined to battle against the cruelties of the convict system.

A great deal of his prison record has suffered from the erosion of time and damp and is indecipherable, but the fragments that can be deciphered show a seemingly interminable list of offences, escapes, crimes, and punishments. He made his first escape in 1831, only a year after his arrival in Australia, and he escaped or 'absconded' a number of times after that.

The prison guards strung him up to the triangle again and again, and he received two or three dozen lashes at a time. His rebellious spirit was yet to be broken. He received many extra sentences of hard labour in chains and numerous spells of solitary confinement. One of these, of fourteen days, was for fighting with another prisoner and threatening to kill him.

Whenever he escaped from custody he took to the roads, and a charge of Robbery and Putting in Fear at last brought the death sentence. It was commuted to transportation for life and he was sent to Van Diemen's Land.

This narrow escape from the gallows did not make him mend his ways. He escaped yet again, and teamed up with another runaway, William Driscoll. They joined the bushranging fraternity of Tasmania and lived by robbing travellers and settlers.

By that time, 1847, the Tasmanian authorities had had plenty of experience in tracking down bushrangers and the police and soldiers eventually captured Driscoll and Wilson. They appeared before the Launceston Supreme Court on 7 April 1847 for robbing Edward Duanesque.

Robbery under Arms usually attracted the death sentence at that time in Tasmania, and the two bushrangers heard the sentence passed upon them. But John Wilson was to escape the gallows yet again. The sentences were commuted and he was sent to Norfolk Island for eight years.

The intention of the Norfolk Island penal settlement was to break the spirit of even the most hardened criminal. It very often failed to do so and John Wilson's record showed that he committed a variety of minor offences during his years on the island. He survived until the settlement was closed and the prisoners returned to Tasmania.

He was granted a Ticket of Leave on 13 January 1857 and nothing more is known about his life story.

Also see William Driscoll

ISAIAH WRIGHT

No. 12313

Born: 1849
Native Place: Ireland
Trade: Labourer
Religion: Church of England
Education: Neither read or write
Height: 5ft 11ins
Weight: 13st 2lbs
Complexion: Fresh
Hair: Brown
Eyes: Hazel
Nose: Short
Mouth: Medium
Chin: Medium
Eyebrows: Light brown
Visage: Square
Forehead: Medium
Particular Marks: Scar inside corner left eyebrow, large scar right cheek, pimple right cheekbone, scar left side of nose and throat, scar back of head, fourth and little fingers contracted, upper joint right forefinger injured, scar right thumb.
Previous History: 02/08/71 18 months Hard Labour. Per the Carlton from Liverpool to Geelong in 1858. Married, wife maiden name Bridget Lloyd in Mansfield. proper name
Sentence: (1st charge) Three years Hard Labour, for Receiving a horse knowing it to be stolen.
(2nd charge) Six years hard Labour for Horsestealing.
Date of Conviction: (1st charge) 13 October 1874, at Beechworth Circular Court, before Mr Justice Fellowes.
(2nd charge) 16 February 1883, before Beechworth General Sessions, before Mr C. Skinner
Details from later records: 25/02/97 Cruelty to a horse 20/- or three days imprisonment (part indecipherable) 20/- or three days imprisonment (illegible) Cororyong Police Station (arrested 18 January 1900).

Most of the legends and stories that have developed around the Kelly country deal with the exploits of Ned and his gang, but there were plenty of other reckless and law-defying Irish people in the district. One of these was Isaiah 'Wild' Wright, who arrived in Australia in 1858, on board the ship *Carlton*. He was nine years old.

He grew to manhood and his reputation as a wild young man was well earned. He continued to appear before the Courts when he was a man in his fifties. He was a big, heavy man, even taller than Ned Kelly, which would have made him an impressive personality in those days when, as criminal records of the bushrangers show, most men were of no more than medium stature.

Isaiah arrived in the Mansfield district when he was in his twenties and he married Bridget Lloyd, of the Lloyd family which had a colourful criminal record and was associated with the Kellys. The stories now told about Ned rather give one the impression that he was the leader of the bushrangers and the horse and cattle thieves in the Kelly country, but these types of crime had become almost a local industry before Ned appeared on the scene. The records contain many reports of cattle stealing, an offence so common that it was almost taken for granted, and if it had not been for the Glenrowan affair then Ned Kelly might have been seen as just another of the bushrangers and cattle duffers of the 1870s.

In March 1871 Ned Kelly would become involved in an incident with 'Wild' Wright, that would result in Ned receiving a three-year prison sentence. Wright said he had lost a horse during his stay at Ned's mothers place, and so borrowed one from Ned. He asked Ned to keep the horse if he found it, and that they would exchange it later when he called next from Mansfield. Ned did find the horse, but was stopped by police Senior Constable Hall, who arrested Ned for the possession of a stolen horse, a fact which Isaiah had forgotten to tell Ned.

In August 1871, Ned, Isaiah Wright and Ned's brother-in-law Alex Gunn were brought before the Beechworth Court. Ned and Alex received three years hard labour. Isaiah received a curious sentence of only eighteen months for the charge of merely 'illegally using' whereas lengthy evidence proved that he was the culprit who had stolen the horse. It has been suggested that although conclusive evidence had been brought against him, the reason for the lighter sentence was a local petition to his good character and the fact that he had not sold the horse.

Isaiah 'Wild' Wright would go on to serve not only this sentence in prison but many others.

On 8 August 1874 Ned Kelly and Isaiah Wright met in what would become known as an epic 20-round fight, and later a famous photo of Ned in boxing pose would be taken. Supposed to have been conducted in Beechworth, it was either to settle the old score for Ned having received the prison sentence because of Wild's horse stealing, or possibly as a sporting challenge match. In any event Ned did win the epic bare-knuckled fight, and his reputation grew. They would remain in constant contact however, and Isaiah certainly assisted the Kelly Gang and their families to the end.

In October 1874 he received a sentence of three

■ *The changing face of Isaiah 'Wild' Wright. No photograph of 'Wild' Wright had been published until the original edition of this book. His prison record gives not one but numerous photographs taken during years of Wright's imprisonment. The complete collection is presented here, and on the following page.*
(Courtesy Public Record Office, Victoria)

years hard labour for 'Receiving a horse knowing it to be stolen'. He served time in Pentridge, on board the hulk *Sacramento,* and in Beechworth Gaol. Entries in his record show he was a constant bother to the authorites with offences listed like: Quarrelling, Away from labour, Improper language, Assaulting a prisoner, Having a black eye, Misconduct, Annoying a prisoner, Having prohibited articles, Insolence, and so the list goes on.

He had entered Pentridge on 27 October 1874, and served thirty months of this sentence before receiving 'Freedom by Remission' on 19 May 1877.

He returned to the Kelly country shortly before everything exploded and Ned took to the bush, but he did not join them. He was far from being a reformed character. His prison pay of £3.2.8d, received when he left Pentridge, would not have lasted very him very long, and he did not have particularly good prospects.

He was a known Kelly sympathiser, and openly defied the police. In Mansfield he rode past the police station and shouted — 'Dogs! Curs! Cowards! Follow me if you want to catch the Kellys, I'm going to join the gang. Come out a little way and I'll shoot the lot of you!' During the chase by police he is also supposed to have yelled — 'All the police in Mansfield can't catch me!' But he was later caught and charged.

The events of the Kelly Gang in their notorious war with the authorities raged and Isaiah Wright kept in touch with the gang and was an active assistant. At the burning down of the Glenrowan Inn and the destruction of the gang, one of the sympathisers in the crowd was Isaiah Wright. He was one of the 'family' that claimed

■ *Photographs of Isaiah Wright were taken from his prison record.*
(Courtesy Public Record Office, Victoria)

the burnt bodies of Steve Hart and Dan Kelly, wrapped the corpses in blankets and carried them away. He kept a high profile in the events after the Glenrowan affair, and at Ned's trial.

He was refused admission to Melbourne Gaol when the family saw Ned for the last time prior to his execution. When Ned was hanged 'Wild' was present with Kelly family and friends when they gathered together at a nearby hotel. 'Wild' was reported to have muttered something about the police. It was probably not of a laudatory nature.

Scratching a living on his small selection or working for other men on the hard, monotonous round of bush labour may not have had much appeal for 'Wild' Isaiah Wright. He took to horse stealing again, but was caught again and sentenced to six years hard labour.

He entered Pentridge on 1 March 1883, and now it seems that the 'wild' man was wild no longer. For the next four-and-a-half years, until he was released on 26 October 1887, he 'kept his head down' and avoided trouble.

His prison records lists only three charges of being disorderly at Divine Service, of having a knife concealed, and of having tobacco concealed. These offences resulted in the loss of nine days remission of sentence.

Once more he returned to the Kelly country, which was a sad and legend-haunted territory now that Ned and his mates had gone. The manner in which he occupied himself is now unknown, but the old spirit was not entirely quenched.

He was arrested again on 18 January 1900 . . . but that is another story.
Also see the Kelly family

JOHN WRIGHT

The bushranging exploits of men like Ben Hall, Frank Gardiner, and John Gilbert inspired a host of emulators, but the majority were small-time bushrangers compared with those famous (or infamous) names in bushranging history. John Wright was one of those who took to the roads in the 1860s, but his career was brief and his end extremely sudden.

The surviving records in the case of John Wright tell us little or nothing about his earlier life. He escaped from Rockhampton prison at some time early in 1864, and by the middle of that year he was robbing homes in the Rockhampton area. Perhaps he would have been regarded as no more than a nuisance, to be tracked down in due course, if he had not stolen a racehorse owned by a well-known landowner, a Mr Cranston.

Colonial law was particularly hard on horse thieves and the police and all honest settlers kept a sharp lookout for John Wright. A mere housebreaker was one thing, but an armed man on horseback could be regarded as a bushranger.

Wright bailed up a few people in the area but met his end when he encountered Henry Oliphant Paton, a Rockhampton auctioneer. Paton took the law into his own hands in the manner described in a 'Magisterial Enquiry touching cause of death of John Wright,' which is preserved in the Queensland State Archives. The enquiry was carried out on 16 July 1864 at the Police Station, Rockhampton.

Paton was a member of a party of civilians which set out in search of Wright, and he told his story in a seven-page deposition containing the statements: '... I saw a man coming on foot as if from the river whom I recognised as Wright. I looked round a second time to make sure he was the man. I then stooped down and picked up my revolver and without saying a word to any of them went towards Wright. I presented my revolver at him saying you are my prisoner, I know your hang ups — I was about 2 yards from him at the time. He said in a saucy manner, all right, raised his hands to his shoulders and immediately lowered them to his belt. I then said again throw your hands up or I'll fire — when I went towards Wright, Mr Bedford came and the two men followed. Mr Bedford had his revolver also presented at Wright. As I told Wright the second time to throw up his hands I turned my head round and said Dan bring up a strap — as I moved my head my pistol being one of Trantor's hair-trigger revolvers, the moving of the body caused my pistol to go off. The pistol going off was quite unintentional on my part — as my head was turned I heard a response from my pistol.

Wright raised his hand to his chest and exclaimed oh what is that for. Seeing no mark on him and him standing I thought he was only frightened at the report and was shamming.'

But Wright then fell down, and he died almost immediately. Paton searched his body and found a capped and loaded revolver which Wright had taken from one of Paton's friends, a Mr Carroll.

The Magisterial Enquiry concluded that 'The conduct of Mr Paton in the pursuit of the bushranger has been meritorious. The accidental shooting of Wright is to be deplored but the result of that accident does not detract from the merit of Mr Paton.'

The Queensland government rewarded Henry Oliphant Paton with £50, but it seems that he thought he might profit by much more than that. He seized the accidental killing as an opportunity to further his profession as an auctioneer.

He sent the reward money to the Colonial Treasurer in Brisbane, asking him to donate it to the Rockhampton hospital, and followed up this request with a four-page letter full of self-praise.

He sought the favour of the Minister for Lands and Works, and suggested that instead of a £50 reward he should be given the post of Government Auctioneer in Rockhampton.

He wrote 'I beg most respectfully to apply for it, trusting you will recognise my claims to some other mark of favour than a mere pecuniary reward. The very appointing of me "Government Auctioneer" would be of the greatest service to me in my business here, as it would give me an additional standing here.'

Two notes on Paton's letter show what the government thought about him. One, by some unknown public servant, states 'I believe this person is not altogether suitable for the office of which he is recommended; if it were proposed to offer such an office.'

The other, probably by the Minister for Lands and Works, says 'Inform that the Govt have declined to make any appointment of this kind in several places and that the arrangement in Brisbane may be regarded as experimental in a certain degree.'

Henry Paton's sordid little attempt to profit from his accidental killing of John Wright meant that he had even lost the £50 reward.

• THE BUSHRANGERS •

TRADES OR OCCUPATIONS

	ENGLISH	IRISH	SCOTTISH	AUSTRALIAN	OTHERS
Baker	1	.	.	.	.
Blacksmith	.	.	.	1	.
Bootmaker/Shoemaker	1	3	.	1	.
Butcher	.	.	.	1	.
Carpenter	3	.	1	1	.
Civil Engineer	.	1	.	.	.
Clerk	1	.	.	.	.
Cook	1	1	.	.	.
Gardener	1	.	.	.	.
Groom	.	1	.	.	.
Hairdresser	1	.	.	.	.
Horsedealer	.	1	.	.	.
Labourer	7	7	1	12	1
Nailmaker	1	.	.	.	.
Painter	1	.	.	.	.
Plasterer	1	.	.	.	.
Puntman	.	.	.	.	1
Seafarer	3	1	.	.	.
Sawyer	1	1	.	1	.
Selector	.	.	.	1	.
Shepherd	.	.	.	1	.
Soldier	.	1	.	.	.
Stockman	.	.	.	4	.
Stonemason	2	.	.	.	.
Tinman	1	.	.	.	.
Weaver	.	1	.	.	.
Unknown	1	2	.	2	14

COUNTRY OF ORIGIN

Australia 30   England 29   Ireland 22   Scotland 3   Canada 1
France (?) 1   West Indies (?) 1   India (?) 1   Unknown 12

NOTE: Two Englishmen, two Irishmen, one Scot, and five Australians have two or more trades or occupations listed on their records. Others are known to have had at least one trade or occupation but none appear in their records. Where any doubt exists the recorded trade or occupation has been listed, or the one commonly known to have been practised by the bushranger has been listed. There is an anomaly in the fact that a number of the Australian-born bushrangers are known to have been stockmen, but the records show them as 'Labourers.' When bushrangers were shown as having two or more trades or occupations they have not been included in the above lists but are as follows:

English
C. Farrell, Printer, Mason   G. Jones, Labourer, Quarryman
Irish
J. Bradshaw, Carnivalman, Professional footrunner, Farm labourer, Shearer, etc.
L. Kavanagh, Stonemason, Quarryman
Scottish
A. McPherson, Shearer, Stonemason, Carrier
Australian
J. Bow, Labourer, Stockman
J. Dunn, Labourer, Stockman
J. Governor, Horsebreaker, Blacktracker, Contract farmer
Musquito, Stockman, Blacktracker
J. Nesbitt, Labourer, Tobacco manufacturer

PERSONAL STATISTICS

HEIGHTS
In imperial measures as listed on records

	ENGLISH	IRISH	SCOTTISH	AUSTRALIAN	OTHERS
5ft to 5ft 5ins	4	6	.	2	1
5ft 5ins to 5ft 7ins	9	5	1	3	.
5ft 7ins to 5 ft 9ins	4	1	.	4	.
5ft 9ins to 5ft 11ins	3	2	.	7	.
Over 5ft 11ins	.	1	.	3	.
Height unknown	4	4	1	10	13
Two heights listed	6	3	1	.	2

NOTE: Heights were usually listed on prisoners' records although there were frequent variations. Sometimes these could be accounted for by the fact that a bushranger's record began when he was very young. For example, the record of Ned Kelly's younger brother James began when he was a mere boy and shows him as 5 feet 5 inches, whereas later accounts, and photographs, show that he grew into a tall man, possibly to 6 feet in height. In other cases the variations apply to grown men, such as Martin Cash or Andrew Scott, and may perhaps be accounted for by carelessness or by a criminal's deliberate attempt to disguise his height.

Records showing different heights are as follows:

English
Dalton 5ft 0ins — 5ft 0½ins
Farrell 5ft 7ins — 5ft 8ins
Roberts 5ft 5ins — 5ft 6½ins
Stallard 5ft 0ins — 5ft 1¼ins
Suffolk 5ft 10½ — 5ft 11½ins
Wilson 5ft 3½ins at 17; 5ft 6ins at 20

Irish
Cash 5ft 6¾ — 5ft 9¾ins
Dunne 5ft 6¾ — 5ft 7¼ins
Scott 5ft 8¾ — 5ft 9¼ins
Scottish
McCallum 5ft 0ins at 15; later 5ft 5¾ins

Australian
Governor 5ft 7½ins — 5ft 8ins
J. Peisley 5ft 9½ins — 5ft 10ins
Others
Hunter 5ft 10ins — 5ft 11ins

EDUCATION

	ENGLISH	IRISH	SCOTTISH	AUSTRALIAN	OTHERS
Able to read and write	4	4 (a)	.	15	.
Able to read only	.	1 (b)	.	.	.
Unable to read or write	.	1 (c)	.	.	.
Unknown	26	16	3	14	16

(a) H. Power, who was said to read and write 'With difficulty'. Later official correspondence in the 1880s shows he wrote very well.
(b) L. Kavanagh
(c) I. Wright

NOTE: Very few of the prison records gave information about education. The records kept in the colony of Victoria gave most of the information listed above, but even these were often incomplete. Isaiah Wright is the only man whose records show him to be illiterate, but it is fairly safe to assume that there would have been many more.

RELIGIONS

	ENGLISH	IRISH	SCOTTISH	AUSTRALIAN	OTHERS
Roman Catholic	7	9	1	15	.
Protestant	10	4	.	3	1
Church of England	3	1	.	5	.
Presbyterian	.	.	1	.	.
Wesleyan (Methodist)	.	.	.	1	.
Religion unknown	10	8	1	5	15

NOTE: Some prison records did not list religions. In others, the different denominations within the Protestant faith were not categorised.

• REFERENCES •
Sources of Biographies of Individual Bushrangers

Abbreviations *used in reference notes*
PRO, V   Public Record Office, Victoria
AONSW   Archives Office of New South Wales
AOT   Archives Office of Tasmania
QSA   Queensland State Archives
VP, PRD   Victoria Police, Public Relations Division
RHSV   Royal Historical Society of Victoria
NSWP, PRD   NSW Police Public Relations Department
MLNSW   Mitchell Library, New South Wales
LC, SLV   La Trobe Collection, State Library of Vic.

Note: Names such as 'J. Sadlier; Charles White' etc. refer to the authors of books listed in the bibliography

WILLIAM ARMSTRONG
Prisoner Register (Males) vol. 7, no. 4402, p. 42, Series 515, PRO,V; J. Sadlier; Charles White

JAMES ATTERALL
CON 3112 and 1813, AOT No. 633; *Hobart Town Courier* 15.6.1838

WILLIAM BARNES
Prisoner Register (Males) vol. 1, no. 387, p. 387, Series 515, PRO,V; Melbourne *Argus* 8.10.1852; Melbourne *Truth* 16.7.1910; Inquest No. 352, 18.12.1852, Series 23, PRO,V; George Boxall

GRAHAM BENNETT
Darlinghurst Gaol: Photograph Description Book 1879 81, AONSW ref. 316043, No. 2172, 1879; George Calderwood

BILLY THE PUNTMAN
J. Sadlier; F. A. Hare

BOGONG JACK
E. Harding; J. Sadlier

ROBERT BOURKE
Return of Bushrangers: Acts of Bushranging. AONSW, ref. 411880--No. 1. Robert Bourke, No. 12; Charles White, *Shortlived Bushrangers*; George Boxall

CHARLES BOW
Prisoner Register (Males) vol. 1, no. 458, Series 515, PRO,V; George Boxall

JOHN BOW
Darlinghurst Gaol: Photograph Description Book, AONSW ref. 3114031, no. 1054, 1874; Bathurst Gaol Entrance Book, AONSW ref. 518492, no. 272; Returns of Bushrangers: Acts of Bushranging, AONSW ref. 411880 – no. 1. John Bow, no. 18; Returns of Bushrangers, Offences by Gardiner &c. AONSW ref. 411880 – No. 5; Returns of Prisoners proposed for Exile or Liberation; Returns of Bushrangers, Offenders Apprehended AONSW ref. 411880– No. 2; Charles White

HENRY BRADLEY
D. Blair etc.; W. Howitt; M. Brooke; *Government Gazette* 24.9.1953 p. 1430

JACK BRADSHAW
Bill Wannan; Wannan, Prior, and Nunn; R. Mendham; E. Dickenson (unpublished correspondence in author's possession)

MATTHEW BRADY
Alphabetical Record Book of Convicts in Colony, A-B, 1807-1830, AOT ref. 21131, p. 898; AOT ref CON 3111 p. 89; Bushrangers tried at Third Session of Supreme Court, Hobart, sitting 25 April 1826, AOT ref. 751804; B. Wannan; K. R. von Stieglitz

WILLIAM BROOKMAN
Darlinghurst Gaol: Photograph Description Book; AONSW ref. 311431, No. 1039, 1874; George Boxall; Charles White

WILLIAM BRYAN
Prisoner Register (Males) vol. 2, no. 693, p. 90, Series 515, PRO,V; R. Mendham; George Boxall

RICHARD BRYANT
Prisoner Register (Males) vol. 2, no. 532, p. 9, Series 515, PRO,V; Inquest no. 292, 29.4.1852, Series 23, PRO,V; George Boxall

ARTHUR BURROWE
Prisoner Register (Males) vol. 2, no. 695, p. 91, Series 515, PRO,V; R. Mendham; George Boxall

JOSEPH BYRNE
Prisoner Register (Males) vol. 24, no. 13890, p.99, Series 515, PRO,V; Inquest no. 833, 29.6.1880, Series 23, PRO,V; Prior, Wannan, and Nunn; J. J. Keneally; J. Sadlier; George Boxall

JOHN CAESAR
Australia's Heritage vol. 1, part 7, p. 162-3; B. Wannan; *Australian Encyclopaedia*

MARTIN CASH
Convict Department Records CON 3511 – p. 133, AOT; letter from Governor Franklin GO 33134 AOT; Frank Clune, *Martin Cash the Lucky Bushranger*

GEORGE CHAMBERLAIN
Prisoner Register (Males) vol. 7, no. 4396, p. 40, Series 515, PRO,V; J. Sadlier

THOMAS CLARKE
Returns of Bushrangers: Offences committed by outlaw Thomas Clarke and Gang, AONSW ref. 411880 – No. 6; Returns of Bushrangers: Acts of Bushranging AONSW ref. 411880 – No. 1, no. 33, Thomas Clarke; John O'Sullivan

GEORGE COMERFORD
Victoria Police – Origin and History VP, PRD, Melbourne – 100177; Charles White

ROBERT COTTRELL
Darlinghurst Gaol: Entrance Book AONSW ref. 511899 – No. 3508 Robert Cottrell; George Boxall; Charles White

PATRICK DALEY
Darlinghurst Gaol: Photograph Description Book AONSW ref. 31140300
No. 310; do. Entrance Book AONSW ref. 511896 – No. 285 P. Daley; Returns of Bushrangers: Acts of Bushranging, AONSW ref. 411880, no. I; do., Offences by Gardiner, Peisley & Others, AONSW ref. 411880 – No. 5 Frank Clune *Wild Colonial Boys*

ALEXANDER DALTON
Convict Department Records CS0112284, p. 106-7, AOT; CON 3119, AOT

JAMES DALTON
Convict Department Records, CON 1813, 31110, 3416 p. 62; B. Wannan; George Boxall

JOSEPH DIGNUM
Charles White

JOHN DONOHUE
Colonial Secretary Department: Special Bundles re Bushrangers, 1830-31. AONSW ref. 417090, letter dated 30.8.1830, *Government Gazettes* (NSW); Aust. Dictionary of Biography vol. I p. 312; Frank Clune *Wild Colonial Boys*; B. Wannan; Prior, Wannan and Nunn

JOHN DONOVAN
Prisoner Register (Males) vol. 1, no. 455, p. 455, Series 515, PRO,V; George Boxall

'BLACK' DOUGLAS
Charles White, *Short-lived Bushrangers*; James Flett

JOHN DOUGLAS
Prisoner Register (Males) vol. 2, no. 692, Series 515, PRO,V; R. Mendham; George Boxall

WILLIAM DRISCOLL
Hobart Town Gazette 20.11.1855 pp 1266-67; Convict Department Records CON 18118, 31110, 3211, 3415 (all no. 1037) AOT

JAMES DUNCAN
Prisoner Register (Males), vol. I, no. 251, p. 253; vol. 2, no. 7403, p. 44, Series 515, PRO,V; Melbourne *Truth* 16 July 1910; Inquest no. 1198, 18 December 1875, Series 23, PRO,V; Royal Historical Society magazine vol. XIV, August 1931, no. 2.

JOHN DUNN
Returns of Bushrangers: Acts of Bushranging, AONSW ref. 411880 – no. I; Returns of Bushrangers: Offences by Gardiner &c. AONSW ref. 411880 – no. 5;
Bathurst Gaol Entrance Book, 1854-1867, AONSW ref. 418493; Frank Clune, *Wild Colonial Boys*

PATRICK DUNNE
Convict Department Records, CON 31/9, 13/2. Other information is contained in Supreme Court Criminal Register lists, SC 41/1, AOT

GEORGE ELLISON
Prisoner Register (Males), vol. 2, no. 540, p. 13, Series 515, PRO,V; George Boxall

CHRISTOPHER FARRELL
Prisoner Register (Males) vol. I, no. 82; vol. 1, no. 108; vol. 39, no. 82, p. 267, Series 515, PRO,V; Inquest no. 1057, 1 September 1895, Series 23, PRO,V; *Government Gazette*, 11 October 1889, Book 3, p. 3382; George Boxall; J. Barry

JOHN FINEGAN
Prisoner Register (Males) vol. 1, no. 454, Series 515, PRO,V; George Boxall

JOHN FLANIGAN
Prisoner Register (Males), vol. 1, no. 434, p. 434, Series 515; *Government Gazette*, 20 October 1852, Book 3, p. 1171; George Boxall; White; Melbourne *Argus* 22 October, 19 November 1852; C. White

JOHN FOLEY
Returns of Bushrangers: Acts of Bushranging, John Foley, no. 60, AONSW ref. 4/1880 – no. 1; do. Offenders Apprehended (1863) John Foley, no. 26, AONSW ref. 4/1880 – no. 2; do. Offenders Apprehended (1865) John Foley, no. 70, AONSW ref. 4/1880 – no. 2; Darlinghurst Gaol: Entrance Book

AONSW ref. 5/1896 – no. 1512
ALEXANDER FORDYCE
Bathurst Gaol: Entrance Book 1854-1867, AONSW ref. 4/8492, no. 271; Returns of Bushrangers: Acts of Bushranging, AONSW ref. 4/1880, no.I; Frank Clune *Wild Colonial Boys;* G. Boxall; C. White. There are also brief mentions of Fordyce in other lists in the Returns of Bushrangers
STEPHEN FOX
Prisoner Register (Males), vol. 1, no. 268, p. 269, Series 515, PRO,V; RHSV magazine, August 1931; George Boxall
FRANK GARDINER
Prisoner Register (Males), vol. I, no. 70, p. 71, Series 515, PRO,V; Returns of Bushrangers: Acts of Bushranging, AONSW ref. 4/1880 – no. I; do. Offences by Gardiner etc, AONSW ref.4/1880 – no.5; Cockatoo Island Transportation Register, 1853-1855, AONSW ref. 4/6573, p. 153; Darlinghurst Gaol: Photograph Description Book, 1874, AONSW ref. 3/14031, no. 1055, 12 June 1874; Frank Clune, *King of the Road;* Joy & Prior
BERESFORD GARRETT
Victorian Police Gazette 20 October 1854, p. 516; George Boxall; Richard Burgess/Ken Byron
WILLIAM GARROWAY
Prisoner Register (Males), vol. 2, no. 694, Series 515, PRO,V; George Boxall; R. Mendham
JOHN GILBERT
Return of Bushrangers: Offences by Gardiner &c., AONSW ref. 4/1880 – no. 5; Justice Department: Register of Coroners' Inquests 1852-59, AONSW ref. 4/6614 no. 17, 805 Edmund Parry; Returns of Bushrangers: Acts of Bushranging, AONSW ref. 4/1880 – no. I; H. Nunn; Prior, Wannan, & Nunn; George Boxall; Frank Clune, *Wild Colonial Boys;* Manning Clark, *A History of Australia vol. 4*
CHRISTOPHER GOODISON
Prisoner Register (Males) vol. I, no. 191, p. 193, Series 515, PRO,V; Ticket of Leave Application 28 September 1853, Inspector General files, Gaols and Penal Establishments, Box 53/6711-11449, no. 9445; *Victorian Police Gazette* 30 December 1853
JAMES GOODWIN
Convict Department Records, CON 31/15, AOT; Supreme Court Register list, SC 41/1, AOT
JIMMY GOVERNOR
Darlinghurst Gaol: Photograph Description Book, 1900-1901, AONSW ref. 3/6066, no. 8194; Supreme Court, Register of Civil Causes, AONSW ref. 4/4594, no. 4; Darlinghurst Gaol: *Diary of Officer doing Duty over Jimmy Governor,* AONSW ref. 6/1029; do. Condemned Prisoners' Daily Record, 1892-1903, AONSW ref. 5/1739; Frank Clune, *Jimmy Governor – the True Story;* Brian Davies, *The Life of Jimmy Governor*
BENJAMIN HALL
Returns of Bushrangers: Offences by Gardiner &c., AONSW ref. 4-1880 – no. 5; condensed notes compiled by John Bond in unpublished material for his appearance on ABC-TV *Mastermind* 1978 (copy in author's collection); reference should also be made to the lists of the Returns of Bushrangers and information in Register of Coroners' Inquests, 1852-59, AONSW ref. 4/6614, no. 18319, Ben Hall

STEPHEN HART
Prisoner Register (Males) vol. 26, no. 14823, p. 106, Series 515, PRO,V; J. J. Keneally; George Boxall; Prior, Wannan, & Nunn

MICHAEL HOWE
Historical Records of Australia p. 122; *Hobart Town Gazette* 11 January 1817; *Historical Records of Australia* p. 98; *Australian Dictionary of Biography vol. 1;* B. Wannan *Tell 'em I Died Game; George Boxall: J. Bonwick*

HENRY HUNTER
St Helena Penal Establishment PRI 2/2, PRI 2/3, Q.S.A.; P. H. McCarthy
The Wild Scotsman – James McPherson the Queensland Bushranger

JOHN JAMES
Prisoner Register (Males) vol. 1, no. 146, p. 147, Series 515, PRO,V; RHSV magazine, August 1931; Melbourne *Truth* 16 July 1910; George Boxall

THOMAS JEFFRIES
Convict Department Records, Indent CON 13/2, 31/23 AOT (note: Con 13/2 is more likely to be correct because CON 31/22 was written up retrospectively beginning in 1827); *Hobart Town Gazette* 6.5.1826 p. 2

HENRY JOHNSTON
Prisoner Register (Males) vol. I, no. 460, Series 515, PRO,V; George Boxall

GEORGE JONES
Convict Department Records, CON 16/1 p. 210, 31/25 p. 226 AOT; Supreme Court Minute Book, SC 41/4, AOT

LAWRENCE KAVANAGH
Convict Department Records, CON 16/1, 35/1 p. 619; Charles White

ANDREW KELLY
Convict Department Records CON 37/5 no. 1539, no. 1039, CON 33/25 no. 6092; Melbourne *Truth* 27.8. 1910

KELLY FAMILY
Father John Kelly, mother Mary Kelly (Quinn), uncle James senior, brothers Edward (Ned), James junior, and Daniel, and relations associated with Quinn and Lloyd families. About 100 books cover various aspects of the Kelly story, and newspapers have mentioned Ned Kelly ever since he first came under police surveillance when he was about fourteen. The Bibliography lists a number of books which may prove valuable to readers who wish to learn more about the Kellys. The Public Record Office (Victoria) holds a copy of Ned Kelly's Jerilderie letter, which is mentioned in various books. The original which was either written by Ned or transcribed for him by Joe Byrne, is still in jealously guarded private possession. The owner's reluctance to release the original is understandable because so many original documents, even those held in such institutions as the Public Record Office, have 'disappeared' over the years. Other sources used in this article include: Prisoner Register (Males) vol. 26, no. 14991, p. 280, (Dan Kelly); vol. 17, no. 10926, p. 287, (Edward Kelly); vol. 17, no. 10861, p. 22, James Kelly); all Series 515, PRO,V; Papers presented to both Houses of Parliament, Session 1881, Legislative Assembly, vol. 3, appendix 10, p. 699: unpublished correspondence in author's possession; particularly detailed material from Ian Jones, recognised as Australia's leading historian on Kelly and associates. J. J. Keneally; J. Molony; J. McQuilton, K. McMenomy.

FREDERICK LOWRY
Returns of Bushrangers: Acts of Bushranging, AONSW ref. 4/1880 – no. I; do. Deaths and Bodily Injuries Sustained by Police. AONSW ref. 4/1880 – no. 7; do. Bushrangers Killed and Wounded. AONSW ref. 4/1880 – no. 3

WILLIAM MACK
Prisoner Register (Males) vol. 2, no. 533 Series 515, PRO,V; George Boxall, Melbourne *Argus* 28.12.1852

FRANK MCCALLUM
Prisoner Register (Males) vol. 2, no. 528, p. 6, Series 515, PRO,V; Convict Department Records, CON 18/17, 31/8, AOT; correspondence and taped interview with Miss E. Biggin, Daisy Hill, Vic., in author's collection; *Government Gazette* 31.12.1852; Visiting Justices of Penal Establishment Reports, no. 177, Inspector General's File, box 53/6711-11449, PRO,V, Criminal Trial briefs, Queen v. Captain Melville and others (1856) no. 2 221 16/17, Series 30, PRO,V; Melbourne *Argus* 13.8.1857

JAMES MACPHERSON
(or MCPHERSON) The Queensland State Archives hold a large file of correspondence relating to 'The Wild Scotsman' and the Petition to His Excellency George Augustus Constantine, Governor of Queensland for his release. The following references are relevant: Col. Sec. In-letter no. 1849 of 1874; 36/2922 SCT/CCI 7 Dep no. 2/1866 of Aug.; COL/A 140 1094/70 (all Q.S.A.); P. H. McCarthy *The Wild Scotsman*

HARRY MANNS
Returns of Bushrangers: Acts of Bushranging, AONSW ref. 4/1880 – no. 1. Henry Manns no. 105; do. Bushrangers Apprehended, AONSW ref. 4/1880 – no. 2. Henry Manns, no. 5; Bushrangers Killed and Wounded, AONSW ref. 4/1880 – no. 3. Henry Manns no. 3; Frank Clune *Wild Colonial Boys, King of the Road,* R. Mendham

EDWARD MELVILLE
George Boxall; unpublished letters and taped interviews from various sources, in author's possession

GEORGE MELVILLE
J. Sadlier; Melbourne *Truth* 6.8.1910; *McIvor Times* 13.6.1962; Joy and Prior (note: most of the official records, including Trial Briefs, letters, etc., indexed in the Public Record Office, Victoria, have 'disappeared.' The author examined the records of numerous Victorian government departments for two years in search of relevant documents but without success; unpublished letters and taped

interviews from various sources, in author's possession

DANIEL MORGAN
The bushranging literature contains many references to 'Mad Dan' or 'Mad Dog' Morgan and the newspapers of the period contain relevant material. However the prison and other records of this bushranger cannot be located. The principal reference used in this book was Margaret Carnegie's Morgan — *The Bold Bushranger*

JAMES MORGAN
Prisoner Register (Males) vol. 1, no. 145, p. 147, Series 515, PRO,V; George Boxall

MUSQUITO
Hobart Town Gazette 13.8.1824, 3.9.1824, 3.12.1824; George Boxall

JAMES NESBITT
Prisoner Register (Males) vol. 18, no. 11251 p. 169, Series 515, PRO,V; Prisoners Description Book, vol. 16, 1875-1878, no. 11251, p. 28, James Lyons alias Nesbit, Series 858, PRO,V; George Calderwood; George Boxall, and unpublished correspondence from the Nesbit Society of Australia, in author's possession.

JOHN NEWTON
Prisoner Register (Males) vol. 1, no. 73, p. 73, Series 515, PRO,V; Frank Clune, *King of the Road*

PATRICK O'CONNOR
Government Gazette, 24.9.1853, p. 1429, bk. 2, 1853; Melbourne *Truth* 27.8.1910

ALEXANDER PEARCE
Report by State Librarian, Tasmania, in which details of Alexander Pearce have been taken from various sources. This report states that 'No record has been found giving details of the crime for which he was sentenced.' Other information from Convict Conduct Register; Description List of Convicts per Castle Forbes; Convict Muster, Buckingham, 1820 1821; *Hobart Town Gazette*

JOHN PEISLEY
Cockatoo Island Transportation Register, 1853 1855, AONSW ref. 4/6573; Returns of Bushrangers: Offences by Gardiner and others, AONSW ref. 4/1880 no. 5; Bathurst Gaol Entrance Book, 1854 1867, AONSW ref. 4/8492; Peisley to John Coutts, jockey, quoted in C. McAllister's *Old Pioneering Days in the Sunny South* (1907) quoted in Bill Wannan; George Boxall

GEORGE PENNY
Exhaustive research failed to discover official or other documents relevant to this bushranger. Material used in this article was derived from Charles White

HARRY POWER
While this book was being prepared for publication the author found an 80-page file on Harry Power, including letters from his sister Margaret, but it could be used only to check relevant facts and may be employed as the basis of another publication. Other material was derived from Prisoner Register (Males) vol. 13, no. 2643, p. 159, Series 515, PRO,V; Melbourne *Truth* 20.8.1910; J. Sadlier; George Boxall. An inquiry was held on the recovery of the body believed to be that of Power but it is headed 'Man Unknown (Henry Power?)' and Power's eventual fate must still remain a mystery. Magisterial Inquiry no. 1489, 2.10.1891; Inquest depositions Series 23, PRO,V

JAMES REGAN
Convict Department Records, CON 18/7, no. 1131, and CON 31/37, AOT; Supreme Court Register SC41/5; Colonial Secretary's Office CSO 1/122a, p. 104

CODRINGTON REVINGSTONE
Melbourne *Morning Herald* 22.1 1.1850

JOHN ROBERTS
Prisoner Register (Males) vol. 1, no. 252, p. 253; do. vol. 2, no. 1116, Series 515, PRO,V; Melbourne *Truth* 161 30.7.1910

WILLIAM ROBERT ROBERTS
Prisoner Register (Males) vol. 2, no. 529, p., Series 515, PRO,V; Frank Clune, *Captain Melville*; George Boxall

THOMAS ROGAN
Darlinghurst Gaol: Photograph Description Book, 1879-1881, AONSW ref. 3/6043, no. 2171 Thomas Rogan alias Brown alias Baker; George Calderwood; George Boxall

ANDREW GEORGE SCOTT
Prisoner Register (Males) vol. 15, no. 10124, p. 454, Series 515, PRO,V; Darlinghurst Gaol: Photograph Description Book, 1879-1881, AONSW ref. 3/6043, no. 2170 A. G. Scott alias Captain Moonlite; George Calderwood. (Note: further research by the author has located substantial quantities of previously unpublished material concerning A. G. Scott, in both private and official collections. This material was sighted when the book was almost ready for publication and could be used only for checking relevant facts, but may be used as the basis of another book on 'Captain Moonlite.')

WILLIAM SCOTT
Returns of Bushrangers: Acts of Bushranging, no. I, Bill Scott — no. 136. AONSW ref. 4/1880; George Boxall; J. O'Sullivan

AARON SHERRITT
Prisoner Register (Males) vol. 24, no. 13891, p. 100, Series 515, PRO,V; Joy and Prior; J. J. Keneally; George Farwell; C. Osborne; Frank Clune, *Ned Kelly's Last Stand*

ALFRED STALLARD
Prisoner Register (Males) vol. I, nos. 54, 190, p. 191, Series 515, PRO,V; Melbourne *Argus* 8.10.1852; George Boxall

OWEN SUFFOLK
The files of the PRO,V, contain substantial quantities of letters and documents relevant to Owen Suffolk and it is the author's intention to use these as the basis for another book. The principal references used for the present work were: Prisoner Register (Males) vol. 1, no. 51 p. 53 and no. 107, p. 109, Series 515, PRO,V; *Victorian Police Gazette* 27.9.1866; Melbourne *Truth* 16.4.1910; George Boxall; J. Graham

JOHN VANE
Darlinghurst Gaol: Photograph Description Book, no. 2279, AONSW ref. 316043, John Vane: Returns of Bushrangers: Acts of Bushranging, AONSW ref. 4/1880 — no. I, John Vane, no. 149; J. O'Brien

FREDERICK WARD
Returns of Bushrangers: Acts of Bushranging, AONSW ref. 4/1880 — no. I, Frederick Ward alias Thunderbolt, no. 150; George Boxall

JOHN WHELAN
Convict Department Records, CON 37/4, no. 1231, AOT; Confession of John 'Rocky' Whelan, original in C.S.O. (Fox Young period) Y94, 10/9. AOT; *Hobart Town Courier* 29.5.1855, 5.6.1855; Bill Wannan

JOHN WHITEHEAD
Convict Department Records, H.O. 26-7, p. 132; Knopwood Diary, May 1815; *Hobart Town Gazette* 13.12.1817, 31.1.1818; George Boxall. (Note: Convict Department files contain records for both John Whitehead and James Whitehead, which may account for this bushranger being described both as 'John' and 'James.' A Sarah Whitehead, possibly a wife or another relation, is listed in the Convict Record immediately after John Whitehead)

JACK WILLIAMS
Melbourne *Truth* 26.3.1910; George Boxall; Joy and Prior; B. Wannan; Ian MacFarlane

THOMAS WILLIAMS (1st)
Prisoner Register (Males) vol. 1, no. 433, p. 433, Series 515, PRO,V; John Barry

THOMAS WILLIAMS (2nd)
Darlinghurst Gaol: Photograph Description Book, AONSW ref. 3/6043, no. 2173 Thomas Wiliams; George Boxall

EDWARD WILSON
Prisoner Register (Males) vol. I, no. 399, p. 399, Series 515, PRO,V; Melbourne *Argus* 8.10.1852

JOHN WILSON
Convict Department Records, CON 34/2, p. 670, no. 1146, CON 18/2, no. 1250, CON 34/2, p. 670, CON 31/46, AOT; Supreme Court Register SC41/5, AOT; *Hobart Town Gazette* 15.2.1859

ISAIAH WRIGHT
Prisoner Register (Males) vol. 20, no. 12313, Series 515, PRO,V; J. Sadlier; J. J. Keneally

JOHN WRIGHT
Magisterial Inquiry held into the circumstances touching the death of John Wright, 16.7.1864. Police Office, Rockhampton; Deposition of Henry 0. Paton, ref. 64/2455, LWO/A 17, QSA; letter from H. 0. Paton to the Colonial Treasurer, Brisbane, dated 31.10.1864, QSA

• OFFICIAL GOVERNMENT SOURCES •

Public Record Office of Victoria
One of the largest collections of bushranging material is contained in the Public Record Office of Victoria, although much of it is not indexed and is diffficult to locate. The following is in various government department files but most of it is in the Social Welfare Department (Prisons Division):

Chief Commissioner of Police In & Out Correspondence
Chief Secretary In & Out Correspondence
Convict Indents
Criminal Trial Briefs
Executive Council Minutes
Governor General In & Out Correspondence
Guide to Development of Prison System in Victoria, 1851-95 (Len Undy)
Inquest Depositions
Prisoners Registers (Males), 1853-1947, volumes 1-39
Prisoners Description Books
Photograph Description Book (1878)
Sheriff's In & Out Correspondence
Tickets of Leave
Victorian Government Gazettes
Other files of various government departments were referred to as general reference purposes required.

Victoria Police, Public Relations Division
Victoria Police Gazettes
History of the Victoria Police — various pamphlets of Divisions
Forensic Science Squad: Firearms of the bushranging era.
Photographs, volumes of Offficial Correspondence, telegrams and other documents related to the Kelly Gang, Photographs of Police, Bushrangers, Officials, Settlers, etc.

LaTrobe Collection, State Library of Victoria
A large collection of Photographs, newspapers, letters, reports, etc. related to bushranging is contained in numerous files, particularly the photographic collection.

Archives of New South Wales
Department of Corrective Services:
Darlinghurst Gaol: Photograph Description Books, 1873-74 (ref. 3/14030-31); 1879 81 (ref. 3/6043); 1900-1901 (ref. 3/6066)
Darlinghurst Gaol: Entrance Books, 1850-1914 (ref. 5/1896, 5/1898, 5/1899)
Darlinghurst Gaol: Condemned Prisoners' Daily Record, 1892-1903 (ref. 5/1739)
Darlinghurst Gaol: Diary of Officer doing duty over Jimmy Governor, 1900 1901 (ref. 6/1029)
Bathurst Gaol: Entrance Books, 1854-1867 (ref. 4/8492, 418493)
Cockatoo Island Transportation Register, 1847 49, 1853-55 (ref. 4/6571, 4/6573).

Colonial Secretary Department:
Special Bundles re Bushrangers, 1830-31 (ref. 4/7090) Returns of Bushrangers:
No. 1: List of offenders, Guilty of Offences known as Acts of Bushranging (ref. 4/1880)
No. 2: List of offenders, Apprehended (ref. 4/1880)
No. 3: List of offenders, Bushrangers Killed & Wounded (ref. 4/1 880)
No. 5: Offences committed by Francis Gardiner, John Peisley, and others, also by the outlaws Hall, Gilbert, Dunn and Gang (ref. 4/1880)
No. 6: Offences committed by the outlaw Thomas Clarke and Gang (ref. 4/1880)
No. 7: Particulars of Deaths & Bodily Injuries sustained by the Police from Bushrangers (ref. 4/1880)
No. 8: Private individuals murdered (ref. 4/1880)
No. 9: Private individuals wounded (ref. 4/1880)
No. 10: Offences committed by Daniel Morgan (ref. 4/ 1880).

Justice Department:
Register of Coroners' Inquests, 1852-59 (ref. 4/6614).

Supreme Court:
Register of Civil Causes (ref. 5/4594).

Police Department:
Convict Branch-butts of Colonial Certificates of Freedom, 1867-69 (ref. 4/4422).

Police Department of New South Wales
History of the Police of New South Wales
Photographs of convicted bushrangers

Archives Office of Tasmania
Convict Department Records:
Convict Registers (Male Convicts) arriving in period of assignment 1803-43 (ref. CON 31)
Supplementary Registers (CON 32)
Convict Registers (Male Convicts) arriving under assignment system and still on strength in 1844 (ref. CON 34)
Convict Registers (Male Convicts) arriving on non-convict ships, and still on strength in 1844 (ref. CON 35)
Assignment lists and associated papers, 1810-1826 (ref. CON 13)
Indents of Convicts locally convicted or transported from other colonies (ref. CON 16)
Alphabetical Record Book of Convicts in Colony, A-B, 1807-30
Bushrangers Tried at Third Session of Supreme Court, Hobart 1826 (ref. 75/804) Supreme Court Register lists (ref. SC 41/1).

Queensland State Archives
(Premier's Department)
Petition for release of McPherson (ref. COL/A198, in-letter 1849 of 1874)
Depositions re capture of the 'Wild Scotsman' (ref. STC/CC17; 2 of 1866)
Report of Attempted escape by McPherson and others (ref. COL/A140; in-letter 2455 of 1864)
H. Paton's account of witnesses at the inquest into Wright's death (ref. JUS/N7; 64/100) .

Newspapers:
Argus (Melbourne)
Bendigo Advertiser
Hobart Town Courier
Hobart Town Gazette
Inglewood Advertiser
Mclvor Times
Morning Herald (Melbourne)
Sun (Melbourne)
Truth (Melbourne)

• BIBLIOGRAPHY •

BARRY, JOHN *The Life and Death of John Price.* Melbourne: 1964
BLAIR, DAVID *History of Australasia.* Glasgow: 1879
BOXALL, GEORGE *History of the Australian Bushrangers (var. editions)*
BROOKS, MABEL *Riders of Time.* Melbourne: 1967
BURGESS. RICHARD *Guilty Wretch That I Am.*
Echoes of Australian Bushrangers from the death row memoirs of Richard Burgess and historical notes by KEN BYRON. Melbourne: 1984
CALDERWOOD, GEORGE *Captain Moonlite, Bushranger.* Adelaide: 1971
CARNEGIE, MARGARET *Morgan — The Bold Bushranger.* Sydney: 1975
CLARK, A MANNING *History of Australia (vol. IV).* Melbourne: 1978
CLUNE, FRANK *Jimmy Governor — The True Story.* Melb.: 1978 (reprint)
_____.*Martin Cash, The Lucky Bushranger.* Sydney: 1969 (reprint)
_____. *King of the Road.* Sydney: 1969 (reprint)
_____. *Ned Kelly's Last Stand.* Sydney: 1969 (reprint)
_____. *Wild Colonial Boys.* Sydney: 1948
_____. *Captain Melville.* Sydney: 1956
DAVIES, BRIAN *The Life of Jimmy Governor.* Sydney: 1979
FARWELL, GEORGE *Ned Kelly.* Melbourne: 1978
FLETT, JAMES *Dunolly — The Story of an Old Gold Diggings.* Melb.: 1956
GRAHAM, JOHN *Bushlife in Australia.* London: 1863
HARDING, ERIC *Bogong Jack the Gentleman Bushranger.* Melb.: 1967
HARE, FRANCIS *Last of the Australian Bushrangers.* London: 1892
HOWITT, WILLIAM *Two Years in Victoria.* London: 1855
JOY, WILLIAM and PRIOR TOM *The Bushrangers.* (p/back) Adelaide: 1975
KENNEALLY, JAMES J. *The Inner History of the Kelly Gang.* Moe. nd
MCCARTHY, P. H. *The Wild Scotsman — James McPherson the Queensland Bushranger.* Melbourne nd
MACFARLANE IAN *1842 The Public Executions at Melbourne.* Melb.: 1984
MCMENOMY KEITH *Ned Kelly - Authentic Illustrated History.* Melb: 1984
MCQUILTON, JOHN *The Kelly Outbreak.* Melbourne: 1979
MENDHAM, ROY *Dictionary of Australian Bushrangers.* Melbourne: 1975
MOLONY, JOHN *I am Ned Kelly.* Melbourne: 1980
NUNN, HARRY *Bushrangers: A Pictorial History?* Sydney: 1980
O'BRIEN, JOHN *Men of 38.* Kilmore: 1975
OSBORNE, CHARLES *Ned Kelly.* London: 1970
O'SULLIVAN, JOHN *The Bloodiest Bushrangers.* Adelaide: 1975
_____. *Mounted Police in New South Wales.* Adelaide: 1978
PENZIG, EDGAR. *Morgan the Murderer,* Sydney 1990
PRIOR, TOM; WANNAN, BILL and NUNN, H. *Pictorial History of Australian Bushrangers.* Melbourne: 1966
SADLIER, JOHN *Recollections of a Victorian Police Officer.* Melb.: 1973
TRAVERS, ROBERT *Rogue's March.* Melbourne: 1973
VON STIEGLITZ, K. R. *Matthew Brady, Van Diemen's Land Bushranger.* Hobart. nd
WANNAN, BILL *Tell 'Em I Died Game.* Melbourne: 1967
WHITE, CHARLES *History of Australian Bushranging.* Melbourne: 1970
_____, *Short-lived Bushrangers.* Sydney: 1911

• ACKNOWLEDGEMENTS •

I doubt if any author can do justice to those who assisted in the research of any book. Words cannot express the gratitude an author feels when material is forthcoming from varied sources. These assistants usually only receive a small mention in the final manuscript, this one being no exception. I can do no better than to simply say a sincere 'Thanks' to all who who helped me with this book, including:

Victoria Police
Inspector George Puckey,(late)(District Inspector)
Sergeant Brian Thompson,(Forensic Science-Ballistics)
Sergeant Bill Morrison, & Senior Constable Tony Dickinson
(Public Relations Division)
State Law Offices, Victoria
Bill Johnston
New South Wales Police Department
(Public Relations Department)
M.W. Diven
Public Record Office, Victoria
Chris Diver, Len Undy, Rod Smith
Archives Of New South Wales
Lauren Catchpool, Laurel Croucher, D.J.Cross
State Library of Victoria
Judy MacDonald, Mary Kehoe, Shar Jones
Queensland State Archives
Lee McGregor
Archives of Tasmania
Mary McRae, Ian Pearce

Australian National University, Canberra
Professor John Molony
Ian Jones, Kellyana historian, Producer 'The Last Outlaw', Melb.
A great help with Kelly history
John Bond, ABC-TV 'Mastermind' 1973, Melb.
Peter Cuffley, author and collector mate, Castlemaine, Victoria
Colin & Dot Nesbit, Bruce Nesbit, Nesbit Society of Australia, Vic.
John LaTerra, John LaTerra Studio, photographer mate, Melb.
Don Bennetts, Producer of 'Ned Kelly-The Making of the Myth', ABC-TV, Melb.
Doreen Carswell, Publicity Officer, City of Benalla, Victoria
Vic Lane, fellow Australiana collector, Bendigo, Victoria
Dagmar Balcorek, author, Adelaide
Janice Daley, researcher, Moonah West, Tasmania
Diana Ward, Carolyn Carver-Gibson (Library Officers)
North Central Goldfields Library, Bendigo.

Thanks to numerous people who supplied many yarns, and cups of tea, over the years.

Special thanks to **Colin** and **Lisa Barr**, of DiGiTYPE Bendigo, and my wife **Janette**, who between them, did the typesetting.

Finally, sincere thanks to friend **Geoff Hocking**, of Geoff Hocking Graphics, Castlemaine, who has worked with me on this, our third project together. As usual his design has brought the material to its final form in just the manner I had hoped. His expertise and commitment is appreciated.

If I have overlooked anyone I can only apologise, for I would not willingly commit such an oversight.

• INDEX •

Note: Numbers in Italics represent the page on which individual bushranger biographies are found.

A

a'BECKETT William Justice 71, 132
ABBOTT Mr (Overseer) 18
AFTER DARK 23
Ann and Amelia 50
ARMSTRONG William *11*, 12, 37, 137
ARTHUR George Sir (Lieutenant Governor) 24
ATKINS William 120
ATTERALL James *13*, 145

B

BANKS Anthony 13
BARNES William *14*, 91, 176
BARRY (Constable) 156
BARRY Ellen 160
BARRY J. V. (Author) 59, 174
BARRY Redmond Sir (Judge) 19, 79, 104, 109, 116, 125, 147, 152, 165
BATMAN John 26, 93
BAYLIE John 19, 51, 60
BELL (Constable) 138
BENNETT (Sherriff) 36
BENNETT Graham *15*, 148, 153, 156, 175
BENNETT MARY (Mrs Martin Cash) 36, 37
BERRIMAN William 40
BIGGIN E Miss 115
BILLY THE PUNTMAN *16*
BLACK JACK 129
BLACK MARY 89
BLOOMFIELD (Constable) 29
BODENHAM Thomas 46, 135
BOGONG JACK 17
BOLDREWOOD Rolf [T.A. Browne] (Author) 43
BOOMERANG 38-39
BOULTON John 74
Bounty 37
BOURKE Robert (Clusky?) *18*
BOW Charles (real name James Clarke) *19*, 51
BOW John *20*, 72, 118
BOWEN (Constable) 131, 156
BOXALL George (Author) 43, 59, 68, 119, 129, 136, 148, 157
BRADLEY Alexander 40
BRADLEY Henry *22*, 133
BRADSHAW Jack *23*
BRADY Matthew *24*, 25, 26, 57, 80, 93, 157
BRICE (Ex Police Cadet) 47
BRIGHT (Constable) 78
BROOK Edward (Horse Breaker) 17
BROOKMAN William *27*
BROWN 26
BROWN James 46, 135
BROWN John 68, 73
BROWN Katherine 73
BROWN Max (Author) 87
BROWN Thomas 95
BRUUN Ludwig W Julius 151
BRYAN William *28*, 30, 52
BRYANT 26
BRYANT Richard *29*, 113
BUCKMASTER (Constable) 47, 97
BURGESS Richard 76
BURKE Mickey 85, 167
BURROWE Arthur *30*, 52, 61, 76
BYERS Bert 83
BYRNE (Joe) Joseph *32*, 107, 108, 111

C

CAESAR 'Black' John 6, *34*
CALDERWOOD George (Author) 148
CALLAGHAN 26
CAMM William 173
CARNEGIE Margaret (Author) 125
CARROLL John (Special Police) 40
CARROLL (Sergeant) 156
CASH Martin *35*, 36, 37, 94, 95, 96, 171
CASH Martin (Junior) 37
CHAMBERLAIN George 11, 12, *37*, 137
CHARLEY (Black tracker) 85
Charlotte Andrews 73
CHARTERS (Dan) Daniel 72
CHEETHAM (Convict) 135
CHRISTIE Francis (see Frank Gardiner)
CHURCHLEY (Constable) 127
CLARK Manning (Author) 78
CLARKE Ellen 40
CLARKE Elsie 81, 83
CLARKE James 40,
CLARKE Jane 40
CLARKE John 7, *38-41*, 157
CLARKE Margaret 40
CLARKE Patrick 40
CLARKE Thomas 7, *38-41*, 157
CLIFFORD Bessie 35, 36
CLUNE Frank (Author) 44, 101, 118, 132
COCKLE James Sir, 117
COMERFORD George *42*, 48, 125, 173
CONDELL James (Sergeant) 72
CONNELL Ellen 40
CONNELL Jane 40
CONNELL John 40
CONNELL Michael 40
CONNELL Patrick 40
CONNORS Pat 44
COOK William 19
CORNELIUS Bill (or Kennelly) 135
COTTRELL Robert (alias 'Blue Cap') *43*
COWEN 26
COX 135
CUMMINS Larry 112
CURNOW Thomas 107

D

DALEY Patrick *44*
DALTON Alexander *46*, 135
DALTON James *46*, 47, 97
DARCY Charles 72
DARGIN Billy (Black tracker) 44, 85
DAVEY Thomas (Lieutenant-Governor) 88
DAVIDSON James (Sub-Inspector) 85
DAVIS (Convict) 135
DAVIS Somes 11, 12
DAVIS William 13
Dawstone 75
DIGNUM Joseph 42, *48*, 125, 173
DOBBIE Dr 95
DONOHUE 'Bold Jack' John *50*
DONOVAN John 19, *51*, 60, 94
DORNAN James (alias 'Long Jim the Taylor') 40
DOUGLAS 'Black' *52*
DOUGLAS John 28, 30 *52*
DREW William 88
DRISCOLL William (William Timothy) *53*, 177
DUNCAN James *54-55*, 90, 146
DUNLEAVY Jimmy 44, 84
DUNN John 6, *56*, 78, 84
DUNN Maggie 56
DUNN Mick 56
DUNNE Patrick *57*
DWYER Father 118

E

EASON (Detective)47
ELLIS Charles 173
ELLISON George *57*
Elphinstone 97
ELSON George 120
EUCALYPTUS 169

F

FARRELL Christopher 7, *58-59*, 163
Ferguson 95
FINEGAN John 19, 51, *60-61*, 94
FIREBRACE Robert (Horsebreaker) 17
FITZPATRICK Alexander (Constable) 103, 104, 158
FLANIGAN John (Owen Gibney) *62-66*
FLETCHER James 40
FLETT James (Author) 52
FLOOKES Thomas 120
FOGARTY Martin 173
FOGG 72
FOLEY John *67*, 112
FOLEY Timothy 67
FORBES (Judge) 16

FORDYCE (Alex) Alexander 44, *68*, 118
FOX Stephen *68*
FRANCIS John 120
FRANCIS Joseph 120

G

GARDINER Frank (alias Francis Clarke) 20, 27, 56, 61, 68, 69, 70, *71-73*, 76, 78, 84, 118, 132, 136, 181
GARRETT Henry Beresford *74-76*
GARROWAY William 30, 52, 61, *76*
GIBNEY (Father) 32
GILBERT Charles 77, 118
GILBERT Francis 77
GILBERT James 77
GILBERT (Johnny) John 20, 56, 72, 76, *77-78*, 84, 118, 167, 181
GILBERT Nicholas 77
GILBERT Thomas 77
GILBERT William James 77
GILBERT William (Junior) 77
GLENNY Mr (Justice of the Peace) 100
GOODISON Christopher *79*, 161
GOODWIN James 26, *80*
GORDON James (alias Mount) 84
GOVERNOR Ethel (Mary Jane) [nee Page] 81, 83
GOVERNOR Jimmy 8, *81-83*
GOVERNOR Joe 8, *81-83*
GREEN Cornelius (Goldbuyer) 11, 12, 37
GREEN William (Constable) 11
GREENHILL (Bob) Robert 46, 135
GREY Joe (alias Nutty) 120
GRIFFIN James 40
GUNN Alex 178
GUNN (Lieutenant) 26

H

HALL (Ben) Benjamin 7, 20, 44, 56, 68, 78, *84-85*, 167, 181
HALL Ben (junior) 84
HALL Bridget [nee Walsh] 84
HALL (Senior Constable) 178
HANDCOCK 173
HARDING Bob 120
HARDING E (Author) 17
HARE Francis Augustus (Police officer/Author) 16, 144
HARRY 'Ballarat' 12
HART Stephen 32, *87*, 107, 158, 180
Harvies 92
HAVILLAND (Constable) 72
HENDERSON Mrs 103
HILL (Inspector) 12
HOBROYD (Justice) 59
HODGETTS 26
HOGAN 168
HOPKINS 92
HOPKINS John 172
HOSIE (Trooper) 72, 136
HOWARD 'Nosey Bob' Robert 83
HOWE Michael 6, 88, 172
HOWITT William (Author) 22, 133

HUNTER (Captain) 95
HUNTER Henry (alias James Russell, alias Dixon, alias 'The Frenchman') 90
HUON Henry 138
HURST Ellen 18
HURST Harry 18

I

Indefatible 88
IRVING W.D. (Magistrate) 44

J

James 71
JAMES John (alias Johnston) 54, *90-91*, 146, 176
Jane and Elizabeth 47
JEFFRIES Thomas 'Cannibal' 26, *92-93*, 125
JEPPS Daniel 173
JOHNSON Joseph 95
JOHNSTON (or JOHNSON) (see Harry Power)
JOHNSTON Henry 19, 51, 60
JOHNSTONE Henry *94*
JONES George (George Davis) 6, 36, *94-95*
JONES Ian (Author) 101, 111
JONES Mrs 107

K

KANGAROO JACK 42
KAVANAGH Lawrence 36, 94, *95-96*
KEIGHTLEY Henry (Commissioner) 85, 167
KELLY 169
KELLY (Constable) 40
KELLY Andrew 47, *97*
KELLY (Dan) Daniel 32, 87, *100-111*, 158, 160, 180
KELLY (Ned) Edward 7, 17, 32, *100-111*, 125, 126, 144, 158, 160, 178
KELLY Ellen 100, 109, 111
KELLY GANG 16, 32, 87, *100-111*, 158, 160, 178
KELLY ('Red') John *100-111*
KELLY (Kate) Katherine 87, *100-111*, 158
KENNAGH Patrick (Special Police) 40
KENNEALLY J.J. (Author) 32, 87
KENNEDY (Sergeant) 104
KENNELLY William 46
KERZ Helen 81
KILROY 50
KING George 53

L

LEE (Police Trooper) 67
LLOYD Bridget 178
LLOYD John (senior) 100, 143, 144
LLOYD John (junior) 100

LLOYD [Tom] Thomas (senior) 100, 143
LLOYD [Tom] Thomas (junior) 100
LOCKYER Major (Superintendant of Police) 50
LONG 168
LONIGAN Thomas (Mounted Constable) 104, 108
LOVELY RILEY 23
LOWRY (Fred) Frederick 44, 67, 78, *112*
LYONS Patrick (Detective) 152

M

MacDONALD Donald 115, 116
MacDONNELL Aeneas (Special Police) 40
MACK William 29, *113*
MACQUARIE Lachlan (Governor) 88
MAGUIRE John 84
MAHONY William (Constable) 90
MALONEY Thomas 174
MANNS Harry 44, 72, *118*
Marion Watson 94
Marquis of Huntley 35
MARRIOTT Henry 74
MASON Thomas 169
MATHERS John 46, 135
MAWBEY Bert 81
MAWBEY Cecil 81, 83
MAWBEY Garnet 81, 83,
MAWBEY Grace 81, 83
MAWBEY Hilda 81,83
MAWBEY John 81, 83
MAWBEY Percy 81, 83
MAWBEY Sarah 81, 83
McBEAN Robert 144
McCABE 24
McCALLUM Frank (Francis McNeish McNeill McCallum, alias 'Captain Melville') 7, 113, *114-116*, 174
McCARTHY P.H. (Author) 90
McCARTHY Tim (Father) 167
McDONALD (Police Trooper) 67
McENROE (Archdeacon) 118
McEVOY Ned 120
McGINNITY David (Police Sergeant) 127
McGLADE Mrs 15
McGLEDE Edmund 155, 156
McGUIRE 118
McINTOSH 168
McINTYRE (Mounted Trooper) 104
McKAY 168
McMAHON (Chief Commissioner of Police) 120
McMONIGLE Sarah 103
McNAMARA (Constable) 27
McPHERSON James (alias The Wild Scotsman) 90, *117*
McQUILTON John Dr (Author) 101
MELVILLE Alfred 119
MELVILLE 'CAPTAIN' (see Frank McCallum)
MELVILLE Edward 119
MELVILLE George 'Frenchy' 119, *120-123*
MELVILLE James 119
MENDHAM Roy (Author) 23, 118
MIDDLETON (Sergeant) 72, 136
Minerva 114
MOLESWORTH (Justice) 55
MOLONY John Professor (Author) 101, 103
MONTAGU (Justice) 36

MONTFORT (Sergeant) 9, 144
MOONLITE CAPTAIN (see Andrew George Scott)
MOORE (Convict) 95
MORAN (Senior Constable) 72
MORGAN (Dan) Daniel 'Mad Dan' 18, *125-128*
MORGAN James (James Gavagan) 54, 90, *128*, 146
MORLEY R. 13
MUGGLESTON (Private) 50
MULHALL (Mounted Constable) 169
MURPHY 25
MURPHY John & Jeremaih (see John & Joseph FRANCIS)
MURRAY (Detective) 47
MUSQUITO 129
MUTTA Miss 11, 12

N

NAIRNE (Captain) 88
Nelson 14, 54, 68, 90, 91, 128, 146, 176
NELSON Elizabeth 56
NELSON Samuel (Constable) 6, 56
NESBITT James *130-131*, 156
NEWTON (Jack) John 71, *132*
NICHOLLS (Police Trooper) 67
NICHOLLS Mary (Editor) 172
NICHOLSON (Police Superintendant) 144
NOLAN (Sergeant) 133
Northumberland 47
NORTON Oxley John (Police Sub-Inspector) 44

O

O'BRIEN John (Author) 50, 167
O'CONNOR Patrick 22, *133*
O'GRADY Miles (Constable) 40
OLD CHUM 146
O'MEALLY Johnny 44, 78, 84, 167
O'MEALLY Old Paddy 68
O'SULLIVAN John (Author) 38, 157
OWENS Owen (Constable) 116, 128, 138, 174

P

PARKES Henry Sir 73
PARRY Edmund (Sergeant) 78
PATON Henry Oliphant 181
PAYNE John 27
PEARCE Alexander 46, 125, *135*
PEARSON William 17
PEISLEY John 20, 72, *136-137*
PENNY George 'Sydney' 11, 37, 137
PERRY 93
PHEGAN John 40
PLATT James 95
POTTINGER Frederick Sir (Police Inspector) 72, 84, 118
POWER Harry (Henry Johnson) 7, 102, 111, 113, *138-144*
PRICE John (Inspector-General) 29, 66, 113, 171, 174

PRIOR Ted 71
PUGH William (Private) (48th Regiment) 89

Q

QUINN 18
QUINN James (Senior) 101, 144
QUINN (Jimmy) James [Junior] 100
QUINN (Jack) John 101
QUINN Patrick 101
QUINN Thomas 74
QUINNS 100

R

RED LANCE 23
REGAN James 13, *145*
REID (Police Sergeant) 17
REVINGSTONE Codrington *145*
RINGLEADER 56
ROBERTS John 146
ROBERTS William Robert (alias Melville)*147*
ROGAN Thomas *148*, 153, 156, 175
Royal Sovereign 114
RUSSELL (Convict) 92
RUSSELL R (Reverend) 147
RYAN (Father) 148
RYAN Jerry 56

S

SADLIER John (Police Officer/Author) 16, 17, 32
SCANLON 104
SCOTT Andrew George (alias 'Captain Moonlite') 15, 131, 148, *150-156*, 175
SCOTT William 40, *157*
Scout 173
SHERRITT Aaron 32, 103, 106, 111, *158-160*
SIMPSON James 151
SKILLION Bill 103
SKILLION Margaret (nee Kelly) 87
SMITH 50
SMITH Henry 174
Sophia 22
SORELL (Lieutenant-Governor) 88
STALLARD Alfred 79, *161*
STANDISH Frederick (Chief Commissioner of Police) 143
STEPHENS Alfred Sir (Chief Justice) 68, 167
STEPHENSON (Senior Sergeant) 112
SUFFOLK Owen 58, *162-165*
SUTTON (Constable) 167
SYMONS William (Cadet) 120

T

THERRY (Archpriest) 118

THOMPSON 93, 168
THOMPSON (Cadet) 133
TILLEY 26
TOAKE 12
TOMKINS (Sergeant) 42
TOMMY (Black tracker) 12
TRAVERS Mathew (or Travis) 46, 135
TROY William 71, 132
TURNER John 116, 138

U

UNDERWOOD Jacky 8, 81, 83
UNDERWOOD William 50
UPJOHN Elijah 100

V

VANE John 44, 84, *166-167*
VINGE George (Constable) 173

W

WALKER Alexander (Mounted Constable) 169, 170
WALSH Warrigal 68
WARD (Fred) Frederick Wordsworth (alias 'Captain Thunderbolt') *168-170*
WATTS George 88
WAUGH Dr 112
WEBB Henry (Detective) 76
WEEKES Anton 160
WHELAN John 'Rocky' 171
WHITE Charles (Author) 62
WHITE Henry (Warder) 100
WHITEHEAD John 88, *172*
WILLIAMS 25, 26
WILLIAMS (Detective) 47
WILLIAMS Edward (Judge) 22, 119
WILLIAMS Jack *173*
WILLIAMS John 27
WILLIAMS Thomas (1st) 62, 66, *174*
WILLIAMS Thomas (2nd) 148, 153, 156, *175*
WILLIS Mary 46
WILLIS Walpole (Judge) 173
WILSON 53
WILSON Edward 14, 91, 176
WILSON Eleanor 77
WILSON George 120
WILSON John *177*
WINDEYER William (Justice) 148, 156
WINSTANLEY Peter (Police Constable) 36
WOODS (Bob) Robert 83
WORRALL Thomas 89
WRENECKIE (Gus) Augustus 153, 156
WRIGHT John *181*
WRIGHT 'Wild' Isaiah 7, *178-180*

■ *Cover Photograph*
The firearms featured on the cover are a Victorian Prison issue smooth bore Snider carbine of the late 1860s, and a Victorian Police trooper 1851 Navy Colt revolver; first issued 1864 to J. (for Jamieson) police station.
Also featured are unmarked police or prison issue handcuffs.
(All courtesy Vic Lane Collection, Bendigo)

• ABOUT THE AUTHOR •

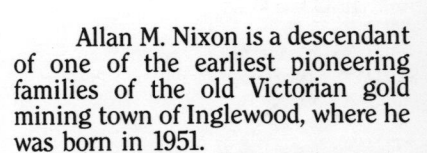

Allan M. Nixon is a descendant of one of the earliest pioneering families of the old Victorian gold mining town of Inglewood, where he was born in 1951.

In his youth he wandered the old goldfields and a favourite spot — Melville Caves, which Frank McCallum, alias 'Captain Melville', reputedly used as a hideout when carrying out his bushranging activities against diggers on the nearby goldfields.

During research for this book Allan Nixon discovered he is a descendant of Charles Grinham, who was convicted several times for cattle stealing and served many years in Pentridge gaol and on the prison hulks.

Allan Nixon combines his time as an author-historian — travelling extensively researching, writing and selling his books — and presenting talks on Australian history to schools, service clubs, historical societies, etc.

Allan lives in Melbourne Victoria with his wife Janette, and continues to add to his vast collection of Australiana, for use on further projects about Australia's social history.

Books by Allan M. Nixon:

INGLEWOOD
Gold Town of Early Victoria

MUDDY BOOTS
Inglewood Football Club

INGLEWOOD GOLD
1859–1982

THE GRINHAM REPORT

THE SWAGMEN
Survivors of the Great Depression

SOMEWHERE IN FRANCE
The War Years of Sgt. Roy Whitelaw, 1st AIF, 1914–1918